Heel to Toe

Also by Charles Lister

Between Two Seas: a walk down the Appian Way

Heel to Toe

Encounters in the South of Italy

CHARLES LISTER

Secker & Warburg
London

Published by Secker & Warburg 2002

2 4 6 8 10 9 7 5 3 1

First published in Great Britain in 2002 by
Secker & Warburg
Random House, 20 Vauxhall Bridge Road,
London SW1V 2SA

Random House Australia (Pty) Limited
20 Alfred Street, Milsons Point, Sydney,
New South Wales 2061, Australia

Random House New Zealand Limited
18 Poland Road, Glenfield,
Auckland 10, New Zealand

Random House (Pty) Limited
Endulini, 5A Jubilee Road, Parktown 2193, South Africa

The Random House Group Limited Reg. No. 954009
www.randomhouse.co.uk

A CIP catalogue record for this book
is available from the British Library

ISBN 0436250993

Papers used by Random House are natural,
recyclable products made from wood grown in sustainable forests;
the manufacturing processes conform to the environmental
regulations of the country of origin

Typeset by Deltatype Ltd, Birkenhead, Merseyside
Printed and bound in Great Britain by
Mackays of Chatham Plc

Contents

Travel; take half the clothes and twice the money

- anon.

ITI SAPIS POTANDA TINO NE

- anon.

To my children,
Benedetta and Sebastian

Acknowledgements

I am greatly indebted to Nicolette James who lives in Lecce (one of George Berkeley's 'faire cities not known to Englishmen') for allowing me to use information from her book *Inglesi a Gallipoli* which is largely about the Stevens family who lived there during the turbulent years of Italian unification. I am also grateful to David Gentilcore for providing me with his unpublished doctoral thesis *The System of the Sacred in Early Modern Terra d'Otranto*, and for taking me to the play written and produced by his father-in-law mentioned on page 61. My thanks also go to Tony Bennett and to Professor Edward Chaney for their generous help, and to the staff of the library at the British School at Rome for their patience in dealing with my many enquiries. My editor too, Stuart Williams, has had to be very patient and understanding.

This book began life as an amalgam of letters I sent home to my wife while I was in the south. If I have offended or made mistakes, I apologise. The errors are all mine, as are the views expressed.

SOUTH ITALY

Gravina

Brindisi

San Cataldo

Lecce

Taranto

Copertino

Sternatia

Bernalda

Otranto

Pisticci

Metapontum

Galatina

Soleto

Rabatanna

Uggiano la Chiesa

Anglona

Erakleia

Badisco

Gallipoli

Valsinni

Leuca

Golfo di Taranto

Trebisacce

Cifti

Sybaris

Lungro

Rossano

Ciro

Santa Severina

Crotone

miles

0 10 20 30 40 50

0 10 20 30 40 50 60 70 80

km

Tiriolo

Capo Rizzuto

Catanzaro

Squillacè

Adriatic Sea

Stilo

ITALY

Caulonia

Rome

Gerace

Siderno

Locri

Brindisi

Reggio

Tyrrhenian Sea

Pentedattilo

Reggio

Melito

SICILY

ONE

Brindisi

When the train stops at Brindisi it tips you straight down the Corso into the sea. You and a thousand others, unshaven and mouth dry; tipped out into yellow eye-bright sunlight and scratched by a rat-catcher tatter of all-night clothes; everyone wanting a boat to Greece. Pilgrims to pleasure. Nobody stays in Brindisi; unwanted and unsplendid, it's *città non grata*; just for leaving and arriving. So dawn-jaws drip on the pavement bars – California, Kennedy, Florida, Waffles, Ham and Eggs; pack a pizza before sailing away. Things have changed since the architectural historian Martin Briggs sighed, 'Oh! for a Joe Lyons in these parts', ninety years ago when he was down here studying the buildings and writing *In the Heel of Italy*. He said Brindisi was dirty and dull and the people did nothing but fleece travellers. They're a lot tougher today: world-trekking hoboes wide as grizzly bears, swollen with body-belts and twice the size of the locals; tower-block Australians with biceps like Sydney Bridge; behemoth baseballers from the USA; bulging Dutchmen; and snow-capped Swedes tall as pine trees. All Parthenon pilgrims heading for the old-world ferry and the land where they know sex and civilisation started.

It's not dull when they shower the dust and sweat off in the Corso fountain halfway towards the sea, all laughs, limbs and loincloths. As it's been swum in, fished in, peed in, danced in, skated on, has drowned cats, killed tropical fish, housed a pair of swans and been a rubbish dump, no one seems to care. Brindisi's like that – Vivaldi variations on an Italian theme; happy tinkles of brightness among the palm trees; careless fun in the morning sun.

Then off they sway down the Corso in giraffe-headed bulk through the massive square buildings yellowed by the sun with geraniums bleeding off balconies; wiping more sweat off and smiling at the motionless locals passing endlessly nodding times of day, or chair-fixed on the pavements all morning over a sip of coffee. Which is much as it was 200 years ago – 'they only work for four hours then spend the rest of the day in taverns drowning their misery,' said one visiting Italian.

It's all down to sun power – God's evil eye, or Phaeton's furnace that blisters time into two separate days here, cockcrow and roost, with six hours of hell-heat between, full of cinder silence, dead-stretch and a long, dry-tongue pant of Gorgon stillness. At midday it bounces off the buildings like balls of fire and the fountain's prostate dribbles, late trekkers snore on mats in greedy palm shade, and the dead Corso's dusty finger just touches the blinding sea.

That's where Old Brindisi was and where little is left; Rome's gateway east; malaria's west; Mussolini's hope; and Virgil's death rattle – *'Mantua me genuit, Calabri rapuere . . .'* (Mantua my birthplace; Calabria my grave); and where they say his last-gasp house is, up the white steps by the sea, with a plaque on it. It was put there by Benito in year twelve of his empire to extol the greatest-ever laureate of nature and dominion power, though they've rubbed Il Duce's name off the bottom now.

Beside it once was the twin-tower end of the Appian and Trajan Ways after a 400-mile march from Rome; two sun-white columns that hailed conquerors, sped out armies, cowed galleys of thirsty slaves; towers that knew Caesar and saw Cleopatra. There's the anklebone left of one, where the fractured tibia says Maradona is a Jew, Lazio football team has AIDS and the Socialists are the prick-party of Italy – *'partito del cazzo'*. No doubt the graffiti-loving Romans did the same: Nero is a fat pig, long live Spartacus, see you

2

tonight Messalina ... The rest of that column is thirty
miles away in Lecce, holding up their pest-purifying St
Oronzo, who is supposed to have saved them from the
plague in 1656 and whose arms are raised so high above his
head in benediction that one traveller thought he was high-
diving onto the remains of his population. And now the
only column left has disappeared too; it has vanished under
a cobweb of boards, iron poles and hoardings. It has been
smothered and deadened by sackcloth; cocooned in a
workforce shroud; scaffolded into oblivion; the last pillar of
Brindisi's history is hidden and mummified by a Ku Klux
condom of rods, nets and placards. The end of Rome's road
has melted away; evanesced; been gulped, and totally
Jonahed.

This morning I met an artist. He was old, grizzled and
endlessly happy, sitting at the top of the Appia steps with a
French beret on his head and a benign smile on his walnut-
wrinkled face, such as children have when dreaming. He
kept looking up over his easel, pondering for a moment,
then dabbing on a little paint. 'Brindisi,' he said, with quiet
confidence. But when I looked over his shoulder it wasn't
Brindisi at all; it was rows of white and pale-brown houses
along a shoreline, with a beach and palm trees and a blue
sea; an undiscovered dream-town; and behind it was an
outline of a castle. '*Tempo fa,*' he said, in case I should ask.
'Years ago' – his eyes on another world.
   I asked him what was wrong with the pillar behind us.
'Nothing,' he answered. 'They can't decide.'
   'What?' I said.
   'Whether to take it down or not.'
   'Who can't?'
   'Everybody. Engineers, architects, archaeologists, the
Comune, Enichem, the Belle Arti ...'
   'So what's going to happen?'

'Nothing. They've gone away now. Soon men will come back and take the scaffolding down again.'

'What's wrong with it?'

'Nothing. It's been there for two thousand years. They should have known better. I've written a poem about it.'

He started to sing in a brittle little voice: '*Sobbra a stu munumento ca la storia ride lassatu . . .*', which was Brindisi dialect for 'History is laughing high above this monument'. Then he wondered where the archaeology park was that the authorities had promised, but which had never arrived. Instead, they had let a pizzeria open just behind the columns, with a purple sign that rotated and flashed on and off in the dark like a lighthouse; a plutonic welcome to a phosphorescent hell.

I watched his brush strokes tipping the waves in white. He knew he was lying; that he was inventing things; fairy tales; reconstructing history; like Canaletto's whimsical romances of Venice when it was a brothelised quagmire of stinking waterways. Brindisi was worse – it never recovered after the Romans; it was all plagues, pestilence, starvation, war and death. It rotted for centuries in a malarial swamp where the Appian columns guarded stench and corpses. Early travellers who came here wanted to leave as quickly as possible. Craufurd Tait Ramage found it full of ghastly people. Keppel Craven sniffed noxious exhalations. Octavian Blewitt, who wrote Murray's first guide, said it was a mass of filth with scrofulous inhabitants. And Janet Ross said it excelled all towns in dirt and smells. Even Sir William Hamilton said it was 'doomed to speedy destruction'.

These early travellers to south Italy were a different breed; they were scholars, explorers, charting the unknown, not tribes of tourists after sun, sea and sex. They wanted information, kept records and had opinions. Henry Swinburne was here in 1777 and, being a classicist, knew that the harbour was a putrid swamp because Julius Caesar had

4

blocked it up trying to trap Pompey's fleet. Swinburne travelled all along the Ionian from here to Reggio, usually with an armed guard in case of trouble, and he was able to recognise ancient battlefields and the remains of Greek cities. He was insatiably curious and an endless note-taker: how many varieties of fish did they catch? How were silkworms cultivated? What did people eat? Was there such a spider as the tarantula? How did the Albanian language originate? Why were there different breeds of sheep and goats? As he spoke Italian, was well connected and knew the right people (the Queen of Naples was godmother to one of his children), he was able to travel from one grand estate to the next and to dine and sleep in relative comfort; unlike the mildly eccentric young teacher Craufurd Tait Ramage down here fifty years later, who often slept on straw in barns. Swinburne had so much to say about the south that his *Travels in the Two Sicilies* spread into two thick quarto volumes, but in spite of the wealth of information they contain, they tend to be dry, stuffy and a bit lifeless. He is a typical eighteenth-century aristocrat; a member of 'the poor will always be with us' school; an aloof and detached recorder of things, rather than an involved or sympathetic commentator. Only once does he mention how the harsh conditions of the 'oppressed peasant' could easily turn him into a robber and assassin; and only once does he dare suggest that 'a wise administration under an ambitious monarch might train up this race to be once more the conquerors of nations', though he quickly tempers this by adding that it would take 'a very fortunate combination of circumstances . . . to bring it about'. As for Brindisi, the fact that the harbour was nothing but a 'fetid green lake', and that more than 1,500 people had died of malaria in three months the year before he arrived, didn't really seem to bother him; it was just another statistic.

But the artist doesn't want that kind of truth. He wants visions of a flower-strewn Hesperides set by a breathless sea in a world of love. He is a poet, praying to vanished spirits and praying to the gods to return past years.

He was there again this morning and invited me into his house. He lives in *Casa Virgilio* and points to the plaque on the wall:

Qui
Ai Termini della Via Appia
Publio Virgilio Marone
Il supremo cantore dei campi e dell' Impero
Or due millenni di ritorno dall' Ellade
L'ultima volta saluto
La Saturnia Terra

which roughly means that the greatest poet ever died on this spot 2,000 years ago, which is pure invention and another fairy-tale, and is about as likely as Horace's house being Horace's in Venosa or Juliet's being Juliet's in Verona. This time he says he can prove it, and shows me a magazine cutting taken from the *Illustrated London News* of 20 February 1869, when that awful disease of Italian unity was spreading. It shows the tottering shell of a farmhouse, with two long-skirted women standing on a balcony; they are watching a girl feeding chickens below them and in the wall behind them are three wooden arches. He fingers the caption – Casa di Virgilio – and then points at the wall of the room we are in. There are the same three wooden arches outlined in the plasterwork. Now I know why he does those paintings; his mind is 2,000 years old, back in legend land. 'O irreporabile tempus,' he whispered.

He had drawers full of memorabilia and started pushing things at me: an advertisement dated 1900 for a Columbia graphophone and medicine to cure malaria in fifteen days for 150 lire. Maria Casalini's obituary notice: she had thirty-two children in twenty-three years. There was even a poster in English. 'Reward. Young lady will be very thankful to the person who will bring back to her, to the Foreign Office, Via del Leo 6, black cocker by the name of Pequenito written on his collar. Lost on Sunday morning in the nearby of the market square. It is a most precious souvenir. 30 January 1944.' A most precious meal too in those days, I should think, doubtless well roasted by supper time. The Brindisians, according to Henry Swinburne, were never averse to a slice of well-fed cur.

He waved brightly coloured old posters at me: tall-masted screw steamers ploughing into the bay with funnels belching, watched by frock-coated men on the quayside and half-bare urchins paddling for shrimps. The triumphant Indian mail train steamed in from London to Brindisi in forty-three hours, full of passengers en route to Bombay, where turbaned rajas waited on elephants. I saw the P&O's SS *Isis* docking on its passage to India, its rails lined with our parasolled great *grandes dames*, tight in wasp-waisted high-necked chiffon, waving at the rows of expectant donkey carts and at groups of costumed girls dancing their greeting with whirling tambourines. He's a total nostalgic.

Then he pulled out a drawing he'd done. He must have been out in a boat one day, looking back at the town, because the castle was there and the crush of muddled houses ringing the shore, but the only thing different was the end of the Appian Way. He'd painted in the two white pillars at the centre and had made them almost silver. They stood there, triumphant and defying reality, because he'd seen them in his dreams, and they had to be true. In this land of a thousand reincarnations he knew that the crowd on the Appian Way was still the same.

Today is Brindisi's *festa* and they're putting coloured lights up in the streets because tonight at sunset St Theodor will arrive. He will arrive by motor boat from across the Adriatic. No one I've asked seems to know his pedigree, but it doesn't matter as saints don't have to have them; they evolve, or you get them on prescription. Brindisi's library – incidentally one of the biggest in south Italy – is suitably cautious. A book I consulted said that he was a Roman soldier called Theodor, who happened to be Christian, and who, after taking part in various victories in Turkey, refused to give thanks to the pagan gods. He also set fire to the Temple of Cybele at Amasea. Following his roasting at the stake, charred bits of Theodor floated round the Mediterranean and turned up at Palermo, Messina and Naples. When part of him arrived in Venice they made him their patron saint, but in the thirteenth century he let them down during a plague so they voted in St Mark as a replacement. Where Brindisi featured on Theodor's itinerary isn't clear, but as Venice did considerable trade down here, perhaps they exported him as being surplus to reliquary requirements.

He arrived tonight in a pool of floodlit darkness. Fireboats in the harbour started spuming skyscraper jets of coloured water, arcs of blues, pinks and greens, and the air was soaked in whoops and whistles, as foghorns blew and a fat Greek ferry boomed out a stomach-full of mad-cow diapasons. It was coloured cacophony greeting a pinpoint convoy white-foaming its holy course from the darkness of sea to the light of land and the swell of roaring throats. A pepper of small boats sped in, led by a radiant cabin cruiser. An armour-clad statue stood at the prow vanguarding a train of swaying clerics on sea-legs. As it hit the landing stage, the fly-swarm of tooting flotilla-flotsam shrieked a caterwaul of ecstasy and whooped off into the surrounding darkness in a frothy stream of exhausted happiness.

Once unloaded, St Theodor was borne away along the quayside in unsteady triumph, surrounded by a dazzle of flashing lights with outriders, patriarchs, priest-attendants, police, pietists, gnostics, zealots, enthusiasts, helots, parasites and camp followers, in a crowd as thick as Oxford marmalade. Coloured rockets exploded over the harbour like God-sperm fertilising heaven; pumping the sky full of shattering stars and spouting out balls of gold and red, each boom of their thunder touching the clouds to chase away devils. Wedged women made finger crosses on black cardigans and thigh-high children stared in a squash of half-comprehension, or bobbed balloons on endless strings among stallholder shouts and the tight-thronged jostle of wondering what to see and do. Theodor's helmet pushed along through them slowly, gold against black, followed by his catafalque – skeleton, heart and sundry leftovers.

No sooner had the sandwich of piety passed than Mammon erupted behind it. Every vendor and hawker in the province had been lying in wait along the route and they closed like a vice behind the throng. Carpets unrolled, arc-lights blazed, stalls rose up by magic as worldly goods replaced holy thoughts. Among the growl of drumbeats and the fortissimo yells of operatic traders, devotion turned to the solid substance of saucepans, fly-swats, screwdrivers, umbrellas, dolls, birdcages, sunhats, or television sets, deep-freezes and car engines. Thick balls of smoke rose from stews of soup, grills spat at frying fish, lambs had their ribs sizzled, and superglue toffee locked your teeth. Theodor's market had erupted in his wake and everyone was happy in the saintly bedlam he had left behind; the holy roar of microphones, loudspeakers, car horns, pealing bells, Guzzi engines and wailing sirens.

'Oompah' boomed the happy band of welcome, after fleeing through a fairy-lit square to the safety of a festooned rostrum, where a coloratura trombone took pot-shots at Puccini and slithered ski-slope grace-notes into every bar. The audience was transfixed with glacial admiration, apart from the *festa*-smart children who bubbled and raced in bursts of energetic competition or popped giant balloons, or just yelled and wrapped themselves in yard-long strings of crisps and candyfloss. Somewhere among the ocean of bobbing heads a barrel-organ churned and tinkled – the very last one perhaps – wavering on unsteady legs and monkey-less, blinking out tinny squeaks of the 1910s and 1920s, pure as fairyland bells, and wistful for the parasols and long dresses of the colonial wives who disembarked here years ago, their pale eyes dreaming of a sweet and greener England only forty-three hours away.

I put 5,000 lire into the man's hat.

I'm worried that my bicycle hasn't arrived. The station master consults an old timetable, but it is so thick and full of footnotes that it doesn't help. One of the porters wants me to kneel and pray. He belongs to a brotherhood called Radio Dio and shows me his membership card. The headquarters are in Grand Rapids, Michigan. He thinks my enforced stay here – it is now day three – is a sign from God that I have a mission in Brindisi. I rather doubt this. If there are paranormal influences working here, it is more likely to be the gibbering spirits of the bulldozed Jews whose cemetery was destroyed in 1860 to build the railway station.

The memory of them is still here. I passed Rua Giudea this morning and then Rua Longobardo, still using the old French for road and showing how Brindisi organised its inhabitants into different areas. Merchants from Pisa, Venice or Genoa were told where to live, and there were streets for different trades: locksmiths, carpenters, wine-sellers, bakers, silk merchants. It saved time when you went shopping or wanted to meet a friend.

I thought I'd better go and see St Theodor in the cathedral. He is appalling; a doll. He is an effete little pansy sitting on a horse, wearing a vapid smile and rouged cheeks. He looks about fifteen; crimson-lipped and doe-eyed, with blond locks sprouting under his helmet; your first instinct is to take off his armour and skirt and give him a cuddle. Instead of that, people kiss his toes as they come in. He is a cross between Goldilocks and Ganymede. Considering what awesome pious icons this country possesses, you wonder where God-fearing art has gone; and where all the godly grand dukes are, the millionaire cardinals and profligate popes who knew that fear inspired worship, and that terror made the ignorant honour and obey. Theodor is devastatingly pretty, the closest thing to a rent-boy on horseback I've ever seen.

I went back to the cathedral after lunch, just in time to see two weddings: couples obviously anxious to be united in Theodor's afterglow. The elegantly spacious square outside gave the families of well-wishers perfect opportunities to perform miracles of contortionist high-speed driving. They arrived in packs, waving out of windows and hurling their chintz-fluttering vehicles around as if demented. With the millimetric precision of bats performing a ballet, they dodged and slithered across the stone into a pandemonium of jumbled parking. The introit to matrimony was a screech of locked brakes, roaring reversals and door slams; the finale was a clamour of celebrating car horns and another catapult scream of rubber. With hands glued to klaxons, they uncongealed themselves and rocketed off out of the square in a one-handed dodgem race and disappeared down skin-tight alleys like a panic of rabbits. For some time their banshee howl floated on the air in diminishing discords, until it faded away to a distant Gregorian wail as if a nest of Walpurgis witches were being drowned on the other side of town.

At right-angles to the cathedral was an older building altogether, a square brown bulk of Norman stone, squat and strong-looking, even glowering. It is said to have been the Templar chapel. Broad-shouldered and rugged, it had shadowed archways that suggested secrets, threats and whispers of champion knights. There was an important clan of them here until Pope Clement and Philip of Spain grew uneasy about their wealth and influence, so they bribed two of their knights to become *pentiti*. Hugo of Samaya and John of Nardo broke their oath and declared that the Templars denied Christ, refuted the Virgin birth, worshipped cats, peed on the cross and buggered each other – '*Unirsi carnalmente fra loro*'. The order was outlawed by Papal Bull in 1312, and members were hounded to death.

But secrecy dies hard in southern Italy. From the Golden Words of Pythagoras and the fish-code of Christ, it flowed through the Albigensians, the Maronites and holy heretics into the Carbonari and Mafia and then into the corrupt masonic lodge P2. Where despotism and tyranny have flourished, so has an underworld of conspiracy and deceit; and it always will.

Then another wedding arrived, another seismic convoy. I knew I shouldn't have stayed, but it was an all-Mozart service, and its softness seemed to cool the sun. So I took my hat off and crept to the side door, just as the Countess was lamenting the Count's infidelity. In my eye-mist under that vast, vaulted ceiling I saw Frederick of Hohenstaufen marrying Jolanda of Jerusalem here 800 years ago, and I saw a cloth of gold and heard trumpets of pageantry. But I shouldn't have bothered. As the vows to eternal love were taken to the melting strains of 'soft winds and calm seas' and I floated on clouds of Amadean paradise, the most overfed of all the cathedral pigeons shat straight onto my head from 100 feet. It was Theodor's revenge.

The artist wasn't surprised to see me again. '*Per Bacco!*' he exclaimed, diving into his imaginary past and summoning up his ancient gods again. 'Now you can see the Art Exhibition.' The Appia steps were invisible beneath a sea of people, easels and canvases; they even stretched up round the pillars and down into the road. It was a blaze of polychromatic brilliance where each colour seemed more vivid than the last; marine-life fantasies of shells, ships, squid, sea-lions, crabs, dolphins and frying sardines. An abundance of mermaids – cherry-nippled ones sitting poised on rocks, giving sickly grins over their shoulders as their ovoidly unclenched buttocks turned tantalisingly into tails. There was the whipped-cream whiteness of tourist Trulli nestling in fields under acres of azure sky, and *contadino* cottages with honeysuckled doors peeping from Puglian glens. All in bilious technicolour brightened by the sun. Brindisi's Venus herself was there in soft-skinned plenty; miss doe-eyed, wistful libido gazed out wet-lipped and pouting with soup-spoon lashes, pleading eyes and Zeppelin-pointed breasts, always stickily stuck in her inch of pale fluff at ever-pubescent fifteen. When they do a thing badly, they do it really well.

Still no bicycle and it has been nearly a week. I've done Tancred's Fountain where the crusaders watered their horses before setting sail, and I've been to the Swabian Castle where a traveller heard prisoners moaning and rattling their chains, and I've walked two miles out to the astonishing church of Santa Maria del Casale standing isolated in a field, where the Knights Templar are said to have sworn their oaths. I've also repelled the advances of the Radio God porter again, and told two American girls how they were cheated in a restaurant when a bottle of wine should have been 3,900 lire not 39,000. Noughts do have their uses.

The artist seemed very happy today. 'Ho-ho,' he chortled. 'My wife was mugged yesterday in Bari.' As he no longer surprises me, I didn't react. 'They snatched her handbag, ho-ho, *Per Bacco*.' So I waited for him to go on. 'She was on her way to hospital and the only thing in it was a full specimen bottle. Ho-ho!' He hates the Baresi; says there are more crimes committed there than in Naples, and thieves leave you '*con culo fuori*' – which means with your arse hanging out of your trousers. A friend of his had his car stolen there three times last year. He had to pay the police to look for it each time, and then pay them again when they found it. He hates the police as well.

As I had just been in the library reading about lawlessness, piracy and the behaviour of tyrannical dukes, I told him about Frederick of Hohenstaufen's *Constitutiones Augustales*, which stated, among other things, that any community failing to solve a local crime within a certain period had to pay a fine to the regional capital. In 1269 Brindisi had to pay Lecce 100 ounces of gold because no one could discover who had murdered the prostitute Zuranella; and even in 1814 Brindisi was fined 700 ducats when a visiting doctor was set on and robbed and nobody was convicted. *'Per Bacco,'* he chortled, as if such efficiency had solved all his problems, but suddenly his face turned maudlin. 'You're lucky to be English,' he said. 'You've got a queen and policemen and you win wars.'

'Well, you've got the Pope,' I answered after a moment, 'and Michelangelo and Ferraris and beautiful women and lots of good food and marvellous weather.'

He gave a little sigh.

'Italy is only Italy when we play football. We hate each other really. North and south; Milan and Rome; Rome and Naples. We're all Arabs, Turks, Greeks, Jews, Spaniards, Africans, bits of everything; we aren't Italians at all.'

'Yes, you are. The Pope's your tribal chief.'

He almost laughed. 'And he's Polish . . . I'm talking about this world, not the next one. That's all a waste of time. Treasure in heaven? What about all his treasure in the Vatican? What's a pope ever done for Italy? Religion doesn't unite people or make a country. Garibaldi called the Pope "anti-Christ" and said priests were the scourge of Italy.'

'But don't forget we're not English, either; we're Danes, Vikings, Normans, even Romans. And we're not very nice; we've been called a pernicious race of odious vermin, and not worth the dirt between someone's toes.'

'Yes, but you've got laws, you've got Prime Ministers, and you've got London.'

'And you've got Rome, while we've got drugs and hooligans and rain and snow; and we've got crowds of miserable people who hate foreigners and think we're the best. In fact we are arrogant, aggressive, hypocritical, intolerant, and compared with you, we're inhibited and repressed. Just look at you. Everyone here is smiling and happy; not a care in the world; happy to be alive.'

He started to chuckle.

'Yes, and there is only one miserable face to be seen here,' he said. 'It's yours.'

I'm off. The bicycle arrived late this afternoon and I've already packed. For a last look round, I went for a night walk along the quayside. It seemed sad watching grey gull-bodies resting on the sleeping waves, the moon scattering silver streaks as they rolled in their nightly requiem; and little boats rocking gently on the lapping breath of sea. The Brindisians go to bed early and they get up early too. In daytime this quayside is like a kasbah market with such shouts and squash and colours you can't even think. The frenzied explosion of procreant Puglia; nature's monstrously fertile and bursting womb. A barrow-crush of oranges, bananas, tomatoes, figs, lemons, pineapples, peppers, corncobs, apples, plums, marrows, chestnuts; and the same number of yells, waves and arguments. It's the noise they love; like Pavarotti. Can any Italian whisper? There are pots and pans too, fishing tackle, CDs, lobster traps, footballs, chickens in cages, T-shirts, contraband cigarettes . . .

But tonight it was different, almost ghostly. The only unsilent thing was the lapping sea. Once there were graceful *palazzi* along here, overlooking the waterfront, rich residences for borghese traders. Now the ground floors are garages or store-rooms. They look mummified in the night shadows, accepting that time has moved on. Their window-eyes are shuttered and blind, their cavernous doorways are dead and sleepy, cloaked by pillars under wind-worn coats of arms: lions, leopards, coronets. All round my footsteps was a hollow silence, then the dart of a bolting cat, and above me stone balconies jutted like feeble, unwanted breasts needing the succour of the sun.

It will be different tomorrow. Phoenix-time. These sleeping tubs of geraniums will be splashed by his golden rays, and will lift crimson lips of laughter or drip tears of blood. Genius will be here again to welcome the sun.

TWO

Towards Otranto

Brindisi's outskirts are really ugly. Endless tower-blocks and dusty roads peppered with potholes and lined with refuse bags torn at by dogs and cats. Far away I heard the *autostrada*'s refrain of howling engines and tortured rubber as they all tried to win. What? I'm not sure. Perhaps an ego-prize or a seat in the next world. Some genie catapults Italians from being pedestrian somnambulists into piston-powered maniacs. It inflates them.

I found a disused lane and after a mile there was silence and the sea stretched out on my left, a powerful and lonely blue, earth burning beside it, dry and level and so well cooked it must be dead. Stream corpses splintered it in wizened cracks, filled with wild reeds and bulrushes; and once-white *masserie* – farmhouses – floated in the distance, flaked and torn and tortured by sunlight, among half-lines of forgotten cypresses. Then a scared bird swooped low and nervous as it bounded on hot currents of air in a bid to vanish; and sometimes sweaty fumes hovered over a power station far away in a dip. All was silent, and the sun-spotted sea danced for ever in silver to the rim of existence and hugged a sparse pollen of tiny yachts.

After Cerano, on no one's map, I sat thinking of lunch on a whaleback hummock of sand to watch an iron-legged fisherman on the beach swinging a tall, tapered cane out two-fisted, and I listened for the invisible plop of bait in deep water. He says he has found a shoal and shouts to his children. His house is fifty yards away over the dunes, with a barking dog, and the children wave and run with buckets; and smoke curls. My sweat runs too at the sparkling smiles of years of ocean, where two blues merge and will merge again tomorrow. Wordless waves, where slave-ships passed; Trojans with bloody prows, Argonauts, quinqueremes, Turkish armadas and Othello's Venetian galley. Now it's rafts of Albanians. Then the sand moves behind me. '*Lutrini*,' she says, quietly. '*Buon appetito . . .*' Then she puts the plate down and runs, hair streaming behind her like a mane. A multi-fish stare at me from a dish; pink and crisp little bodies with heads and tails, and barely dead; the size of fingers, so down they go, bones and all; and then she's back with more of them, and a glass and a jug of wine, coal-black: '*Casa recc*' . . .' she bobs, and flees again, feet spewing sand. It slides down like velvet and my stomach is a sponge.

Two glassfuls and midday stands still, silent and unfocused, with sweat dribbling into eyes and the blue-bellied pool of sea rolling in elastic slow motion, danced on by silver sparks. The bare sky bends to touch it; melts, descends, turns icy-white . . . Then she's here again, black-haired and dwarf-like, tiny feet puffing a sandstorm, handing out bread to mop me up and a bunch of grapes; she stands in a Puck shadow against the sky, then does an Arab haunch-squat on a dune-top to sit and watch, windless and still as a goblin-eyed beach sprite. How old is she? A flimsy ten? Flesh-folds of sand stretch away in a swaying plain of buttock-bumps and rolling thigh shapes . . . lumpety, dumpety . . . dwindling through heat-haze and salty tears. Can anything matter in this sun? Will I ever reach San Cataldo?

'We're one family under God,' the mother says, when I'm swaying at the door, half-hoping to pay or wash up. But instead she gives me more grapes, and wine and a plate of *ricci* – those beastly little black cacti you step on in the sea. The girl opens them with a knife and scoops out the orange roe with her fingers straight into her mouth. I try it too, but she's expert and I'm drunk. They won't let my glass empty, and the dog is on all fours by the door eating a bowl of spaghetti; and I just wish there weren't such beautiful people in the world with hearts much bigger than mine. The artist was right. We're miserable, we think too much; our souls are mean and dangerous; we live in a web of fear.

Then the girl finds my bicycle, lost somewhere in the dunes, and laughs as I wobble away, waving each other out of our separate lives.

I had to stop at Cerate, a mile further on, and have a rest. Pedalling was hopeless. The sun was like an attack of razor-blades. I sat in the shade of a tiny Norman abbey perched in a field in the middle of nowhere, watched curiously by two custodians playing cards in a shed. The French art historian Emile Bertaux, who was down here in 1895, called this 'a little Basilica' on account of its delicate cloister of arches, its nave covered in twelfth-century frescos and a carved doorway as intricate as Ruvo Cathedral's. In his monumental work *L'Art dans L'Italie Meridionale*, Bertaux – a member of the French Academy in Rome – referred to the south as 'the land of unknown art'. He's right. Not long ago this was a ruin. Janet Ross's friend, the Duke of Castromediano, pleaded for its restoration in 1880, but nothing happened until 1965 when a group of local enthusiasts overcame '*notevoli ostacoli di natura burocratica*' and started work. They bulldozed their way through the initiative-sapping swamp of Italian bureaucracy, and turned the abbey of Cerate into something delicately beautiful but completely unknown.

There should be more people like that. Enthusiasts prepared to fight their way through the quagmire of official apathy and negation. The writer Norman Douglas who lived and died in Italy called civil servants Italy's army of official loafers, specialists in administrative suffocation and obstruction. Even their own countryman, the journalist and author Luigi Barzini, said they were incapable of doing anything efficiently.

★

Before I reached San Cataldo it got dark and my headlight fell off when I hit a large pothole. The place is named after an Irish saint who landed here after visiting the Holy Land sometime between AD 300 and 900. He had proven his miraculous powers on the voyage here by calming storms, curing seasickness and bringing back to life a sailor who had fallen from the crow's nest and broken his neck. It is said that Puglia was so guilt-ridden that the earth howled as he landed. (This could be true, as there are some small caves in the coastline that sometimes give out a resonant booming sound as the waves wash into them.)

Now I wanted to howl too. San Cataldo is large on the map, but in reality it is minimal. No street lights, shops or hotels. My only hope was a news-vendor just rattling his shutter down, who thought I was a brigand come to rob him until he saw the abject despair on my face. He said he would drive me into Lecce, where there were plenty of hotels. On the way he changed his mind and said I could sleep in one of his apartments, as he had two flats in Lecce, as well as a holiday house on the coast. He had taken an early retirement pension from the Ministry of Finance, and had invested in property and the newspaper business, and was still being paid by the ministry for doing nothing, which suited him down to the ground.

So we rattled along nine miles of dead-straight road, originally built by the thoughtful Ferdinand of Bourbon to help the stifled and overheated population of Lecce get to the sea occasionally for a healthy, cooling dip. It was even called Strada Cristina in memory of his popular and pious queen, who was famous for her good works; and special conveyances ran along it to help people escape from summer suffocation into the fresh air. Unfortunately they had overlooked the greedy habits of *Anopheles*, the malaria mosquito, so the death rate of holidaymakers soared and San Cataldo became known locally as the Malaria Torture

Chamber, and any public conveyances were nicknamed Nuremberg Specials.

So there I almost ended the night, settled in one of his apartments, six floors up in a Lecce tower-block with him, her, twin daughters of seventeen and a huge bowl of macaroni; then a bath and a long, full-stomached sleep in a private bed, until the bomb went off outside at about two o'clock. We all squeaked and shook in the kitchen, spilling coffee into rattling saucers, while blue lights spun eerie circles on the ceiling, sirens howled, running people yelled in night-shirts, dusty smoke drifted and red lights flashed. Outside among the arm-waving there was a shop without a wall, and a big black space steaming gently . . .

'Who did it?'

'*Tangente. Pizzo.*'

'Why?'

'Extortion. Threats.'

'What for?'

'Protection money.'

'Why?'

'Pay, or else . . .'

'How much?'

'Millions.'

'Who then? Mafia?'

'Yes, Camorra too . . . Sacra Corona . . . probably Foggia.'

'It's local gangs,' chips in a trembling twin.

'How often does it happen?'

'Forty this year.'

'Where?'

'Shops, cafés, little businesses.'

'Christ! How?'

'Telephone calls or letters. Pay, or we'll blow you up.'

'Jesus! Police?'

'Useless. Take a cut.'

'Bloody hell.'

What did the artist say? Hate thy neighbour? There's a

bomb almost every night somewhere in Puglia: Nardo, Soleto, Ruffano, Maglie, Ugento. It's the new road to riches. Extort by threats or violence. Parliament sets the example, so the people follow. *'Il pesce puzza dal capo,'* he says – it's the head of the rotting fish that stinks. 'I'd rather have a whore in Parliament than a bunch of thieves', which was a nice tribute to the old antics of La Cicciolina, the people's favourite porn-star whom they even voted into government; a friendly pat on the ex-parliamentarian's bare bum. It still decorates the book stalls. At least she was honest about her service industry, which can't be said of the others, using bribes and backhanders. About a hundred of them are under investigation at the moment. VIP here stands for *Visto in Prigione* – seen in prison. Italians only go into Parliament out of self-interest. Stuff the country! Down here people know the Mafia is government-run; that's why they don't pay taxes and only deal in cash.

I hadn't meant to be in Lecce at all; an off-the-track accident. In spite of the oven-heat, which is almost breath-stopping, I went to the square to eat ice-cream and look at St Oronzo. He is precariously perched on bits of Appian pillar, enormously mitred and hand aloft in blessing. He didn't look very safe. This one is Oronzo II, as his predecessor melted during a fireworks display in 1739 and they had to get a replacement from Venice. According to my notes, his real name was Orontius, a Puglian of noble birth who was a bit weird and went to live in a cave near Ostuni. One day it seems he met a man on the road hurrying towards Rome with a letter. It came from Corinth and spoke of terrible things going on there: lust, fornication, wickedness, unnatural acts, murder, deceit and backbiting; it was signed by someone called Paul. Orontius was so impressed that he hurried to Corinth to meet him and as his reward was appointed the first Bishop of Lecce, so on his return he promptly converted the Roman garrison to

Christianity. Nero didn't approve and had him thrown to the lions in the amphitheatre here. This must be a lesson not to read other people's letters.

You can't walk round Lecce for long without blinking in amazement at some of the buildings. They're either grotesquely over-decorated or stunningly beautiful. They seem to compete in reckless ornamentation; inventive madness in stone. Martin Briggs, the architect, who was down here studying them for his book nearly a hundred years ago, thought they were splendid; so did Sacheverell Sitwell. He said Lecce was unforgettable. An English article that I read somewhere referred to them as 'those silly south Italian churches'. George Berkeley, a pioneer visitor to Lecce in 1717, was amazed by them. 'The profusion of alto-relievo,' he enthused, 'the incredible profusion of ornament ... gusto in the meanest houses.' The Marchese Grimaldi said the façade of Santa Croce made him think a lunatic was having a nightmare. His interests were more worldly: the girls were the most beautiful he had seen in all Italy and their eyes flashed so intensely that they seemed to leap out of their sockets.

Martin Briggs was here in 1909 and Sacheverell Sitwell in 1920. Two hundred years before that George Berkeley was here on a tarantula hunt. This original and eccentric Grand Tourist bear-led fifteen-year-old Thomas Ashe into the dangerous and unexplored regions of south Italy looking for spiders. He didn't find any, but instead – being a lover and enthusiast of architecture – was amazed to see 'five fair cities in one day ... the most part built of white marble, whereof the names are not known to Englishmen ... the most beautiful city in Italy lies in a remote corner of the heel'.

Although Berkeley's notebooks often read like stream-of-consciousness sporadic jottings, one can understand why he was made a bishop later. His enthusiasm, excitement, concern and even occasional disapproval burst out of every page. One can almost hear him growling as he scribbles, 'shrubs on right, pasture left. Vines round reeds on the sides of ye hills.' His notes bump along in time to the primitive chaise in which he was travelling and read like a fledgling Baedeker; remarks dashed off about terrain, inhabitants, food, buildings, priests. Although Berkeley was down here sixty years before Henry Swinburne, his account is more lively and intense, doubtless because his notes are original and not 'written up'. 'We were stared at like men dropt from the sky ... slew a black serpent four feet long ... fleas innumerable ... inhabitants of Terra di Bari reckoned somewhat stupid ...'

His enjoyment is obvious, his observation acute, and little of importance seems to escape him: herbs, gorse bushes, goats, churches, bumpy roads, sour wine, ignorant priests. But while amazed at some of the buildings and disquieted by the poverty of the people – who often stood in rows to catch a glimpse of him – Berkeley was less successful in his search for tarantulas. Sometimes he was told they were scorpions, or they never bit within sight of a church, or they avoided Franciscans because of their clothes, or spitting down a straw would draw them out of their holes; then a wise doctor assured him that the hysterical dance performed following a so-called spider bite was only done 'for lewd purposes' – which is probably right. Berkeley's own view of the dance he witnessed was definitely sceptical; although the person whirled around 'with cheeks hollow and eyes somewhat ghastly', he thought it was 'too regularly and discreetly managed for a madman', especially as the dancer thrust a sword at him. He was surprised at how many Jesuits he came across and wasn't very pleased to meet a murderous English sailor prize-fighting the locals in Brindisi harbour.

Whatever early travellers may have thought of the strange architecture, it is not easy to comment on it today as most

of the old buildings are hidden by scaffolding and monstrous sheets of green tarpaulin. Whether or not this
conceals a genuine process of repair and maintenance is
hard to say; activity seems minimal. It could be a veil of
persuasion that restoration is imminent. It could be to
prevent you seeing what a shocking state things are in. The
Florentine publisher Pino Orioli saw scaffolding in a church
as a young man and found it was still there twenty years
later when he went back on a second visit.

There is an amazing new museum in Lecce: air conditioned,
hidden lighting, spacious rooms, mirrors, vast display cases.
Statues line the walls and exhibits are laid out chronologi-
cally; Palaeolithic through Neolithic, Iron and Bronze Age
into Greek and Roman. The display of bones, pots, tools,
coins, weapons, jewels and ornaments is never-ending, and
the inventive shapes of the figured vases seem infinite –
elbows, hips, necks and spouts everywhere. As for the
designs, there are dancers, musicians, heroes, gods, athletes,
lovers, satyrs, wrestlers, armies, sacrifices, weddings and
death. You're forced to remember that the land you are in is
10,000 years old and you're only a tiny part of it; and you
see that exploration and travel are nothing new either.
There is a breath of the East in the cabinets, ideas from
India and China, and the lure of Africa as well, dark heads
with fuzzed hair and enlarged lips, and no shortage of
Nilotic cats and tall Pharaonic hairstyles. This is a land of
mixed fertility and all the mongrel elements that started
civilisation.

It was too hot outside, so I went into the library next
door. Lecce's library is not for browsing; you know your
title, look for the card in a filing cabinet and present it at
the desk. I was looking for useless gossip to pass the time
and found some in Pier-Fausto Palumbo's *Storia di Lecce*:

    1. In 1350 Lecce sent King Louis of Anjou in Naples a

gift of 1,500 lb weight of richly carved silver, three racehorses, two beautiful slaves and one camel.

2. The medieval lords of Lecce owned all the rain that fell on the town and all the donkey-droppings. They could also screw any girl they wanted; a privilege called *cunnatico*. (Some members of Parliament still believe in this.)

3. Around 1690 a native of Lecce called Antonio Verrio was supposedly in England painting the stairway at Hampton Court. (This makes Berkeley's journey that I mentioned earlier seem less remarkable. It also shows how much travel went on years ago on the Continent.) I seem to remember there were also Italians in Russia building palaces for the Tsars around 1500.

4. Part of a ship's manifest dated 21 January 1690 reads as follows: 'Isima, a Turkish slave girl aged twelve with fair skin and chestnut hair; daughter of Isuph and Atiphaz from Buscima, forty silver ducats; and Usso, a fair-skinned Turkish boy aged nine, eight ducats.'

5. On 2 September 1742 an elephant arrived on a sailing boat: a present from the Sultan of Turkey to the King of Naples. It left Brindisi on 18 October with six Turks to look after it, and it walked ten miles per day.

I could find no mention of 'the infamous plague of 1656,' but there was one in 1466 that killed 12,000 people. I also came across a quotation about Lecce by the leading Decadent, Arthur Symons: 'Here one dreams of light music, of masquerades, of voluptuous and easy feasts' – which, were I staying, I might possibly agree with.

Instead, I shall retire to the news-vendor's apartment, pray for a bombless night, and see if his twins' eyes 'leap from their sockets'. He guards them like a Rottweiler. The eyes of southern girls have caused problems to travellers before. They can give glances of gentle salutation, or of heavenly rhetoric. The impressionable young Ramage might have abandoned his journey through the south on account of one young lady's glances.

THREE

Otranto

I can hardly remember that ride, it was all uphill; except that one cyclist overtook me on his way to Otranto and then waved at me on his way back. They take pedalling seriously over here.

The news-vendor had taken me back to San Cataldo earlier. I didn't like what I saw; it was a sprawling settlement of exclusive bourgeois, double-sized villas, almost palaces, each discreetly enclosed behind high walls; fortress-like. A secret spa-town of the 1890 post-Risorgimento wealth earned by the exploiters and those who could afford quinine. You could glimpse their money and magnificence through massive wrought-iron gates or over wall tops through veils of palms, firs and monkey-puzzles. A very private and defiant rich-ville, with tightly shuttered windows cloaking years of guilt.

So I went on pedalling to get away, while cicadas kept rattling invisible thrills at me in the trees and in more trees further on, and the sun was brutal. Little men waved oranges and grapes hopefully from shaded huts beside the road; or sweat ran down my chest; or the sea crunched into rocks a few yards away or lay far out of sight beyond parched fields. Trees webbed the horizon at fancy's random – some patches, some prongs; platoons of them spread in neat little ranks, or running up halfway like soldiers at war, giving spiky shape to things shapeless. In land hollows there were shimmering stretches of water, inland lakes bouncing the sun.

That's Puglia for you; a plateau dwindling to the sky; limbs of red earth rolling for miles in an everlasting flatness of soft ups and downs, each different and beautiful; brown belly-curves, biceps, buttocks and bent backs; limbs stretched with exhaustion and swept by sun, all the same but varied around every corner. And God it was hot. Everything caught under a cauldron dome of blue sky and blurred by heat. 'A land without shadows' someone called it.

Then suddenly, a vision: olive groves and orange trees swept down in a gentle dip to the left; a spread of buttons glowing on a sea of green among specks of white houses. It was the Abbé Saint-Non's 'earthly paradise . . . drowned in the song of nightingales'. (That was in 1770; today they shoot them.) He had found the Elysian Fields, '*un lieu délicieux*' where the untouched beauties of nature were indescribable. But the Abbé Saint-Non was a fake; he never went near the place. This distinguished cleric, friend of Voltaire and of King Ferdinand IV of Naples, and one-time Abbot of the Benedictine Monastery of Pothières, remained in Rome and Naples while others made the ninety-day journey through south Italy and Sicily for him. And if he didn't like what they had written or drawn on their return, he changed it. The actual author of the five-volume elephant-folio *Voyage Pittoresque, ou Description des Royaumes de Naples et de Sicile, Paris* 1781, with 380 engraved plates, was Baron Dominique Vivant Denon, scholar, explorer (*Travels in Upper and Lower Egypt*), pornographer (*Point de Lendemain*) and co-founder of the Napoleonic Louvre. He was also highly popular as a socially and sexually active diplomat in Naples. Among the artists who accompanied him to the south were Fragonard, Robert, Chatelet and Renard. But the enterprise was so massive and proved so expensive that the Abbé was bankrupted; nobody wanted to know about south Italy. Today you'd be lucky to find the work complete for less than £10,000.

Otranto still shines like a beacon as it lies in a hollow by the sea. Its ancient nucleus is perched on a hill, where

Charles V's castle climbs on top of the one built by
Ferdinand of Aragon, who in turn built his on top of
Frederick of Hohenstaufen's. It is little more than a village,
and they say the hill is hollow, full of caves and dungeons,
crammed with skeletons, which wouldn't surprise me.
Otranto was the main port to the East for a thousand years
and has suffered a brutal history. There are tales that King
Minos was here with the Cretans long before the Trojan
Wars; Pyrrhus planned to build a bridge of boats fifty miles
long across to Apollonia; St Peter arrived to celebrate the
first Mass in the Western world at the top of the hill; Sultan
Mohammed II sent an army of 18,000 Turks over to
massacre Otranto's inhabitants (which was an unhappy
accident, as they had meant to land at Brindisi but had been
blown off course); and until 1890 there was a British Consul
here. There are cannonballs twenty inches across lying in
the streets being used as doorstops, and in the quiet,
blinding whiteness one senses exhaustion; a plea for peace.

The sea has attacked it too. Used to sliding in on silky
sand, it has now met the harshness of Puglia's eastern
coastline; solid, unyielding and defiant from here to the
Cape; a defence work of jagged cliffs and saw-toothed rocks
with claw-like toes stuck out underwater where waves
swirl and chafe at dark razor-points. Neither element yields;
they fight everlastingly, angry and baffled; the sea hates the
land and the land hates the sea; as one sighs and sucks in
relentless motion, the other tears it to so many pieces that
the froth runs like a snow queen's blood.

Today, Otranto has leaked beyond its protective walls,
and white houses now curve round a little bay up to a
northern point where hotel lights wink, scooters roar and
cafés pound out magnetic sounds. Another invasion has
begun. The dry inland plain of Puglia has discovered the sea
and Otranto has become a Mecca; the pop-muezzins are
calling.

So I cycled in and had to stop because the sea-front road

was blocked. It was a solid wedge of cars and people, and it was Sunday afternoon. Aldo had brought Otranto to a standstill. Aldo owns a bar and had put two television sets on the pavement outside so that everybody could watch Napoli playing Bari, and he had two jukeboxes inside so that anybody else could hear Michael Jackson screaming 'Beat-it, Beat-it'. The result was a congealment of impenetrable humanity, accompanied by a fury of car horns and a smoky rage of choking engines. There was also the hubbub of a hundred commentaries and happy murmurs of close body contact, in which Italians delight. Having achieved this staggering success of condensing a large part of Otranto's 4,000 inhabitants outside his bar, Aldo should have been happy, but Aldo wasn't. His audience had discovered that while his television was free, ice-cream and drinks were cheaper across the road, so nobody wanted to buy anything. When I eventually reached the counter, he was bewildered and angry, while his wife sat immobile at an idle till.

'Orangeade, please.'

'It's her fault, silly cow.'

'Orange?'

'Stupid bitch, two televisions, two jukeboxes, she's mad.'

'How much?'

'Crazy! She's *pazza*, she can piss off back to Pisa. Shit, who'd marry? . . . Hundred lire.'

'You don't have rooms, do you?'

'No. Silly cow, sod her, my aunt does.'

'How much?'

'Hang on, God! What a cretin, she's mad. That your bicycle?'

'Yes.'

'It's crap.'

'I'm cycling to Reggio.'

'Reggio on that thing? Reggio Calabria? You're mad, take my motorbike.'

That's the problem with Aldo. He's impetuous and wants to be loved. He's not getting enough appreciation. Nor is his aunt. She has a small farmhouse half a mile out, with two rooms to let, and her husband has disappeared. He's turned priapic, and gone on a cunt hunt. Even before I've unpacked I know all about it. She won't stop telling me. And now I've got to hunt him out, which shouldn't be difficult because he's only got one leg. It all started when he fell off his tractor and it ran over him, since when, it seems, he has gone rampant, turned into a satyr. Did I see him in Aldo's bar? No, I didn't. He's very short – was he with a blonde? This is all highly confidential; whispered; fingers-to-lips stuff, so I mustn't tell a soul. It's secret. It's also disgusting. 'He never stops,' she says. 'At it night and day. He's horrible.' She hardly pauses for breath. 'Filthy. Whores all the time. Do you do that in England? He's short with a wooden leg. You won't tell, will you?' I start mumbling assurances, but she interrupts; she won't stop talking, and he won't stop screwing. 'He's over sixty, it's shameful, *"puttane, puttane"*. Did she have fair hair? You mustn't say a word. It's horrible.'

I won't. I'm going to look round Otranto and I've promised to keep an eye out for peg-leg Pan, hop-along Don Giovanni, the insatiable satyr who wants to get his wood over.

I'm rather uneasy about this. There are three little fields outside the farmhouse, each one allotment-sized, and the injured madam has a swarthy young Albanian looking after them, invariably stripped to the waist and well tanned. I've now discovered he is twenty-six years old, a qualified doctor, trained in Tirana; but, being of the wrong political colour, he floated to Italy. He also speaks excellent English, quotes lengthy passages of Shakespeare and Milton, enjoys Dickens, supports Vaclav Havel and says Byron is his favourite poet. To prove it he looked eastwards and said, 'My native land goodnight, sad relic of departed worth.' I think my landlady may be doing better than screw-happy peg-leg.

Things worsened rapidly this evening when I went to telephone home in her hall, failing to notice a bulky shape beside the receiver. It only registered halfway through our conversation. It was a large revolver, and fully loaded; so I'm not surprised he doesn't come home.

'It's a dovecote,' whispered Aldo.

'Don't talk rubbish – it's underground.'

'Well, look at those holes then.'

'They're niches for candles . . . offerings . . . bones. It's a chapel.'

'It's for doves.'

'Well, how did they get in?'

'Up there. That hole in the roof. I can see the sky.'

Our voices were muffled by the damp stone closing around us, hewn out smooth and flat into two long chambers in the shape of a cross. We were twenty feet down and could only just see each other. Aldo was showing me some of Otranto's caves. The land here is like a sieve, a soft lump of geological cheese that has been maggoted and riddled ever since man learned to dig. There are holes everywhere: pock-marks, mouths, tunnels, sockets, fissures and slits gaping from the hillsides in pepper-pot darkness. They're old, black, dirty and cold, with hidden histories of blood and terror, used by hermits, brigands, goatherds, runaways, lovers and secret gods; savage lives and unknown deaths. The rough walls show the faded hieroglyphics and scratched names of today's partners and yesterday's damned.

Otranto is the centre of a mole-run; it's hollow underneath; a warren. When they find a new hole or passage below them, they fill it in. One of the biggest is under the police station – a labyrinth where they used to store tobacco to keep it moist. There are still coloured frescoes on the walls; a procession of cowled monks with eye-slit hoods in chalky blue, each holding a taper, is seen walking round a corner into a pile of rubble. They look like the Ku Klux Klan, tiptoeing to a mystery assassination.

We had to struggle through brambles and crawl in darkness along a smooth pyramid tunnel to get into our hole, which must have been some kind of chapel or shrine, though Aldo still insists it was a bird sanctuary. It was a cruciform cave with smooth walls, big enough to stand up in; a faint beam of light seeping in from a hole yards above, showing a pale-blue sky like a peeping eye of God, and every surface covered in a regular pattern of triangular incisions.

'Who did it then?' he whispered.

'I don't know. Hermits . . . monks . . . priests . . . Byzant-ines?'

'Why?'

'I told you, people's bones – ashes – memories . . . It's a chapel, a columbarium.'

'Crazy. When?'

'Ages ago. A thousand years maybe, probably more.'

'Mad. I think it's for pigeons. Want to see something really crazy?'

Aldo meant the floor in Otranto Cathedral, which was still in its final stages of restoration. It was protected by a barrier of planks and by notices forbidding entry, none of which hindered Aldo who climbed over the barricades, urging me to follow. We stood in a vast expanse of multicoloured terracotta tiling sweeping in all directions, with Aldo waving his arms like a windmill, staring at it in bewilderment and saying, '*Crettini! Pazzi! Imbecili!*' I could see what he meant. It was an unintelligible display of misshapen figures covering nearly 1,000 square yards of flooring. There were nightmare monsters floating among trees, humans hanging upside-down, heroes from myth and history suspended in air. It was a religious metaphor; a fantasy message thought up by the Archbishop of Otranto to show that there was only one true God, because the heathen were in Jerusalem again. He gave the message to the young monk Pantaleone to execute, and he started work on it in 1163; a technicolour vision of heaven and hell, good and evil, hope and despair, the present and eternity. Among the confusion of shapes were elephants, monkeys, camels, snakes and sea-serpents, some of which were eating each other. Samson was there somewhere, and so were Adam and Eve, Hercules, King Arthur and fighting crusaders; every detail shining with a rainbow brilliance. When Henry Swinburne saw the floor in 1778 he called it 'barbarous', and Emile Bertaux, the French art historian, said it was an 'astonishing menagerie' – '*un bizarre fouillis de figures*'. No one has fully mastered its message yet, or interpreted all its symbols, though copious learned theses appear at regular intervals in French, German and Greek, explaining its mysteries and interpreting the medieval mind as it struggled with a confusion of beliefs and invading theocracies. Myth, history, nature and fantasy mix in sweeps of vivid colour; a bedlam of crabs, centaurs, saints, unicorns, kings and prophets, tangled among sea-serpents. They are all suspended from trees supported by elephants, and among the compress of branches are camels with wings, birds turning somersaults and trumpeting humanoids upside-down. Aldo keeps pointing and shaking his head over Noah's ark, which is surrounded by two-tailed mermaids, eagles riding lions and donkeys with human heads. Somewhere else Jonah is fighting a whale, a chicken is swimming, and four lions are joined to a single head. Among the chaos are kings in ectopic colours – Alexander on a throne, King Arthur waving and Nebuchadnezzar performing a dance next to a sea-serpent swallowing its own tail. Pantaleone's pandemonium of what to believe was created as East fought West, Jerusalem was invaded, new gods swept through Puglia, and truth shuddered and crumbled like an earthquake. Could it mean anything?

Then we were caught by an angry priest, swirling his cassock like a wounded bat. *'Via, via!'* he whispered. *'Fuori!'* Then suddenly he softened. 'Look,' he whispered, 'the Tree of Life. God coming down to man, expelling Adam and Eve . . . Arthur seeking the Holy Grail . . . The zodiac is everlasting love . . . The single-headed lions are God's world united . . . The woman with snakes is man's downfall, the whore of Babylon – it's in the Bible.'

'Alexander isn't,' I said.

'A symbol. He united the world.'

'Elephants?'

'God's strength and patience. He supports us for ever.'

'Is that hell?'

'Yes . . . look at it.'

Irregular letters spelt *'Infernus Satanas'* where a man with his hands tied was being garrotted. Below him naked bodies were diving out of branches through space, with limbs at all angles and gaping mouths – diving into flames where Satan was waiting. He looked very happy, sitting on the back of a sabre-toothed monster with nothing on except a crown and his toes curled up in pleasure.

'Lunghi baffi,' whispered the priest, pointing to Satan's long, Daliesque moustache sticking out like a propeller. *'Il vero Satano.'* But I didn't agree. I think it was Satan's forked tongue.

They are lucky to have the floor there at all after what the Turks did in 1480, sailing in with 130 ships and 18,000 soldiers. They stabled their horses there. There followed the famous battle which the Pope thought was an invasion and which made him flee from Rome to France, and it was bad luck for Otranto anyway as the Turks hadn't meant to land there at all. As the inhabitants were all Christians, they were told to convert to Mohammed or have their heads chopped off. Most of them chose the latter course, as a large stone behind one of the altars in the cathedral bears witness: *'Hoc Lapide Hydrunti Cives Sua Guttura Turcis Truncanda Ab Christi Deposuere Fidem, MCDLXXX'* is engraved on it – this stone is where the Hydruntines were beheaded for declaring their belief in Christ, 1480. Some chronicles talk about boilings alive, trepanning, disembowelling, roasting, lynching, strangling, sawing in half and bodies being burst open by water pumps. The cleansing was followed almost immediately by numerous miracles – headless trunks were seen walking about, severed heads continued to praise God, and voices from heaven were heard chanting *'Con Gioia Abbiamo Visto/Madre Maria E Gesu Cristo'*. One account says that the Turkish executioner was so overcome by the people's faith that he turned Christian on the spot and was promptly beheaded by his understudy. Not only did the blood run into the sea, but the corpses lay on the ground for a year without rotting, and neither bird nor beast would go near them.

This all happened at the highest point in Otranto, where there was once a temple to Minerva but there is now a church of St Francis, with plaques on the wall commemorating the 800 martyrs. Among them are Matthew of Capua, Theodor the German, Girolomo of Spain, Alberico the Sicilian and Alfonzo of the mountains. And, if you're ghoulish, you can open some glass-fronted cupboards in a side chapel in the cathedral and look at the skeletons: 500 of their skulls are ranged on shelves. The rest are in Naples in the church of Santa Caterina a Formello, taken there by King Alfonso of Aragon, after his army had driven the Turks out of Italy. It has even been reported that some martyrs' bones are in Venice, Tivoli and Spain.

As Aldo was leading me up the hill to see where it had all happened, we passed a railed enclosure protecting a single lonely pillar. It was about six feet high and nine inches in diameter. 'What's that?' I asked.

'Oh, they impaled them on that,' he replied.
'Who?'
'The martyrs.'
'What do you mean? How?'
'Well, into their bottoms and out of their mouths.'
'Don't be silly. It's too big. You said they were beheaded.'
'Oh, yes. They were beheaded afterwards,' he said.

FOUR

Otranto II

It's leap-out-and-kiss-baby time. Warm evenings bring it on, when the sun has gone, dust settled, sweat dried, and the streets flow with rivers of strolling people fresh from their pupae of afternoon sleep to parade in slow motion on newly laundered wings. They're all displaying their spick-and-span offspring.

Beyond them are palm trees, fronds bent in the half-dark lamp glow, where murmurs rise and men at barrows with hissing gas lights sell nuts or crêpes or melon slices as the throng of bodies wanders by – an uncertain tide always on the turn; pausing, passing, waiting, swinging round, unstable; languor in motion; and the prams are halted every yard for a kiss and hug. Vast mouths swoop down to smirch on tiny infants – peck, nip and nuzzle with croons of love; bodies dart over roads for a hungry buss; some are held in the air for adoration; wide eyes shine with saturation and surprise; loud cuddles stem the tidal flow; giant heads bounce low in dips and stoops. Bill, bill . . . coo, coo . . . and yum-yum, snuffle, kiss . . .

Bambino is king. He seems to expect it and so does she: triumphs of babydom – gurgling, ogling, chuckling goo-goo, smile after liquid smile, toe-kick, giggle, imperial wave, beady rolling eye – every amorous inch. Adore me, you rabble; bring frankincense, myrrh and lollipops. Is this a mass Magi adoration of the infant Christ – or a love of lost innocence? Is it a heartstring we no longer pluck? Proud father has a reborn self, and mother has a toy to spoil. The cradle controls the world and tiny-tot bedlam reigns at last. In five years they'll cause havoc in restaurants, rush in crowds under busy feet, elbow past you in shops, fight you off buses, barge you out of doorways, push you off pavements, put their tongues out and kick you when thwarted. And this is the origin; the infant epicentre; the witching hour of *bambino*-beatification.

It's evening and I'm sitting on Mario's terrace beside the sea, smugly watching it. Mario cooks the best fish in Otranto; you can watch it sizzle straight out of the sea while his pale wine ends the day's dryness. It also liquefies vision. Mario has two outrageous daughters who are pocket-sized versions of the priest's daughters of Babylon. They are mini-sirens and keep filling my glass up, and should be pickled until they're old enough. They have vibrating hips, squirm like hooked maggots and have bedroom eyes. But sparrow-tits are quite the rage in Italy. Half a boob and you're winked at; three-quarters and you're a sandwich in a rush-hour bus with a well-pinched bum. These two can't help it; it's an extension of baby-art learned in the pram, and it is in their blood. They semaphore with their hips as if Satan was on fire between them, but in twenty years they'll have bodies like shirehorses and legs like traffic bollards. It's their *carpe diem*. They're Juliets waiting on the wings of the night; they're deliberately delinquent, Delores Hazes. A glow-worm star starts to wink as the blue sky darkens. Gather ye rosebuds, it says, there's world enough and time . . .

Then a loathsome pygmy example of infant horror arrived at the next table, plus adoring mother.

'Do you want an ice-cream?'

'Yes.'

'Stop swinging your legs then, sit still.'

'I'm not.'

'Yes, you are, so do what you're told. Stop it.'

'I wasn't.'

'Do you want that ice-cream?'

'Chocolate.'

'Stop it, I said.'

'Why?'
'You're kicking the table.'
'No, I'm not.'
'Do what I tell you. You won't have an ice-cream.'
'Stupid [under his breath]. Don't want one.'
'You said you did.'
'Didn't.'
'You won't get one if you kick. Sit up.'
'Cretin [under his breath, but louder].'
'Do you want me to hit you?'
'No.' He slides off his chair. 'You can't.'
'Where are you going?'
'*Toiletta*.'
'Come here.'
'Why?'
She grabs at him. He ducks and puts his tongue out.
'You can't, so there.'
'Do you want that ice-cream?'
He shrugs.
'Idiot [quite audible].'
'Peppino, I'm going to slap you.'
She gets up. He cowers away, arm shielding his head.
'Can't.'
'You're frightened.'
'Not of you . . .'

He gives a gargoyle grimace from under his arm, tongue wriggling, then sees too late the chairs barring his escape and squeals as she grabs him. He kicks her, bites her arm, stamps and whimpers. She raises a hand to smite him as he cowers against her, but it slows as it starts to descend. It pauses and stops. It reaches around him in an armful of monstrous motherly hug, and all subsides into love and cuddles.

If he'd been mine, I'd have kicked his teeth in, even though he was only six.

'*Sciammune vagnone*,' hisses shrimp-siren Erica as they

finally leave and she wipes the table, which is Hydruntine for 'bugger off'. This probably explains why the Italophile and philologist Gerhardt Rohlfs' Salentine–Italian diction-ary extends to three volumes. Wine is *mieru*, good evening *navespera*, pocket *poshia*, let's go *shimmo*, cheese *casu* and girl *vagnona*. More mongrel evidence. Erica says she can write it as well: '*Caru Francu. Ieu te aiu mutu bene e tie? Tie me monchi motu vaiu nu bacu. Quannu tie vieu u core meu sarte e face lu fessa. Dum ussi me pu pe culu...*'

Which I suspect to be somewhat indelicate for a girl of twelve, but if I were Franco I would get over here as quickly as possible, or he'll get his arse kicked.

Sounds like these words will be dead in a hundred years. There are already about twenty European languages dying. Maltese won't last long, nor will Gaelic or Catalan, and you won't find many Sardinians speaking Sard or Corsicans speaking Corse. Yankee screen-speak will wipe everything out and we will mutate into linguistic dough and become talking Coca-Cola cans. Roman mothers want 'baby-seeters', computer men say '*clic sul mouse*' and Italian newspapers have 'stress', 'business', 'fitness', 'racket', 'kill-er', 'gangster' and 'sexy' jumping off the pages like flying zits. As Wilfred Thesiger, the great traveller, said – televi-sion has replaced the tribal bard. The only hope is for us all to return to Latin; the Vatican is already trying to keep up. A one-night stand is *lascivia brevis* and a page-three girl is *exterioris pagina puella*.

This is Marvel madness. Sitting in sunshine on a mount of olives outside Otranto while Aldo lies on a dolmen sucking figs. I'm in an endless green ocean, floating on thoughts and shades; a pea-green soup mixed with waves of malachite, jade and lime. The treetops coagulate in a hundred mix-tures; a patchwork disappearing into skies, horizons, dim misty seas of sage, spruce, Lincoln green, bilious pea and Joyce's snot; a grease-green Deucalian flood of olive tops.

They're not happy underneath. Their trunks are wizened; they knot and twist in the agony of age, with rough bark tight as a frozen scrotum. Black branches dip in mourning with thin, clawing fingertips. Some are like spider-legs or witch-talons, and some like corpse-hair waving in the wind.

Aldo's dolmen is a grave. It's prehistory. An enormous slab of granite supported by two upright granite pedestals. Once there was a body in the space beneath and it was covered with earth; probably the body of a king or chief; and once these things were all over Puglia. They were all over the world as well, and probably still are: France, Spain, Ireland, Portugal. Now they're in the way here – anachronisms – and so farmers knock them down. There used to be menhirs as well, granite totem poles as tall as trees that may have marked graves or battlefields; there aren't many of them left. Tractors topple them and drag them away. Bring out your Messapian dead.

Unhistorical Aldo is supine and has juice running down his chin and neck from an Indian fig plucked off a cactus. It is purple and looks like a monstrous and bloated tick, but Aldo is happy. To him a fig is not just a fig. He has dirty thoughts and dreams it is a maiden's postern; which is precisely why it's called a fig.

Aldo's aunt worries me. I had assumed a certain poverty, with her scratching chickens and two goats around the house, plus Albanian Adonis. But she owns another farm a few miles away that her brothers look after. It is called Nicola di Casole. Once upon a time there was a huge and famous monastery near Otranto founded by the Basilians in the tenth century, a hundred years before William was disembarking at Hastings; it was called San Nicola di Casole and was destroyed by the Turks in 1480. She didn't know that.

We drove down a shadowy avenue of needlepoint cypresses still as sentries, and under a square archway into a yard of bright pandemonium full of fleeing children dressed in dust, barking dogs, chickens bolting through scattering straw, and cats vanishing at speed behind ploughs and tractors. It was obvious the Turks had never intended God to return; they had left only scraps of wall for someone to lean a few bricks against and start a new life. It must have been more an abbey than a monastery – even a cathedral. Bales of straw rose in piles under domed ceilings, stone gables leaned into space, a buttress protruded from breeze-blocks, ribbed columns bulged out of walls and cracked cupolas sheltered flapping doves. Against them the farm seemed puny, something ordinary and insignificant, a trifle among vaultings, groins and chopped mullions. Tractors were parked among stumps of pillars and a goal had been chalked over a bricked-up arch. Another remnant of holy madness; faith dismembered and blown away; not even memories to be chafed at by the yellow and burning sun.

She wasn't interested, in spite of my invention and poetic unlicence. I told her it must have been like St Peter's – even bigger – and that there were saints here, bishops, perhaps a pope or two, and even monks who wrote the Bible. Her eyes stayed stony. Later on I asked the priest about it, the one who'd caught us in the cathedral, and I think his hyperboles outdid mine, on scribes turning Homer into Latin and lettering bits of the Gospels onto parchment in blue and gold. He said there had been a copy of the *Iliad* in the monastery library and an epic poem on the rape of Helen and that they'd studied Aristotle's 'Sophisms'. He didn't know it was a farm now, but said that it was once a great centre of pilgrimage and had been a resting place for crusaders. One day I will look it up.

Behind the main farm buildings there was a long shed built of breeze-blocks and there were thirty-six tail-flapping Friesians in it being electrically milked. In another building there were two gleaming Fordson tractors. I couldn't help wondering if Brussels had had an input, or perhaps they'd

come across a cache of gold chalices or crucifixes studded
with gems that the monks had buried before fleeing. I
looked over a wall at a pen full of large, hairy goats, all
horned like Old Nick and fiercely bearded. They stamped
impatiently and had gold-green gloating eyes that seemed
fixed on memories of ancestral orgies. Over another wall an
infestation of pigs wallowed in glorious mud, snuffling and
churning like pink hippo-skins, each waving roseate flanks
and whirling its tail as if it was an odalisque swooning on a
swan's-down bed.

It was a mystery; old wine, new bottles; half-creation,
half-corpse; and my landlady owns the bones.

I think I've seen him. A short man trying to hop himself
sideways into a Fiat 500 beside a Hiroshima-bright blonde.
He seemed to have a leg problem and had to pull it in. In
that space it won't be his only problem. Having it off in cars
is quite a common occupation in Italy; it nearly happened
to me once on a drive back to Rome from Frascati, but my
horrendous swerve of surprise across two lanes put an end
to it. There are car parks nowadays – I know the one in
Naples – almost specifically for this purpose; they even
have wardens to allocate time and space and to keep away
peeping Toms. They get quite busy at weekends; there are
often queues. I've heard that one impatient driver let his
foot slip off the clutch, rammed the car in front and caused
an unwanted pregnancy. I don't think cars make for
comfortable or patient and protracted passion – inflamed
effervescence perhaps. But I suppose if you've been looking
forward to it since Mass, then a conflagration in a car park is
better than nothing.

It's the fault of the parents, particularly the mothers.
They're jealous. They keep their young living with them
until their libidos must be bursting. Their houses aren't
built for it anyway, and apartment blocks have nosy porters.
Bedrooms have such paper-thin walls that they sound like

echo-chambers, neighbours are notoriously inquisitive, and
windows have to be left open to avoid heatstroke. So the
only reasonable alternative to the motor car is *coitus al
fresco*, which in a country as large as Italy needn't be
difficult – apart from the risks of sand, pine needles and a
variety of inquisitive insects.

Aldo has taken me fishing because he thinks he is a
fisherman, which he isn't. He isn't really a success at
anything: marriage, restaurants, bars, money. We started off
in a boat, me rowing and him trying to snorkel, splashing
about at random and his body looking like an egg-yolk burst
in water; ungovernable bits trailing off everywhere. He
didn't get anything. Then he said he knew where a wreck
was, so things began to get serious, and he commandeered
two fishermen he knew who had an outboard motor and
yards of rope.

I sat in the scorching sun, with the sea going up and
down, in a trying-not-to-be-seasick motion; also feeling
guilty because this is the kind of thing you can get arrested
for – watery tomb-robbing – while the three of them kept
disappearing somewhere underneath, occasionally popping
up for breath. They wanted more rope, they said, as they
were going to bring something up, and would I mind pulling
when they signalled. It was totally impossible; they'd
obviously tied the rope to the sea-bed. Then they all
clambered aboard excitedly and the four of us started
heaving at something, which almost tipped the boat over as
it started to move. I hoped it was going to be another Riace
bronze, as recently they've been finding lots of pieces of
bronze statues in the sea near Brindisi, but it wasn't; as it
neared the surface it looked like a giant sea-slug. It was so
heavy and unwieldy we couldn't get it on board, but tied it
to the side and limped back to base lopsided. It turned out
to be part of an old cannon, and after a lot of de-scaling and

de-coking it said on the top that it had something to do with
EREDI DE BERNARDI N COLLETA in 1556.

Poor Aldo is in trouble. It is evening and I ought to leave
soon, so he is giving me supper in his small, *al fresco*
restaurant down some steps behind the bar, and we're
sitting at a table under a canopy of orange and lemon
branches inextricably twined, like overcooked spaghetti.
There are fireflies sparking among the sag of fruit, and
insects crawling through the leaves before dropping into my
soup.

Natasha, the only waitress (under age, I suspect), is
slithering between tables looking worried and delivering
wrong orders to wrong tables. Aldo explains she is a trainee,
but I think his interest could be in her wobbling figure and
complete absence of brain. When I asked her yesterday what
her pay was she had no idea. The customers don't mind
getting the wrong dinners; more chance to enjoy her liquid
smile of apologetic panic and more time to admire her waist
and nubile bottom. Mrs Aldo is on the steps surveying
possible wealth and Aldo is beside me, glum and frustrated.
He is thinking about pussy-power.

'*Disponibile*,' he mutters.

'Available? . . . Who? Where?'

'Women.'

'Where?'

'Everywhere.'

'What? I can't see them.' (The English usually can't.)

'It's obvious.'

'What is?'

'Stroking their hair . . . thinking about it.'

'Where? How do you know?'

'See them every day. Body language. Sitting on the
pavement having coffee. Swinging their legs. Wanting it.'

'Not true.'

'Dying for it. Husbands are off fucking someone else . . . *disponibile.*'

He sighs gloomily and slices a lump of cheese from a block as Natasha passes, then munches it. Aldo's wine is 17 per cent proof and nearly black and it works like a medium-paced anaesthetic, so I drink a pint of it to dilute my bowl of *pasta con pecora* spiced with hot peppers. This is followed by sliced peaches warmed in more wine, and Mrs Aldo begins to dim in the distance, out-of-focus, and waves of sound from a tinkling pianist blur. They blur conversation and diners' bodies swim among tables, and comatose satisfaction and warm otherworldliness descend like sleep. I shall leave in the morning.

I'm sure I didn't see it – not in this dreamy contentment – but a man climbed over the restaurant wall . . . nonsense . . . it doesn't matter . . . probably can't pay . . . Natasha's cat-walking somewhere at a trot . . . and customers are standing up . . . now what? . . . Natasha beside us, agitating her hips . . .

'They won't pay,' she squeals.

'Oh,' says Aldo.

'They say put it on Antonio's account,' she wails.

'Oh,' repeats Aldo . . . And there are new bulky customers coming in . . . they've got big pockets . . . they're looking for something . . .

Mrs Aldo skitters up. 'Aldo,' she squeaks, 'they're animals – *bestie* – get them out.'

'Who?' says Aldo.

'Them,' she squeaks again, 'they're here.'

'Where?' asks Aldo dreamily.

'Here,' she almost screams, 'they want Antonio.'

'He's not here,' says Aldo, still in his chair.

Mrs Aldo jumps an octave. 'They've got guns, they want to kill him . . .'

Christ! This isn't happening. But up Aldo gets, shouting 'Shut . . . shut.' And me as well, standing in an empty restaurant – only a darting chef-shape running out through a gate and Natasha following, and Mrs Aldo flitting like a frightened moth as the lights go out. Aldo starts pulling me through the gate among muttering voices: run . . . go this way . . . be careful . . . quickly . . . go home . . . panic-stricken sibilants and racing footsteps . . . *ciao* . . . *ciao* . . . disappearing into darkness . . .

Aldo drags me at a run through midnight Otranto, soot-black silent streets; fear is a very quick way to get undrunk. At a last-gasp bar he chokes a brandy down. 'Tonino?' he asks, but the man shakes his head with eyes that won't look.

'Oh-oh, Antonio, he's gone away . . .'

We can hear our echoes, we pant down alleys, round tower walls and jump at cat-shadows. Then we sit on a rock by the dark, sleeping sea and Aldo shivers as it laps at our feet.

'They're bastards.'

'Who?'

'They think I pay him.'

'Who? Why?'

'Him. For protection.'

'Antonio?'

'He's just a friend . . .'

'Who does?'

'Those others . . . I don't.'

'What's the problem then?'

'He's just a friend . . . I give him a meal sometimes, a drink.'

'Who are they?'

'They're from Poggiardo . . . He's from Maglie . . . They don't like him.'

'Tell the police then.'

'Get my car smashed in, kids done over at school, staff beaten up?'

'Would they?'

'He could wipe them out if he wanted – he's got big friends in Maglie and they're powerful. I only give him a meal.'

Poor Aldo! His kindness will kill him. Generosity and humanity are not virtues in Italy; they're weaknesses. The old artist in Brindisi said they hated each other, and they really do. The bully rules in Puglia. You need a gun more than God here to protect you from your friends.

FIVE

Salento

Aldo's moped takes after its owner; it needs to be appreciated, all sweetness and light until things go wrong. It is fast on the downs, reluctant on the ups and bewildered on corners. There are plenty on the way to Finibus Terrae, Land's End – a contortion of elaborate twists, with the sea growling on one side and red limbs of parched land on the other, corrugated and erratic; furrowed crags and dark rock masses, all buffeted by wind and splashed with bent-over trees. The road snaked along the coastline, one minute towering above a mile-down sea that crashed with hunger and flailed white tails, the next minute beside it, damp with sand and spray. It bumped and dipped and I was saddle-sore.

Uggiano La Chiesa made me jump. Out of desolate scrub straight into tarmac bursting with town life: car horns, shops, barrows in the road, dogs, bent pedestrians, potholes, swerves and dashing cats. Then a head-on church right in the face. Smack! It jumped out of nowhere, huge and yellow and festooned in sunny drips. The old man watching sucked his pipe. 'They couldn't write,' he said, 'but they knew how to build.'

It was a triumphant square, all gold and bold, with crusts of carved riches oozing down every inch; a holy house in court dress. Made in Spain. There were bobbles, sconces, crests and capitals; funicle wisps and fascia saddles and a rash of stone pimples. Every village has one. A bubble-bath of pop-eyed baroque stands at the centre, where sandstone weeps crusted tears of exuberance, saints teeter for joy on impossible pinnacles and rose windows erupt like sunbursts. It's sacred scrambled egg with its portals coiffed, crimped or curled and walls of filigree, rhomboid or scalloped, pulsating in the sun. The outer form of inner space, someone called it.

Then, Badisco. A few houses teetering round a tiny inlet where Aeneas is said to have landed after escaping from Troy, but there are no white horses and no temple to Minerva on a hill. Nothing; only wind and trees on a slope with their backs turned. But Aeneas, like St Paul, landed everywhere in Italy except Genoa and Venice.

It is older than Aeneas, anyway. There are miles of prehistoric caves under Badisco full of wall paintings. Professor Graziosi from Florence University said it was the most spectacular late-prehistoric site in Europe. A fisherman thought I'd come to open the archaeology park.

'What park?' I asked.

'The one they promised when they found the caves,' he answered. 'They said there'd be lots of tourists, like that place in France.' Then he blinked sadly in the sun, his brown face creased as olive bark.

The caves were found by some speleologists from Maglie in the 1970s. It was an accident; they were scuba-diving. They found an underground warren that stretched for miles and had tools, pottery and bones in it, and yards of wall paintings. 'Come on, I'll show you,' the fisherman said. We went in by torchlight, bending and then upright, dampness touching us, through puddles and caverns full of echoing drips, past cathedrals and chimneys. Then the walls came, with splashes of designs on them in red and black. Prehistoric pop-art. Lots of blobs, lines, squiggles, dots, dashes and early shapes; a panorama of stickmen with bows and arrows; stick beasts with horns; stick herds of sheep and goats; sun blobs and moon blobs with circles and dots; walls of graffiti weirdness and a sheet of black fish-shapes, animals, crosses, genitals, fantasies, things unknown. An aboriginal art gallery.

Puglia is an appendix of land built on holes; caves everywhere; a very old warren that no one knows about; its bowels hide a past of grunting half-men. There's a cave at Romanelli with a carving on the wall that could be Apis, the giant bull; at San Caesarea there are pictures of lions, leopards, bears, wolves and a hairy horse. The caves at Parabita are called Grotta Veneri because fat mother-figures are found clutching swollen bellies; they've even found hippopotamus bones . . .

'It should be an archaeology park,' he said, in daylight.

'Yes . . .' I agreed.

'Nah, but it won't be. Not with that lot. They'll chop the pictures off and sell them to Germany. The Americans should have stayed after the war.'

You can't argue with southern despair; it's ancient and irreversible. I didn't know what to say, looking at his sad old face, cracked by the elements. They've already got the Mafia, McDonald's and atrociously dubbed Hollywood bin-ends. What else do they want?

The road gets worse after Badisco; pointless curves and serpentine bends where invisible winds whistle. They're silent and sudden and they hit like a punch. '*Caduta massi*' signs suggest imminent rock-falls, and watch towers teeter on ledges as if ready to overbalance; there are supposed to be more than 300 along the coast; then ridges, scarps, tumbling stone walls, and trees huddled like cowards. Sometimes vine-strewn meadows slip down to the sea and there are pockets of unmapped sandy inlets. Now and then I pass secret places; half-hidden gateways that slide down to private villas, invisible behind roses and bougainvillea, where boats bob on the water; homes of rich exclusives.

They don't have planning regulations in Puglia. I'm not sure they have any regulations at all, Italians tending to consider most restrictions as invasions of personal liberty. You build a house down here and, if you can be bothered, you ask for permission afterwards. Should any problems arise, you either wait for the next Building Amnesty to come round, the Condono Edilizio, or you walk into the local *comune* with a *bustarella* and confess, 'Father, I have sinned and built a mansion of many rooms without permission.'

'Five Hail Mary's, son,' comes the answer, 'and twenty million in cash.'

At last I swept down a curve into Capo di Leuca and wished I hadn't. There was a banner strung across the road saying 'Welcome to Radio Venus'. Everything else was rusty brown; the end-piece of Puglia was a barren tongue of rough earth stuck a mile out into the sea, broken only by a line of six white holiday bungalows that looked like lavatories. It was unpeopled desolation. So much for 'the lovely and lonely shore of Leuca' where a gleaming white temple to Minerva once stood: a beacon of safety and welcome for Greek sailors venturing westwards. Now, her role has been taken over by ubiquitous Mary, and my booklet says that in spite of her shrine having been destroyed countless times by the Turks, if I pray at her feet I am already halfway up the ladder to heaven. The notion of Jacob's ladder being stuck on this promontory is not attractive. Far from showing any celebration of safety and welcome, Mary's expression is one of undisguised lachrymose woe, as if wishing she were somewhere else.

The Cape is being developed. Archaeologists and historians wage useless war against speculative builders and officials who have plans for settlements. They headline their articles 'State Vandalism' and 'How to Bulldoze History'. But nobody in authority is interested. Like the Merchant of Prato, who dedicated his diaries and accounts to God and to Profit at the same time, they'd rather see a thriving development here than investigate a Bronze Age settlement or the bay where Cicero landed. So paper bags waft in the wind, old cans glint in the sun and nobody cares that there are more than 100 Messapian inscriptions in the caves; or that Trojans fled here; or that Hercules wrestled with giants. It's all unimportant – and that Idomoneus sacrificed 100 white bulls while a choir of virgins with scented hair sang praises to Jupiter. The sound now is of barracking vendors round the sanctuary selling mini-Marys in plastic, and a thin, sopranoish wail of piped music seeps out of the sanctuary as if a nest of nuns was being pleasured inside.

I've arrived by accident in Copertino, the home of St Joseph, Norman Douglas' 'flying monk', and it looks as if he is taking off again. There's an enormous festival going on; lots of people, noisy bands and arc lights everywhere. I didn't know where I was till I got here, because Puglian roads can be misleading. They may be as straight as the strands of a cobweb, but they never end up where you expect. Villages supposedly on your right emerge on the left, and what few signposts there are point forward to where you've just been or behind to where you are going. Without meaning to do so, I drove straight into a crowded and *festa*-happy Copertino.

For those who have never heard of Joseph the Flying Monk and wish to know something about him, I suggest Norman Douglas' *Old Calabria* (pages 71–6 in the 1915 first edition). A less inspired account can be found in H. V. Morton's *A Traveller in South Italy*.

One can't travel far here without thinking about Douglas and the best book ever written on the south of Italy. *Old Calabria* is a masterpiece. But as Harold Acton said, he always had to have some 'affair of the heart' going on as inspiration for his writing, and this time it was twelve-year-old Eric Wolton, a London 'pick up'. The result of that attachment is a voluminous work of adventure and observation, great erudition, copious research and often vicious comment, as Douglas rambles without system through the south, and through history, myth, rumour and reality, be it Turkish invasions, local wine, peasant costumes, brigands, werewolves, cures for malaria, saints, demons, fleas, musical instruments and even Milton. Sometimes the book spins out of control as he shoots off at tangents to discuss classical authors or the origin of dialects. No foreigner knew the south of Italy as well as he did or has written such a scholarly and all-embracing book about it, yet it is by no means a favourite with Italians. He makes them feel guilty because he knows more about their country than they do, and they suspect him of piss-taking.

Douglas wasn't always a favourite among the English, either. Conrad dropped him on account of his affairs with juveniles, some people wouldn't allow him in their houses, and he could be irascible enough to throw a meal out of a window if he didn't like it. Yet he could also give generously to the people of Reggio after the 1908 earthquake that, together with Messina, killed 90,000 people. He was a loved and hated person; adored by friends and detested by enemies. He liked to shock and to provoke, and he may have pursued most of the youth of Capri in his time, but he is still the only Englishman to have been granted citizenship of the island.

In spite of some hints of gentle mockery in the book, particularly of Italian officialdom, there is a constant undercurrent of affection and enjoyment. He obviously loved the south in spite of all its discomforts. Yet there have to be contradictions. Pino Orioli, the Florentine book dealer and publisher, who was with him in the south, says that Douglas would often swear at the filthy food, the unbearable accommodation and the pestilential bugs. He even called southerners 'a pack of ferocious idiots'. But as Jonathan Keates writes, travellers are 'poseurs' and 'all travel narrative traditionally embraces the art of lying', so Douglas is no exception.

He certainly enjoyed discovering the simple peasant of old Copertino who was so remarkable that he could not only fly, but could talk to sheep, cure them of rabies and reanimate them when struck by monstrous hailstones. As a minor Franciscan brother (he was too mentally retarded to be a major one), Joseph would welcome flocks of them into church to join in services – he saying '*Sancta Maria*' and they answering after their manner 'Bah'. He was also a thought-reader, knew people's sins before they confessed them to him and, with the nose of a Labrador, could sniff out evil intentions. All this, and more, can be found in Domenico Bernino's *Vita del Bea Padre Fr. Giuseppe Da Copertino di Minori Conventuali* (Rome 1722); and the bare details are in a pamphlet that a priest has just thrust at me.

Giuseppe Maria Desa was born on 17 June in 1603 – 'In a stable, like Christ and St Francis, a sure sign of an extraordinary future'. This overlooks the fact that any peasant at that time would have been glad to bed down among his beasts for warmth and safety. The holy birthplace is now a two-storey whitewashed building clad in fairy lights. 'This vacant and unintelligent child,' continues the pamphlet, 'had to flee into a chapel to escape a mob chasing him because his father owed them money.' It was then that the first miracle occurred. He was 'suspended in air', described as 'an ecstasy', not mentioning the reaction of the onlookers. From then on there was no controlling him. Giuseppe began to fly through the air at will and would even grab friends by the hair and pull them up with him. When it was found he could also summon up thunderstorms, cure fevers and smell out people's 'most hidden secrets', his fame spread so rapidly that the Church decided to investigate him for 'false sanctity'. In 1639 Pope Urban VIII witnessed his flying powers and was impressed enough to absolve him of 'simulated holiness' and as Giuseppe was a minor Franciscan, the Pope sent him to Assisi. This was not a success, as his frequent levitations so distressed the inhabitants that they insisted he should be banished, particularly as at one performance the wife of the Spanish Ambassador fainted. He was sent away to the isolated monastery of San Lazzaro in Pietrarossa, then moved on to a deserted hermitage in Fossombrone. In 1657, the pamphlet records, he was 'pardoned' by Pope Alexander VII (without saying what for) and was then sent for 'rehabilitation' to the Franciscans at Orsino, where he died in 1661.

When St Joseph was finally beatified in 1767 it caused riots in the neighbourhood of Copertino as every hamlet, parish, brotherhood, guild and faction wanted a share of his relics. They even fought to the death for them. Those that are left lie in a small vestibule inside the church here; among them his hair shirt, iron girdle, middle finger, some bones, two hand-written letters dated 1650, and a stole given to him by the Princess of Savoy after she'd seen him fly.The crowd is almost impenetrable outside the church, and worse inside. There is a compress of swaying and chanting bodies so tightly packed that you couldn't slip a Garibaldi biscuit between them. An all-human solid of pious intoxicants is rocking, swaying, muttering, mumbling, pushing, praying and making hopeless efforts to cross themselves. What sinful odours Joseph might have sniffed here I hate to think, but they're most thankfully being neutralised by a priest and two acolytes waving incense burners like metronomes in a panic.

It is fresher outside and Copertino's carnival is under way; a much-changed congregation is now filling the narrow alleys, welcoming release and a chance to sin again, hearing the whispers of ancient paganism – *veteris paganismi vestigia*. A pell-mell crowd of the confessed, confused, shriven and satisfied surge towards the thousand festive lights performing their exultant requiem to their airborne saint. All the streets are alive and multicoloured; each canopied by sprung arches of gleaming fairy lights twinkling into endless tunnels of colour. Bright dome-shapes hover, and crescents, spirals, pillars and towers turn night into brilliant rainbow day. Arcades of stars are flare-lit warrens that filter to distant peacock points, as the shadows of heads float past in muttering armies. The lights are as bright as a second sun and sweep darkness away from St Joseph's night.

Tucked under them in wrapped-up cloaks are pin-thin Africans, moon-eyed at midnight, all dressed as tribal chiefs with flash-bulb teeth. They are selling purses, corkscrews, raffia mats, watches and penknives laid out on rugs; fish tanks to take home, or balloons or canaries or top-of-the-pops . . . or splintered coconut and hot donkey sausages. Italian festivals are like an exuberant contagion of madness breaking out. It is post-piety fun-time in Copertino, so go forth and multiply. Glorify, satisfy and liquefy; eat, drink, mumble and push; congregate, luxuriate; slide down the celestial chute into Hedon and fill St Joseph's money-box. The oracles and sybils were big business too.

I needed to eat; I pushed my way through oozing, earth-clinging crowds as thick as mulligatawny mud; *festa*-expectant bodies meshed into impenetrable slow-motion. Ten-abreast coagulants, they turned back to go where they had come from and made arm-locked barricades, wandering in a dazed euphoria, grunting emulsive mumbles, a glue of happiness-humans; jelly people; breaking only to watch a pop group twanging in a square under a dome of flashing bulbs; all twitching themselves at odd angles for an ocean of hypnotised eyes.

I found a bedlam-restaurant with wooden wine-soaked tables under the stars, invaded by a pizza-mad crowd driven by hunger and happiness. All joyous jostles and shouts; strewn-out bodies, lolling, flagons in the air, giving raucous airborne orders with tummies in turmoil. Fully fat men with hairy shirts open and arms awash, giving belly-slaps and grins among rivers of wormcast kids. Gargantuans of gluttony. Above the hunger-howls, fireworks popped orange balls into the sky, cascading tears of happiness because it was feeding time in Giuseppe's bear-garden; so we all sit, shove, grab, nod, wave, smile, bump and yawn.

Then finally we stuffed ourselves, gulped at yellow wine and crossed eyes gently in the half-dark delirium of *pranzo* for the populus.

Nothing stays still. Excited children with tinkling voices and in carnival dresses scud round the tables like a liner's wash. They bubble in races, then disappear; they phosphoresce into darkness. Lost parents lunge; dog-sniffs tickle and laughter peals; frantic girls dart with high-held platters of festival food; jugs, bottles and clods of bread the size of rocks. At a nearby table friends arrive; they are toasted, bear-hugged and kissed, with jubilant glasses waved to the sky and welcomes bawled. Tonight we're all Lucullan lookalikes; God's gourmets sating our senses; we're blown as bladders and filled to fart-point. Thanks to Joseph, we're pan-happy and piously pissed.

Golden flares floated past on parachutes; they honoured all celestial flights; exploding angels. They hovered like hawks over upturned bright-eyed infants and the spawn-crawl of children vibrating round my legs in mini-merriment. Midnight went and the day was dying. Somewhere above us St Joseph's ghost was flighting homewards across the sky with fireworks to light his path. I could almost see him. I gave him a drunken wave. God bless you, my man . . . and thanks for the party.

I have reached Galatina somehow and seen a play. Galatina is not to be confused with nearby Galatone, which is similarly old and yellow and is the birthplace of Galateo, Puglia's most famous historian and scholar. He was born in 1444 and, as well as writing a history of the area, he was one of the first to describe and try to explain the *fata Morgana* – the mirage that sometimes occurs here, but more often at Reggio in Calabria.

These optical illusions happen occasionally when the conditions are right. Changes of heat can affect the density of air so that the light is refracted enough to produce an hallucination. Castles can appear among the clouds, fleets of ships approach, armies of soldiers are seen. Once, it is said, this kind of apparition sent a Turkish navy hurrying for home. Douglas called these unearthly visions 'diaphanous as a veil of gauze'.

The play was called *Arcobaleno – The Rainbow –* and was written by a doctor friend of the artist in Brindisi. It was Virgil, Theocritus and conservation mixed: the tale of an innocent visitor to an idyllic farming community who turned out to be a property developer in disguise. Described as 'city-slicker' in the cast list, his devious schemes of financial and physical seduction in fields, orchards, kitchens and bedrooms were finally foiled after various romps and near-misses, until in Act III he disappeared through a smoky hole in the floorboards to join Faust and Don Giovanni. This victory of pastures old over the urban sprawl drew thunderous applause and I lost count of the curtain calls.

The good doctor had skilfully woven local lore, personalities, places and customs into it, also chases, fights, frolics and songs. While shepherds lamented, housewives threw saucepans; as money changed hands, couples made bumpkin love. There were harvest dances, milkmaids lullabying sleepy goats, and plenty of impromptu vocal repartee in impertinent *stornelli*. 'What do you girls do in the fields all day? You go out thin and come back fat.' To which the girls answered, 'Don't come to bed tonight, you old fool; just pass your prick up.' Such unequivocal instructions didn't worry the children present – under-age Puglians have known from birth that silk purses are only sows' ears in disguise.

The audience participated vigorously throughout; abuse, encouragement and delight were shouted in turn, their uninhibited involvement inspiring the local cast to skyscraping thespian heights, whether it was Ettrick Shepherd, Buster Keaton on bedsprings, or woolly mutton. There must have been 500 extras in the cast that night, though as Orson Welles said, 'They're all born actors; it's only the bad ones that go on the stage.'

Afterwards, the doctor told me that the play he is working on for next year is the life story of Galatina's saint. Called Margaret, she denied the Turkish commander the full hospitality rights he expected when his forces captured the town in 1480. One encouragement he used was to have her tipped into a cauldron of boiling water, but this simply sprouted a bed of lilies and tipped her out again. In the end he had her decapitated, but when her head was brought in on a silver salver and paraded in front of him, it went on praising Jesus as if nothing had happened.

There is a myth that St Paul came to Galatina, having been blown ashore nearby on his journey from Malta. As Galatina was infested by a plague of tarantulas at the time, in return for the hospitality he received, he blessed a well in his host's garden with anti-toxin powers. A sip of its waters, or even a touch, could cure palsy, epilepsy, chorea and rabies. Such was the daily congregation of the sick and afflicted that in 1793 the church asked the landowner, Signor Nicola Vignola, for permission to consecrate it, thus being able to convince the hydra-headed multitude that any cures came from God.

The priest I met wasn't anxious to talk about the possibility of simple well-water having such power.

'Um, doubtful,' he said, 'it was their faith, really . . . Belief can perform miracles.'

'Ah, but there were pilgrimages, records of people being cured.'

'They were simple people. Ignorant. They persuaded themselves they were better, and they were paid by the well-owner. Only God performs miracles.'

'What about the dances round St Paul's statue?'

'Why not?' he smiled. 'Celebrations. Thanking him,

thanking God. People dance when they're happy – giving thanks.'

I was getting curious. 'Do they dance now?'

'You mean today? No. Newspaper stories about crazy women? Dancing in church? No, it's a holiday, the feast of St Paul, they dance in the streets . . .'

'Not in church then?'

'Well . . .' and he laughed uncertainly. 'It's a festival, the churches are open, people come in from the villages outside, simple countrywomen – perhaps one or two of them, they do it for God . . .' and he crossed himself.

The old antics of *tarantismo* – in Galatina, the frantic dance to exorcise the spider's poison – are not a matter the church enjoys discussing; such archaic rites don't exist; they've been subsumed. Bacchic orgies are devotion mis-directed. There are accounts of frenzied women in Galatina dancing on the altar in wild abandon, tearing their clothes off and attacking any person they see wearing red. It is a hysteria that has never been explained; a vibration of ancient and dormant genes fighting to live again after 2,000 years; a folk-whisper warming the blood; a metamorphic transformation; a corybantic cancan . . .

The Italian anthropologist Ernesto de Martino, who has studied southern superstitions and accounts of witchcraft and magic, has come nearest to explaining it. He has interviewed witnesses, read descriptions, heard confessions and taken sworn oaths; he has questioned historians, other anthropologists, doctors, psychologists and musicians. Yet he remains mystified. He knows that in Ancient Greece most dances were performed by women, and concedes that music can calm victims of scorpion and snake bites; he has also found that tarantism is only mentioned after the influence of Islam, when 'sinister stories of poisonous spiders spread through the land'. So he falls back on history and deduction. There are no poisonous spiders in Puglia, he says, and the summer heat is unbearable. Also the marriage system is repressive, while sexual attitudes are outspoken and uncompromising. Furthermore, most victims are young females in an excitable state and many so-called bites occur in the area of their genitalia. So it must be a hormonal hysteria then, allied somehow to a folk-echo of a summer-festivity celebration practised long ago in Magna Graecia.

I found some lines in a booklet that I came across:

> It wasn't the spider
> But the wine inside her
>
> O Paul of the Tarantula
> It has bitten my quim
> O Paul of the Tarantula
> For God's sake kill him.

Later I stood in the shade staring at two competing churches – they faced each other across a square like fat sumo wrestlers, squatting and glaring for the final bout. Each was broad-shouldered with yellow flesh furnaced into crusty stone; each was rippling muscular chestfuls of warty ornaments at the other, like dribbles of apprehensive sweat. They're amazing; Marlovian hyperboles in stone; deistic bombast. They pop up everywhere, magnificently incongruous; saint rivalling saint; patron outdoing patron; monuments to immortality.

I had to retreat from the furnace of the midday heat, when there's not even strength to pant, and I crept into the shady peace of Santa Caterina. There wasn't an inch of wall or ceiling that wasn't a mass of colour, depicting every Bible story you've ever heard of and several you haven't. Apocalypses, redemptions, births, betrayals, resurrections, deaths. A dazzle of panels, picked out in the brightest reds, greens, golds, blues and yellows, showed miracles, mercies, salvations, visions, revelations, adorations and victories. Chromatic scales of colour filled every space: the walls, pillars, arches, roof – angels, Satans, sinners, monsters and martyrs, and nearly a hundred Christs. My eyes drowned in a technicolour banquet. Most of this dates from the 1400s, when the Spanish sent down painters from Naples and the north to educate these distant southerners; there's even a faint signature 'Franciscus de Arecio – 1436'. 'What writing is to the learned, paintings are to the ignorant,' Pope Gregory the Great had said; 'art is for the intellectual capacity of the lowest'. When you'd seen it, you were forced to believe it. I went on gazing at the rainbow of colour that stretched from end to end, each picture alive with movement and luminous light. This tiny basilica of Santa Caterina contains the whole of God's world in pictures, and its inside shone with the radiance of a summer's day.

Then, when I got to Soleto, I wasn't sure the Pope was right. The first thing I saw from miles away was the *campanile* sticking up out of nowhere like an excited phallus or a Brobdingnagian lighthouse. All fifty yards of it have been hanging up in the sky since 1397. The cone at the top is a shining mirror of green and white that turns in the sun into blinding silver. It's a muezzin tower, made up of carefully rolled butter-pats that melt skywards into barley-sugar twists, and the whole thing shines like a golden candle dribbling crusts of wax. Stupendous! Every town here has something that makes you stop and look – a gateway, an arch, church, tower or castle.

There was an old man sitting by some railings smoking a pipe.

'You haven't come to see the paintings in the church, have you?' he said.

'No. Why?'

'That's good. They've gone. All stolen last week.'

'Jesus!'

'Done to order. They all are nowadays. Blokes in Lecce . . .'

'Have they found them yet?'

'No. I don't know why they're bothering. They were awful.'

Ah well, so much for paintings educating the ignorant.

Later, I shot over a bump straight into Sternatia, and I think it was as surprised as I was. In old Greek I'm told it means 'breast-beating women'. Minutes earlier I'd been out on an empty road – just space and disappearing tarmac ahead, sending up ripples of wobbling heatwaves. And before that, miles of ochre-coloured, lead-heavy land with wild cacti sprouting; giant ones, higher than a man. And those awful little bullet-nosed stone *trulli* kept popping up like muddy bubbles; brown beehives smoothing upwards to a nipple point. Molehill memories lurking in dark groves and orchards. In ones and twos they're bearable, but further north they've turned Alberobello into a Disney-town for tourists: acres of pop-up pixie people in virgin-white with silly high-ho hats on. It's a nauseating field of munchkin mushrooms with *trullo*-burgers, *trullo*-bars and *trullo*-hotels.

I found myself coasting down a wide avenue with old palaces on either side, grave and serious, and I imagined they were bowing at my entry like ancient aristocrats lost in a time-warp, raising pillared eyebrows. 'How nice of you to come; it's been so long.' It must have been too much sun. They were all so silent, dignified and formal; full of effortless grandeur. Arched gateways big enough to take two Sherman tanks opened into sunny gardens with striped lawns, where old men played cards in the cool of shaded loggias, white doves cooed in eaves, and children ran to drink at crystal fountains.

Turning left through the narrow houses I was in a lane paved with giant blocks of stone. There are leftovers of old Greek in this village – the lane was called Via Platea and it met with another one called Via Arpano, both converging on one of the old town gates called Porta Filia. In a doorway a silver-haired old lady wrapped in black was rocking in her chair, mumbling a dirge of non-stop prayers and rattling her rosary with parchment fingers, so I asked her to say something in Greek for me, but she turned away . . .

Then I met a student from Lecce University. He was tall and interested, concerned about my enquiries.

'No, they won't do it. They're ashamed. They think you're making fun of them. Why do you want them to?' he asked.

'I'm interested. To see how much of the past is left . . . Why are they ashamed?'

'It's old-fashioned. Out of date. They think you're laughing at them.'

'It's their past; they should be proud of it.'

'They're not. They want to forget it. Their memories are painful: poverty, disease, wars, you don't understand . . . I do, but you don't; the world's changed . . . Their children haven't got time for them. None of the young ones here speak Greek. They think it's silly. Italians are "now" people, they're not historical. They want to speak American, chew gum and listen to pop songs . . . I'll take you to my grandmother.'

She was frail and old, crouched in a chair with a rug over her. It was only a few words that she spoke, barely audible, the croak of a dying bird. *'Pame sti Luppiu,'* she whispered . . . I want to go to Lecce.

'I'll show you the past,' he said afterwards, 'if you're interested. It might help you to understand.'

We went out into the sun again, back to the Porta Filia, and he opened an iron door in the wall beside it – just big enough to go through bending. We were in a cave with stone steps running down into darkness . . . until he switched the light on.

'This is the one we keep open as an example,' he said, 'to show the school children. It's a *trappidu* – an olive press; there are fifty-two of them here underneath Sternatia.'

It was a monstrous cavern going deeper; full of cold, still air; the rough walls hard and forbidding. Down fifteen steps we were in a chamber where shapes had been cut out of the rock. There were slabs to sit on, a bench, narrow bunk spaces hewn from the wall; ledges, troughs, recesses and somewhere else a stall for beasts. It went on – a confusion of openings and shadows merging into darkness, stepping over drain channels dug in the floor, our figures flitting along walls like Eisenstein monsters. It was gruesome and claustrophobic; like wandering in stone bowels full of dull echoes; through into galleries, halls and bat-hung passages where the ice-cold ghosts of the past walked. The press itself was near the entrance; impossibly huge; a great slab of granite with a drain cut round it and two vast stone wheels standing on it, solid as rock, with bar-holes in them so that the donkeys could push them round and pulp the olives.

'You see, this is the real past of Sternatia,' he said. 'My grandmother remembers her brother working in a *trappidu*. It sent him blind.'

I'm glad I met him. He was sympathetic and interested, and is trying to start a local museum with some friends, housing their small collection in a ground-floor room of a seventeenth-century *palazzo* that has been converted into apartments. He's half-proud of it, half-apologetic. 'You see, they don't like giving us things,' he explained. 'They'd rather throw them away; bury them. They don't like being reminded of the past. Those donkey harnesses, milking stools, that useless old gun – we have to buy them. We find things on rubbish dumps. My grandmother has her old traditional peasant costume with a crimson skirt and a bonnet. It's beautiful. She hasn't worn it for fifty years, but she won't let us have it for the museum; says it's going to be buried with her. It's very difficult.'

There wasn't much to see in the museum. Just the start of something: a few objects struggling against resentment, a loom and some photographs, a soldier's cap, wine bottles, pitchers, medals in a cabinet and two old dolls. 'What's that?' I asked. It was hanging from a hook on the wall by a strap; a slender wooden tub about two feet high, tapering at the base.

'It's a baby-holder,' he said.

'What do you mean? How?'

'Mothers had them strapped on their backs when they worked in the fields, like a rucksack. The baby was in it . . .'

'What? Standing up?'

'Yes, it was to keep their legs straight, make them strong. You see pictures in books . . . Pinelli, I think.'

Yes, I had seen them. Costumed mothers at the side of wells or leading donkeys, tiny heads peeping out of the tubes behind them. It didn't make their legs strong at all; it did the opposite. The poor little sods had no muscles left when the day came, their legs bowed like croquet hoops. You can still see the results of it sometimes – old men walking along slowly as if they've just got off a Thelwell pony.

We stepped outside into the *palazzo* courtyard as evening started. It wasn't loved or looked after. Weeds and long grass sprouted, and the occasional bramble; and there was the faint musk of wild oleander and rhododendron, both spreading unkempt branches, sagging and unwanted. In a corner stood a forgotten well-head; slender coils of rusty ironwork climbed up through scrolls and twists of leaves and fruit shapes towards a broken leopard's head, the futile frills gathering ivy. Round the four walls there were windows watching, all blind with age or dust, but keeping their evening vigil over long-gone palace sounds. They remembered the jewelled laughter and the velvet dreams as carriage wheels faded in the light of dawn after minuet courtships and the light-lipped kiss. They'd seen all the coronets, the princes, the diamonds, the silver and gold of Lampedusa land. They remembered the lamplight too; the oil lamps that flickered through the night like glow-worms shining on fragile happiness; oil sweated from the fetid bowels below them.

The big ballroom eyes could just remember it. They were grey and misty and nearly sightless, straining to see things no longer there, vanishing like time. *Chora ma*, our homeland.

SIX

Gallipoli

There are ghosts in Gallipoli. The remains of seven English sailors lie in one corner of the cemetery, their grey-gravelled resting place spotted with weeds. Messrs Bremner, Grierson, Crosby, Gillard, Smith, Rendall and Faithful went on their final journey in the dying months of 1918. One wonders how. There could be a worse resting place. Gallipoli is beautiful, like an island set in a silver sea; and the cemetery is sunny and peaceful, open only at certain hours for flowers to be strewn. It is set quietly apart on a hilltop, with all the due care and reverence southerners show for the dead, overlooking the little white town that Saint-Non said is an island anchored among the waves; one of the Isles of the Blessed, where all the other graves are weed-spotted too. But their journey wasn't easy; plain wooden crosses marked their burial places at first, until gravestones were sent down from Vicenza in 1921; and even then there were difficulties: hot-country delays, claims of sloth followed by excuses and recriminations. The situation wasn't resolved for another three years. There's just a name on each headstone now, and 'At the going down of the sun we will remember them'. I did so for a moment, but it sets very rapidly in Gallipoli, like a dark trap closing. There's barely a second of twilight.

More flamboyant spirits float nearby. A bulky, austere private mausoleum, with columns and a pyramid on top, and large enough to house a family, announces: 'Erected by Alexander Zarb esquire, for himself and for his beloved wife, Hannah Bona Hutton, British subjects 1898'. A bald statement that discourages interfering flights of fancy and suggests they would rather take their secrets with them, of life and death in such a forgotten corner. But the other ghosts know them and so does the ramshackle pile of Gallipoli's dusty archives. Zarb was Her Britannic Majesty's last Vice-Consul here before the post was abolished in 1900, for by then the railway had arrived from Naples to Brindisi, removing Gallipoli from the trade routes, so it sank back into white and peaceful oblivion – a silver pimple on an azure sea.

Today I looked for another grave, but it wasn't there. I'd read a book of poems once in Naples – *Canti Di Sofia Stevens*, Napoli, 1879. The introduction had said she was the daughter of the British Vice-Consul in Gallipoli, Henry Stevens. He was there at the worst time of all, from 1853 to 1867, the strangling of a kingdom and the abortive birth of Italy that followed. In Lecce I had met Nicolette James, who had written a book about Sofia. She tells the tale of a gifted yet doomed young English girl with a restless romantic spirit, who sought freedom from a repressive society, and who yearned for love after being forced into an unwelcome marriage. In my mind I had composed a brief tribute to her: an English girl in Puglia who had disappeared.

Sofia Stevens, born 22.12.1845 in Gallipoli; died 10.8.1876 in Naples of breast cancer. Daughter of Henry Stevens (HM Vice-Consul) and Carolina (née Auverny). Poetess, naturalist, supporter of women's rights, infant prodigy and staunch republican. Publications: *Canti di Sofia Stevens*, Naples, 1879; *Educazione della donna* (manuscript lost); *Flora in Provincia de Lecce* (manuscript lost). Physical description: dark-skinned with brown eyes and long chestnut hair in ringlets. In her own words:

Ho bruno il volto e le pupille brune	(I'm dark skinned with dark eyes,
Castignina la chioma in folte	My hair is chestnut, full of curls)
anella . . .	

Gallipoli

She translated poems by Longfellow and Byron, for example:

Qual lupo sul gregge discende   (The Assyrian swept down like the
l'assiro   wolf on the fold,
Di porpora e d'oro le coorti hanno   And his cohorts were gleaming in
pondo   purple and gold,
Scintillan le lance, son stelle   And the sheen of their spears was
d'empiro   like stars on the sea,
Nel mare, riflesce d'azzurro   When the blue wave rolls
profondo . . .   nightly . . .)

Sofia loved England, yet she never visited it:

Patria degli avi miei, nobil paese   (My homeland, a noble country,
A te un saluto mando da lontano   I salute you from afar,
E bagna il ciglio mio pianto palese   And I have tears in my eyes,
Mentre penso a te con senso   As I secretly think of you)
arcano

And she loved the idea of a united Italy:

Sorgi Italia, dal crudo letargo   (Rise up Italy from the lethargy
Che t'impose il francese tiranno   Imposed by French tyranny)

There's a road here called Via Stevens. In the preface to her poems, written by Dr Barba, a family friend, he says that she was a precocious and lively child who could make up rhymes when she was eight, and would recite impromptu verses while sitting up a tree. Also, she knew all the names of the local birds and flowers, and was so bright they called her *Una Enciclopedia Parlante*. But it didn't last. She grew up and love entered her life; so did death, hatred, disillusionment, regret and awful sadness. It all comes out in her poems.

Her father had been appointed by our Consul in Naples, Henry Lushington, who was once famous for complaining that being boiled and roasted every summer in Italy on £300 per year was only slightly preferable to starvation in England. But it was even hotter in Gallipoli. It was a major port for exporting olive oil, and the area was full of political unrest – the Bourbon twilight. Then in 1856, perhaps because she had outgrown her local school, ten-year-old Sofia was sent away to complete her education in Naples. Here, at some stage, she met and appears to have loved one of her teachers, a young poet and republican called Federico Villani. But this is only supposition. He wrote love lyrics to 'a friend', and one dedicated to 'Sylvia Sventes'; she wrote a poetic plea that one day he might find his soul-sister in the stars – *'Ne la tua Stella, l'alma sorella'*.

It didn't happen. In 1867 her father died, and a year later, aged twenty-two, she was married off to a man from Ancona, Settimo Barlocci; but within five years she was desperately ill with cancer and back in Naples for treatment. It was here that she met Villani again, but it was too late, she was dying.

It all spills out in her poetry: anguish, sadness, thwarted longings and dreams of a golden past. 'Sweet sentimentalism and languid pathos', as Mrs James puts it. A caged nightingale born out of time. *'Molto mesta è la vita'* she laments in one poem – life is so sad – and harks back to the lost hours of happiness in her childhood: to the flowers, birds, rivers, trees and the sea. She longs to see her brothers and sisters again – Ada, Elisa, Riccardo, Giovanni; and she longs for her father: *'Padre gradisci il cantico/Che a la tua tomba Io dono'* – Father, accept these lines that I am presenting at your grave. In another poem she castigates libertines and seducers and pours scorn on the 'obscene idiot' – *'Ebete osceno'* who is unaware of her soul. Marriage, she says, instead of being a bed of roses, is a

prison: *'Ne le sue catene . . . Non oso dir di fiori . . .'* – It is
chains . . . I would never say flowers. And in this abyss of
pain and betrayal she still yearns to be loved: *'Come vorrei
essere amata . . .'* she calls out – How I long to be loved.

Sofia Stevens died in Naples in 1876 aged thirty, and Mrs
James has looked in vain for her grave. Sofia Stevens has
vanished.

But there are still Stevens memories in Gallipoli. And
Gallipoli knows that name very well; they still talk about
one of the family, the colonel on the radio who always said
'Buona Sera'. Sofia never knew she had a nephew called
Harold Ralph Gaetano Stevens, son of her brother Richard,
who broadcast 1,198 messages to the Italian people from the
BBC in London between December 1939 and February 1946.
Our one-time military attaché in Rome who, in October
1941, said in a broadcast, *'Io non sono mai stato in Puglia'* –
I have never been to Puglia – yet knew that his cousins and
aunts still lived there. So the name is still whispered with
gratitude in Gallipoli because they say his family connections must have saved it from attack. Allied bombs were
dropped harmlessly into the sea, bullets raked the waves,
and not a person or building was touched. Asa Briggs's
history of the BBC says that Harold Stevens 'became the
most popular figure in all Italy'. But this also caused
problems. When the Allies landed they heard the crowds
shouting, *'Viva* Colonel Good Evening', but no one knew
who he was.

Edward Hutton, who wrote more books about Italy than
most people, didn't like Gallipoli. I love it. You can walk
round it in half an hour; right round the sea-wall perimeter
as the sun bounces back off the curving white houses and
soaks you in sweat. It's a sea-circle round a spongeful of
rabbit runs. You go from church to church, fort to fort,
dodge children, and step over strings of nets and men

basking in the solar heat weaving lobster traps. The old walls lie drowning at the edge of the sea, cannoned to bits by invaders, now ugly heaps in the water; careless hunks of stone gently wave-washed where crouching fishermen squat with tight toe-holds and watch as the water swells under their yards of drooping cane.

The ravenous eye of the sun burns the town white and yellow; then at night it turns luminous and silver. One night in 1828 an eccentric young traveller called Craufurd Tait Ramage turned poet here as he sailed by 'through a liquid plain of sparkling stars'. He knew it had been called Kalis Polis – beautiful city. It is a limpet circle sitting in the sea where nothing is ever straight and all alleys touch. They're a wriggling honeycomb of pin-thin passages that twist their way to the sea edge before turning back, all tall and shadowy, to hide from the sun. With hands out-stretched you touch both walls. They hide old palaces too; merchant palaces from the wealthy olive oil days, where stone gateways open into courtyards and heavy dogtooth doors loom in shadow. Barred windows glare from crusted walls – giving glimpses of coloured Pompeian ceilings – and dark balconies bulge overhead like snouts. Then a pealing dart of children comes as they run through zebra-streaked shade and sun like a flash of minnows. Black doorways are hung with fishnet skirts, chromatic washing hangs, vendors shout out their vegetable cries, and your feet ring out on harlequin slabs of stone. Icons glow dimly through bedroom doors where hand-weaving hags watch the flicker of televi-sion. Then round any corner you may bump into the fretwork front of Sant' Agata's Cathedral and hope the tiptoeing trumpeting saints don't fall on you. If they did, they'd demolish two hairdressers, a cake shop and a café.

I asked a man this morning how many churches there were in Gallipoli, and he said thirty-three. He got his fingers out – Cristina, Carmine, Teresa, Purita, Chiara, Crocefisso,

Angelo, Anime, Angeli, Maria del Caretto, Immacolata, Domenico, Francesco, Antonio, Luigi, Francesco again, Cuore and Sant' Agata. That's eighteen, I pointed out, but he shrugged. Who cares?

They all have a common factor. Blood. It flows everywhere; from nooks, niches, tapestries and paintings. Sant' Agata with her breasts cut off. Gallipoli's patron saint was demamillated in the third century AD for being a stubborn Christian. She is also one of Norman Douglas's 'amoeba' saints, split between here and Catania in Sicily. A certain imbalance arises, as all that Gallipoli can claim to have is one of her breasts, though even this has disappeared. It seems the *'sacram mammilam'* was carried off as booty during some local wars, either by Taranto or Galatina, although they both deny this.

Miss Agatha Guisilberto was an innocent Catanian aged fifteen (hagiographers seem to have a fixation with pubescent girls) when a certain Quintianus was a Roman governor of Sicily; and she was suitably shocked when he demanded routine favours of her. Hoping she might change her mind, he enrolled her in a Catanian Academy of Love run by one Signora Aphrodisia and her nine daughters. This had the opposite effect to the one expected and she informed Quintianus after a week that the 'licentious entertainments' filled her with 'great nausea'; also that he was 'a vile slave of Satan' for sending her there. In addition she advised him to leave her alone as she already had 'a husband in heaven'. Quintianus's reaction was to lock her up for non-cooperation and have her breasts cut off; this didn't work either, as St Peter appeared in her cell during the night and replaced them – *'Mammilam meo pectori restituere'*. Death could be the only answer to such intransigence and, depending on which source you read, Agatha was either burned at the stake or 'roasted on a bed of red-hot coals'. Within moments Etna erupted, Catania suffered an earthquake, a mob invaded the governor's palace and Quintianus rushed headlong into the sea.

So, what part does 300-mile-distant Gallipoli play in this? Well, some thousand years later on these shores a suckling mother happened to be sitting by the sea with her infant when she drifted off to sleep. Her tiny offspring, feeling hungry, spotted a familiar shape lying washed up on the sand nearby and promptly applied himself to it enthusiastically. At the same time the mother dreamed that a heavenly voice was scolding her for allowing her child to suck at such a sacred breast, because it was St Agatha's. It was so firmly fixed in the infant's mouth that the two could not be separated, and they came apart only hours later in the cathedral when the whole population gathered there and sang '*Ora Pro Nobis Sant' Agata . . .*'

The advent of this '*Sacram Mammilam Gloriosae Virginis Agathae*' is remembered here in two ways: bloodsoaked effigies in all the churches, and breast-shaped bread rolls in spring, called *minuzzi*. Trays of firm, nipple-pointed buns are baked in Gallipoli each year as the weather turns warmer, lovingly created and extremely lifelike. So when you nibble a roll here in May or June, remember Miss Agatha Guisilberto and just where her obduracy got her in AD 251.

Considerably more about this 'most beautiful girl of all Catania' can be found in *The Book of Saints and Martyrs*, although in his *Lives of the Saints* the commentator Sabine Baring-Gould could find no mention of her before AD 800 and dismissed the story as a 'pious fraud' and just as bad as Chaucer's Pardoner selling 'clouts and pigges bones'. But then if the BVM's milk can turn up at Paris, Chartres, Toulon and Avignon and locks of her hair in Venice, Bologna, Padua, Assisi and elsewhere . . .

In a side chapel in the church of San Franceso d'Assisi there is something much worse than tortured effigies of Sant' Agata. The guide book calls it 'the ugliest statue in

Christendom'. It's the Malladrone, a life-sized model of the thief who died beside Christ on the cross. It is a demonic Goya-grotesque. It has a Frankenstein face with a gleeful grin and huge eyes bulging with savage hatred, and it leers down like a snarling lycanthrope enjoying death. A nightmare face of ghouls, goblins and grim reapers in the dark. It's worse than anything in the London Dungeon. D'Annunzio called it an object of 'sublime horror'. It's goose-pimply. Its *'Terribilità . . .'* defies description, says the book. The Spanish marshal Giuseppe della Cueva had it made in 1681 by a local priest, and it is outrageously hideous.

There is a tiny museum here, a curious assemblage of memorabilia; a bedlam of unlabelled Gallipoli bygones; anything from a pincushion to a First World War mine. The one room is so thick with curios that a duster couldn't get near them, and the whole collection of unrelated impedimenta is looked after by Signor Z. It hasn't always been like this. Martin Briggs saw an embryonic display in 1908 when it was also a schoolroom, complete with 'dozing priest and a knot of noisy schoolboys'. He left for 'a more abiding attraction; the beauty of Gallipoli's maidens'.

The whole clutter is crowded into the main hall of a disused *palazzo*, lofty as a cathedral with galleried walls and a Brunelleschi glass-domed ceiling shedding light. Sharks' teeth snap happily at Roman coins, old muskets aim at butterflies, and a blackshirt truncheon strikes out at a figured bell-crater from ancient Greece. The unities of place or time are irrelevant; the ectopian disarray blends forty centuries, and Signor Z pads along behind you to make sure you don't steal his baby whale or the lid of a Messapian sarcophagus. He loves every item and his voice rotates like a worn-out seventy-eight jumping grooves indiscriminately from stuffed birds to iron crosses, ammonites to amphorae and bugles to ballgowns. In five minutes I had mental indigestion, eyes blurred by uniforms, stamp collections, oil

lamps, medals, half-torsos, swords, maps by Bleau, mando-
lins and a wind-up toy piano with 100 keys. At least it's
novel, a lucky-dip museum. It makes other museums look
like mausoleums; this one is alive and vibrant; fascinatingly
mad – a chaos of ancient entertainment.

Signor Z starts waving aloft at shelves of 10,000 books in
the gallery, whispering mammoth sums as if they were
rows of Gutenberg Bibles. In fact they are miles of dead
clerics' refuse; holy tons of pious tracts, bound sermons and
religious commentaries that the beetles have gorged on for a
hundred years. As I touched one, the vellum spine snapped
like an angry crisp, and pages fell out as if sprayed by
grapeshot.

Now he wants me to go up into the roof space, making a
mystery 'hush' sign with fingers to his lips – a secret tour. It
is a roomful of some of Dr Barba's experimental leftovers.
He wasn't just a medical friend of the Stevens family, he
was interested in the origins of the human species and
collected faulty examples of it. There are rows of them in
jars on shelves; misshapen foetuses, aborted forms, hideous
terminations. They sit there in fat bottles of mummified,
pre-natal shapes with curly tails, infants with heads the size
of melons, a face without eyes or nose, a skin-doll with a
single leg; the monsters of miscreation from the dark days
of village isolation and loneliness, and the sad and desperate
unions to which it led.

Signor Z hasn't finished with me. There's a cabinet in the
room with two wax dummies side-by-side, each with the
stomach cut open showing purple entrails. One was a he
and the other was a she. This is supposed to date from 1620
and is the rather nasty brainchild of an equally nasty priest
called Padre Gennino; his unequivocal proof that man is
superior to woman. He had arranged for a man and a woman
who had died within hours of each other to be buried side-
by-side on the same day. Exactly two weeks later he had the
bodies dug up, and was delighted to find that the male

corpse had hardly rotted at all, while the woman's had decomposed badly. Eureka! He was right. Not only had Pope Paul V decreed that men were superior to women, but hadn't St John Chrysostom said that female beauty was 'nothing less than phlegm, blood, bile, rheum, and the fluid of digested food'? (He also said some remarkably stupid things about Jews.) But Padre Gennino had now proved it and he was thoroughly satisfied. Woman was incontrovertibly 'God's greatest blunder' and man was definitely superior; never mind the female he was supposed to revere most of all ... *Semper intacta* ... *Prae partu, in partu et post partum.*

This morning I wanted to visit Gallipoli's little theatre and opera house, but it wasn't easy. There wasn't a key. It's supposed to be a miniature version of the San Carlo Theatre in Naples, and I wanted to see where the spectacular anti-Bourbon riot had started one night in 1856 during a performance of *Ernani*. It was the night Henry Stevens had been warned in advance, so he wasn't in his usual box. On the night of 31 July – the Queen's birthday – his box was hermetically sealed ('*ermeticamente serrato*').

Signor Z at the museum said that the opera house was a valuable historical monument and I'd find a key in the Town Hall. I didn't. Nobody had seen it for years. There were shrugs and 'behs', and determined escorts from room to room to ask questions and have cupboards searched, heads scratched and drawers ransacked. Hopeless. Someone thought the last caretaker had taken the key to America with him when he emigrated. Somebody else suggested trying the police or the fire station. So I did and they all thought I was a lunatic. One fireman said, 'What theatre? Have we got one?' One official thought the key had been given to a building firm in Rome, which was thinking about restoring it. He gave me their address. It was now afternoon and running-sweat time. At half-past three, after the holy siesta, a posse of Town Hall employees assembled beneath the top-floor window of a one-time opera-house cleaner, and with necks nearly breaking at ninety degrees, began shouting up towards the roof. An equally shouting female head eventually emerged and said he'd gone fishing; and as he'd never been paid anyway, the *comune* could go and screw itself. This led to a circle of apologetic misery and waves of convulsive shoulder-wobbles all round, and a lot of lachrymose faces going soggy bloodhound, so I crept away in case they all burst into tears.

I went and stood in the shade of the opera-house portico, staring unhappily at the doors that would never open; then a man came by and propped his bicycle against the wall beside me . . .

'*Bellissima*,' he said, eyeing me sympathetically.

'I know,' I replied, 'I'd love to see it.'

'Yes. It's lovely inside, really wonderful.'

'Yes, I'm sure it is,' I said miserably.

'Beautiful,' he went on. 'Go on in . . . it's not locked.'

He calmly rolled the big doors back on their tramline runners, switched on some lights and disappeared with a happy smile.

'Don't forget to shut it afterwards,' he called.

It was quiet inside. Nothing but red, white and gold in a three-quarter circle pointing at the stage – almost doll's-house. Rows of red stall-seats and then a display of boxes in an arc with curtains, balconies, golden colours. Tiny candle-cup lights pinpointed the walls like pale ochre flames, proud and significant, illuminating the three tiers of boxes and brightening each balcony with its carvings of ox-blood and gilt, its swathes of velvet curtains. There was emptiness. The flames were the dead eyes of silent memories. Laced among them were moulded figures: trumpeting angels puffed at heaven, celestial putti flew with bare-bummed smirks, martial coats of arms shone on walls, and gilded shields blazed family escutcheons. On the ceiling twelve panels of Graces and cupids played games among cottonwool clouds in a faded sky and smiled down on Gallipoli's ghosts. They smiled at the long-gone golden days, when olive-oil sheikhs had rustled in silk as they bowed from box to box or bent to kiss gloved hands; they smiled at Sofia's happy laughter among the bright spark of diamonds; and they smiled at the scent of jasmine being blown in by the warm sea air over a land of peace. And they even smiled while the hooded bands of 'New Brutuses' prowled the dark streets outside, waiting to plunge their daggers into the tired body of their own kingdom.

On the creaking stage sat a Schiedmeyer concert grand, bulbous and grey with dust; it looked lonely; chords lost in the past, and now mute in the silence. Above it the dead hands of the auditorium clock were fixed at three minutes to midnight. It would soon be the hour for graveyards to yawn again; time for Gallipoli's ghosts to walk.

I had a terrible dinner last night. It wasn't the food, it was the company – two of them; they came and sat next to my table. Italian girls don't mess around; they come straight to the point – 'Do you want to fuck me, or don't you?' English girls are a little more restrained. This one was blatant. We all got an eyeful of lust in action over a three-course meal. If she'd been less attractive it might have been bearable. This one was a raver, a real catwalk underpant-popper, sex on legs . . . fork-stopping-halfway-to-mouth stuff. It wasn't just eyes popping out of sockets this time, for she was popping all over . . . boiling . . .

Within a minute of her sitting down I thought her chair was going to catch fire. He was nothing: diminutive, seriously spectacled and crinkle-haired, with Groucho legs and bar-mitzvah skin. What's he got that I haven't? Probably money and a foreskin. She was sheer bedroom: tall, willowy and 100 per cent carnal; pop-up nipple thimbles and bursting thong; her black hair was straight

Chinese-sleek and touched her buttocks; her mouth was half-open and her big eyes gobbled him. She wanted him before the meal, during it and immediately afterwards.

I was trying to eat *spaghetti alle vongole*. It's usually lovely – the taste of tiny seashells adds a soft fishy succulence to the pasta. I couldn't get it down. He was the only person in the room who hadn't noticed what was happening. Nobody was talking. He was going to be the *spécialité de la nuit*, and she was starving. She'd ordered it already: *tourne dos Rossini, suprême de barbue* and fillet of one-eyed fish. He considered the menu and talked through her, with mutters about trials, pleas, briefs and discharges; stony as a garden gnome. Bloodless. She was rampant and boa-constrictal; she kicked his feet, nibbled his fingers, stroked his cheek, swept her hair away, pressure-cooked her thighs and squirmed on her seat to check for leaks. Two thousand years ago, Arnobius, an African rhetorician of some skill, called it *Clunibus fluctuare crispatis* – to fluctuate with wriggling buttocks ... The shockwaves hit every table in the room.

She spooned up her soup with sucking gobbles, fellated *fettuccine* off her fork with slow-motion goldfish lips, dangled courgettes in the air for nibbles, and lollipopped banana bits out of his salad. We all sat in trouser-tight famished agony waiting for her to explode and rape him or for the heat on her chair to melt the seat. After she'd dragged him away in a hurry, we pecked at our cold food and mourned our fantasies. Some women are strange feeders.

Outside in the street the last shutters rattled down as cats ran, and the lone Vespa circled, purring on its way to sleep. Quietness came with a warm sheet of overhead stars and night-light fishermen bobbing brightly far away on an ink-black sea. They say one of them spawned the town before Troy was born by loving a mermaid. Soft *grandes dames* clucked and whispered in shadowed doorways, muttering their last goodnights, and the Vespa circled again in a final night-watch. The old daytime men on the sea-wall had beetled through darkness home to bed, and all was quiet.

This morning a man caught a squid. I watched him darting along the edge of the rocks, balancing barefoot from tip to tip and dipping his handline. He was teasing each crevice to find something greedy below, leaping between sun and sea, and swaying his wrist up and down to dance the bait. He spasmed a strike, but missed. He missed seven times. He crept over the rock rims that were hiding his hungry hunted prey, sliding his line up and down – down, up again – hand and heart moving in deep-water hope.

Then he got it!

One yell, as greedy octo-beak grabbed it; snake legs pulled up flailing; swung and smashed on rocks in a thrash of tentacle twists; a worm-writhe of hopeless, rolling squidge, yellow with fury. Grabbed and smashed again like wet jelly sprayed on stone; one more soggy splash; a splosh of emulsoid mucus rolling over; squashed again into a pulp of yellow, wriggling and only half-living raging snot. Smashed again in a last leaky roll-over with tentacles curdling; a final glue-turn in sticky death. Wham! Poor yucky cork-screwing was once octopus in a clammy ball of wet squirms, and with one more smash the tendrils are dead. Eight legs hang still in the air and it limply dies.

Faces grinned as he ran up the rocks barefoot holding his damp Medusa head, laughing with excitement, then ran all the way to the fish market. Once they used to cut the tentacles off and dry them brush-brittle in the sun to beat the schoolboys' legs with when they misbehaved. Signor Z remembers. There's a birch of them hanging in the museum beside some butterflies; octo-nine-tails, and rough as dry wire.

The fish market is hidden under the castle walls, where

those thirty-four Hohenstaufen barons beat off the Angevins for seven months. It stinks and roars with rancid sea-
smells and waves of calloused voices: do you want it alive
or dead? Pink shrimp bodies tremble and flick in bowls,
white fish shapes are threaded on string, or on slabs of silver
with cut-up swordfish, finned, tailed, gut-ripped open or
grinning like gargoyles. Or you can split your own needlepoint *ricci* and suck the soft orange pulp out, or lick your
dipped fingertips. Suited lawyers are doing it, bandying
words, fastidiously sipping at silver oysters or gorging
whelks beside fat old matrons who push them back.
Nostrils are full of fish stink; tin buckets are dark with eel-
squirms, and watery fish-eyes are popping in bubbles of sea-
soap, all topped by yells in wellington boots. Today's haul is
spread over slippery tiles of scaly slime under big sun
umbrellas, where the salt stench wafts up your nose like
rancid fog and greedy housewives barter the price down
with gimlet eyes . . . a thousand, seven hundred, five, stuff
it up . . . Spray-bitten faces dance, chapped with salt and
rough as boat-keels. Silver fish streams and eels in mucus,
or wet whelks in froth or gasping coelacanths, and all
slapped down on slabs and drowned in shouts. But no one
wants his squid; there are plenty here already, stuck in dark
big-eyed buckets and no hope.

'Look!' shouts a salt-weathered face and hangs one up,
dangling limp. It spouts out a spiteful bladder of black ink
in a terminal orgasm, straight on a watcher's pale trousers,
who puppet-dances in surprise to see his legs turn a
dribbling piebald. He backs off baffled, fisting the air,
muttering curses and laundry bills, jumping to shake the
Dalmatian dots off his trousers while watchers laugh
without malice. It could have been them. Greasy squid-
knots flop back in the bucket as he turns to flee, shouting
vengeance and fluttering his galaxy of ink spots, and his
face glum with woe at looking such a fish-filthy *figura* with

speckled leggings dowsed in a dose of octopox. Nobody
wants another squid.

SEVEN

Taranto

I should have known better. I lived here once and loved it. I loved the sea on two sides, everlasting blue with streaks of silver, the tall yellow stuccoed buildings, the coiffed matrons with poodles in the park, the endless air of loitering idleness in the sun. Ramage called it 'enjoyment of the passing hour'. Like Rose Macaulay, one can't help imagining things in Taranto: honey, figs, leeks, pears, sheep, purple dye and diaphanous clothes. '*Molle Tarentum*'; the wanton bride on a blue gulf that Horace said was dearer than all other worlds. There aren't any remains of one of the largest Greek cities, as the Romans pulverised it after they'd been down for negotiations that didn't go particularly well; and a Greek had deliberately shat on one of their togas. The gold in the museum is spectacular.

I did the journey along the coast in a day. It was varied; occasional small towns got in the way, all with memories of Turkish or pirate landings to loot, rape and take prisoners. Otherwise the road was open and windy through sand-duney swamps and fields of reeds, with the sea somewhere out of sight. The shore was flat this side; placid, unaggressive, full of wet gusts and salt-stings on the face; perfect for the corsairs to land and make mayhem. Acres of flatness slid away towards the sea, until now and then waves came to nibble fretfully at the roadside. They had bobbles of white froth on them and danced in all the way from Africa like demented pygmies in albino wigs, then chattered in hurt surprise as they died on the sand in bubble-strings. The wind bent the bulrushes over them in sympathy, lamenting their wasted efforts.

In the evening there was another *festa*. The whole of

Taranto was corked solid outside the cathedral waiting for something to happen, but no one seemed sure what or when. I was part of a welded throng of expectant compression, with hip glued to hip and elbow to elbow: an all-round sandwich, and squeezed as pips. I was totally cemented, like a Mafia coffin caught in a sweaty straitjacketed sardine-hug. No body power at all. A loathsome dwarf behind me was using me as a ladder to get a better view of what might be happening. We were so homogenised that his scrambles were useless, so he stuck like a passionate burr, giving the odd pogo-stick leap in the hope of seeing something. Then, as a crucifix appeared and the tops of saintly heads passed somewhere in front and we all surged in a tiptoe thrill, he gave his final jerk of excitement, fell back with relief at glimpsing his vision and disappeared. So did my wallet.

The police inspector at the *questura* wasn't interested. It was the seventh since six o'clock that evening, he said, a bent cigarette brewers'-drooping out of his mouth. He paddled through papers with a sigh of boredom to find a *denuncio* in pidgin English; until he saw my camera. He sat up suddenly, filled his chest like a balloon and fastened his shirt buttons. On went his tie and tunic, out shot his cuffs, down went his sleeky hair, and he smoothed his moustache and then put his cap on. 'OK, I'm ready,' he beamed, puffing out his chest.

Crime isn't romantic any more in Italy. It's cheap and deceitful. Either the Mafia is dynamiting sitting ducks or computers are fixing corruption and fraud. The last of the romantic brigand heroes, Sicily's Salvatore Giuliano, is dead; so are his predecessors, Marco Sciarra, Mammone, Pezza and Ronco, all half-fighting for their king and half for themselves. At least they thought they had a cause. Today's bandits are sleek-suited, travel first-class and are tucked safely away in Parliament or in multinational air-conditioned offices.

Puglia did have a brigand once, a real one. He was a priest

to start with (not unusual in these parts), but his spirit was too weak and his flesh too willing; bodies appealed more than souls. He liked money too; treasure on earth being better than hoping for it later. So he took to looting, whoring and murder, after which he'd usually kneel down and say a Mass. *Carpe diem* into *Carpe Deum*. Don Ciro Annichiarico's exploits are legendary hereabouts, and a little confused. When he'd shot the suitor of a girl he wanted for himself and was hunted by the authorities, he gathered a gang of ruffians together and started a reign of terror stretching from Maglie up to Foggia. Pretending he was an anti-Bourbon Carbonaro fighting for a republic and for justice, he embarked on a spree of extortion, robbery, threats, torture, arson and murder, and his attacks were so ruthless and rapid that he became known as Don Diavolo. He massacred everyone at a wedding party because he didn't like the host, and he raped the Princess of Martano when she refused him, then murdered her and stole 96,000 ducats. All members of his gang had to have committed at least two killings, and in order to terrorise intended victims, advance warning would be sent by means of a note decorated with skulls and the words 'Death, Terror, Sorrow and Mourning'; one in each corner.

The anonymous *Memoirs of the Carbonari*, thought to be by Giuseppe Bertholdi and published in 1821, describe his eventual trial and show how many pseudo-Masonic lodges of revolutionaries there were throughout the country, complete with rituals, oaths and secret signs – all of which have seeped into the Mafia, and into higher places.

Don Diavolo wasn't finally dealt with until King Ferdinand sent his Irish mercenary, General Sir Richard Church, into Puglia to catch him with 1,200 soldiers, but even then it wasn't easy. 'He was a very Proteus in his disguises,' recalls the General ruefully in his memoirs, having found that the Don had dressed up as a woman once and served him at table in his own headquarters. Eventually, on

25 January 1818, Church cornered him in a farmhouse at Scaserba near Francavilla – 132 soldiers against Don Ciro and three companions, and it was only by bringing up a cannon to demolish the building that he was finally caught. He laughed on hearing the death sentence; he also swore at the priest sent to comfort him – 'Stop nattering . . . I'm a priest too . . . Push off – you're making me laugh.' And then he was shot by firing squad on 8 February 1818.

I know a number of Italians who would be very happy to see quite a few of their leaders today go the same way.

Crime is much easier nowadays. It's all plausible lies, cunning, deceit, and knowing the right people. There's an organisation in Rome paid and given grants to send 'Culture' to south Italy: orchestras, ballet companies, art exhibitions. But sometimes the advertised events don't happen; there's illness or travel problems, so a local attraction is put on – much cheaper. The organisation keeps the change. There was once a bright developer who sold off bits of the coastline near Brindisi for holiday homes, mainly for expatriates. It was only when they'd bought the land that they found he didn't even own it. He disappeared to Switzerland to spend their money.

I think it was Bill Bryson who said that if you had a heart attack in a bank in Italy they'd only push you along to the next counter. As they are supposed to have invented banking 600 years ago, you'd expect some efficiency. A lot of customers don't go in for money, they go in for a chat. There are metal detectors to get past first: entry capsules that imprison you till you've emptied your pockets. As the tellers have got your money they're in a powerful position and they don't really want you to have it, so they talk to friends instead about babies, cars, football or what they did last night. What we call queues they call scrums in which the weak, hungry, hesitant or polite go backwards. If you do ever reach a teller, you have to remember he's dealing in millions, which is why he feels so important, while you only want a hundred pounds of your own money, so you'd better be grateful.

This morning I went to see San Cataldo in the cathedral. There was a group of school children on a routine visit, a decidedly undisciplined mob doing anything but revere their saint. A schoolmaster chaperone carried a hunting crop and was quite nonchalantly using it on any young back that came within reach. Its effect lasted all of ten seconds. Italians can't really be bothered with legislation. There are about 200 European Union directives they are happily ignoring at the moment.

According to Morone's *Vita Et Miracula St Cataldi Episcopi Et Confessoris*, this saint was born at Rachan in Ireland sometime in the second century AD of parents called Euchu and Athena, who 'lived together in honest matrimony'. At his birth there was such 'a commotion in the stars' that his mother died and dropped him on the floor 'of very hard marble' (*durissimo marmo*). Unaffected, he stood up and brought her back to life. In due course tales of his wizardry reached the King, who had him imprisoned for sorcery, but on the instruction of angels in a dream, he released Cataldo and made him a bishop and a duke. When he finally came to Italy – in AD 166, Morone insists – he was divinely summoned to Taranto to cure them of their 'pagan abominations' and their 'most appalling wickedness'. His achievements included making a dumb shepherdess speak and bringing a squashed bricklayer back to life after a building had fallen on him. He also resuscitated a dead baby and restored a blind man's sight. He seems to have vanished after that; until a thousand years later another bishop, by the name of Drogon, was clearing a cemetery in order to build more houses, when one of the exhumed corpses was found to be 'smelling of roses'. It could be none other than their missing saint, so they embalmed him, coated the body in silver and put it in the cathedral.

EIGHT

Metapontum

I have arrived in Bernalda. François Lenormant, the French archaeologist and historian who knows more about south Italy than most people, says this is ancient Camarda, a suburb of Metapontum. It is a small white village on a hilltop about six miles from the sea. I have two very good reasons for being here: Paola and Fiffina.

Paola is the daughter of a friend, which is probably a good thing. She is nineteen years old. She is also, in the words of another friend, 'so beautiful it is pain'. Paola's pain starts for the male viewer about ten inches below the solar plexus and lasts for hours. Figures like hers should be on the Index. Her method of communication is by body language, with an elastically supple shape that makes serpentine movements as it slides and radiates fantasies of fluff-pink mirrored bedrooms. Today she is wearing shiny black and her thighs are seething like an overheated kettle stifling steam. She is also short-sighted; when she talks, she puts her face within breath-reach, makes monstrous suggestions with big brown eyes and pouts oyster-wet lips out – as plump and glossy as swollen inner tubes. I don't think she can help it. A lot of Italian girls have the same problem with their solenoid shapes and bodies like gravity. Pulsars on endless legs. They're gift-wrapped incendiaries that semaphore carnal explosions the moment they move. Paola's back-view ticks away like a cutaneous time-bomb, and I'm glad she's going back to Lecce tomorrow. Someone can defuse her at university.

Fiffina is different. I went to see her today. She lives at the other end of town and runs an exclusively female establishment frequented by lots of expectant men. There are brass chandeliers, discreet pine-panelled walls, and the rooms are always crowded and buzzing with the noise of impatience or satisfaction. Three women satisfy the needs of forty eager male customers between midday and three o'clock, then from seven in the evening onwards, and when it gets too crowded the last arrivals have to wait upstairs. I have only ever seen one female customer.

Tonight I started with *melangrano*. That was on Fiffina's advice: a salad of funghi and peppers that scorched my palate and brought my scalp out in a pinprick pox of sweaty tingles. The wine was nectar. Followed by *orecchini*, tiny curled-up pasta flakes, soft as guinea pig's ears, in cream sauce. Followed by whatever Fiffina said. She and her sister cook everything themselves, both trundling out from the kitchen through a curtain, then trundling back in again. They take orders, advise, listen, comment, ponder, then go to cook more; everything is done to order, all matey and democratic, but there is no doubt who's in charge. Nothing is forgotten; clean napkins at every table and the fish fresh today from Metapontum – only six hours dead; and the tables are big enough to eat at, and far enough apart to let you stretch your legs; not like those claustral English jungles where you perch like a wrung-out lemon nudging elbows and knees and spear someone else's soup. The Italians like to indulge their appetites; food should be enjoyed for hours. Meals are banquets, real occasions of importance; and they need time, space and comfort. Every mouthful is a feast. (Except for breakfast, which they don't bother with.)

A niece does most of the serving – she's poised and efficient, with everywhere eyes and nothing missed. Forty men would like to take her home afterwards and every night they offer to. The power delights her, flipping gallantries aside with a laugh and a knowing head-toss on the move, a confident combatant in pseudo-courtship and light-hearted lechery. Between opening time and midnight she's beautified a hundred times; a laughing Lars Porsenna on her untakable bridge. Game, set, match to Fiffina's niece, with the losers' crotches inflated by huge ego and libido boosts.

I knew someone who did the same kind of thing in Milan's Galleria years ago; he'd sit sipping coffee all morning and make pleasant remarks at passing women. I told him he needed his face slapped. He said he averaged three a day and it only cost a cup of coffee each time, and wasn't I stupid. They fuck for fun – he said.

The Italians are different. We don't think of ourselves as body bits. They do. They regard gender as fun and differing genitals as even funnier. Dalliance is a sport here, almost as important as football. They elevate it to an art form. Bodies semaphore signals and eye contacts are like electric shocks. We feel guilty because our flesh is foul, a humming hive of sin. To them it's an exquisite engine of delight. Screwing is a healthy recreation, not just a holy procreation (which is not original). That doesn't mean they're particularly good at it, however. Italian men don't make love, according to the French writer Jean-François Revel, who lived here for five years; they just want to stick it in as quickly as possible and get it out ten seconds later. And having listened to a few bedroom confidences and complaints in years gone by, I can confirm that.

Today Paola's father took me down to Metapontum and left me to sit on the beach. I began to have George Gissing visions of palaces, temples, palms, gold statues and rows of oars dipping into the sea. He sat here musing on how nature had triumphed 'over the greatness of forgotten men'. Lenormant sat here too, more than a century ago, among the mew of whirling lapwings, and he watched two flamingos poised in a puddle, each on one leg, 'like philosophers in grave meditation'. Long before that Keppel Craven rode past here on horseback with an escort of four policemen and blamed the 'incredible ignorance' of the locals for not being able to show him any remains.

Craven was here forty years later than Swinburne but was much the same type of traveller; another aristocrat and classicist who had useful connections in Naples, as he had been chamberlain to the unfortunate Queen Caroline of England during her stay there. (During her trial the opposition called him a 'jack-pudding'.) Very much a key figure among international society that swarmed in Naples during the early nineteenth century, he owned a house in Salerno and a villa on Posillipo, where he held musical soirées for the wealthy; he was also a member of the Society of Dilettanti and an intimate friend of the erudite archaeologist and historian, gouty William Gell. So it's not surprising Craven managed to have an escort of police during most of the journey that he recorded in *A Tour through the Southern Provinces of the Kingdom of Naples*. When you read 'I rested at the house of one of the richest individuals' and that Lecce is full of 'innumerable absurdities', with churches of 'incredible bad taste', you feel you know just the kind of person he is: superior, unfeeling and condescending. Individuals he meets have 'pretensions to knowledge', pieces of merchandise are 'far beyond their merits', and towns offer 'little or nothing to arrest the attention'. The only thing of beauty he notices on his journey is a girl washing in a river near Bagnara – 'the most perfect specimen of human loveliness,' he says, which must have taken quite an effort, as he wasn't that type. Most of the rest is a prosaic and uninspired airing of his historical knowledge, giving some detailed accounts of all the 'generous hosts' he stayed with and disdainfully dismissing Cassano (near Sybaris) as 'amply furnished with all that minister to the necessities of the poor, and gratify the superfluous luxuries of the richer class'. But one has to admire his diplomatic caution when it comes to mentioning the ravages of the 1783 earthquake. Beneficent efforts were made, he says, through 'the paternal solicitude of the sovereign, and the attention of his government', but 'the political vicissitudes to which it [the region] afterwards was exposed, have probably retarded the improvements'. He hedges his bets carefully too when, in an appendix, he talks about 'the honour or disgrace of' the 1820 revolution in Naples.

The reason why Craven didn't find any remains at Metapontum was because there weren't any, and there aren't any now, except for one small minor temple standing beside the main road, called Tavole Palatine. This was the temple to Hera that the locals didn't know or care about; there is a delightful illustration of it in Saint-Non's *Voyage Pittoresque* showing a lively bucolic celebration in progress, full of animated figures such as Thomas Rowlandson might have drawn. The revellers have draped a huge sheet across between the rows of pillars, to provide shade, and some of them are actually standing on the architrave where there is drinking, dancing and rustic merry-making. Just a handy lump of ruin to have fun with.

Metapontum appeared, then vanished. It was probably an outpost of Sybaris, to act as a buffer against the rival might of Taranto. One legend says that Poseidon mated with Demeter here, and that she bore two sons, Aeolus and Boetius, but the god found her lust insatiable so put her eyes out. Perhaps a prelude to Metapontum's everlasting night. Others say that Metabos arrived here in 1270 BC after the Trojan Wars and founded a colony. Or it could be that Lybos, the wolf king, reigned in the forests here and carried virgins off to hell with him. If he did, says Lenormant, 'the demon has returned to reclaim his ancient lands'.

There is nothing now. Breathless air with heat in it trembling over the sand, and the dumb sea moving in a mystery of blues, purples and gold. A slow-rolling, speechless and uncaring sheet. Silver shines into black; frosts of pearl glint on it; or eyes of steely and jealous green, and sparks of diamonds and firefly tails. In the remorseless murmurs the sun threads gold onto it, then a mirror of blinding glass as each belly-swell breathes. But the waves say nothing; theirs is a private history.

Then the Germans arrived. A bunker-truck on rubber swept down the sand and dustily halted.

'*Ach. Guten Tag . . . sehr schöon . . . wunderbar . . . Ja?*'

'I'm English.'

'It's beautiful. No?'

'Beautiful. Yes.'

'Is der sea hot?'

'Warm probably.'

'The kinder vish to svim . . . Komme, Heidi . . . Hans . . . Gretel . . . *schnell* . . .' clapping fat jovial hands. The back of the camper van exploded, loosening a diarrhoea stream of extended juvenescence from three to fifteen, two dogs and a super-efficient iron-maiden mother bearing folded towels and gross picnic hamper. At the water's edge the squealing pack did a rapid shell-pea pop from clothes and, minus all camouflage, began disappearing towards Africa with tinkling shrieks . . .

'You don't object they svim naked? . . . Ja?'

'No . . . *Ja*.' What else?

'Italians are strange about it, ha-ha. Catholics . . . guilty bodies . . . Ve don't mind . . . ha-ha . . . Der papal phallusy . . . ha-ha.'

He said he was a chemist from Bremen University, and he already had his laboratory spread out on the sand: guide books, maps, rulers, compasses and binoculars, plotting times and distances from *schloss* to *schloss*. A symbol of Teutonic efficiency; Belsen and buzz-bombs. In six minutes he clapped his hands and the skin-quintet squirted out of the sea like champagne corks, hands by their sides to attention.

I went to watch a dig this morning about a mile outside the old city walls. The remains of them are just visible in some places: great blocks of stone peeping out of the earth, the original line of defence of the first established settlement. But the land was so fertile, and so many other Greeks from the mainland heard the news, that Metapontum exploded; by 500 BC it had spread far beyond the two rivers Bradano and Basento and even reached well up into the inland hills. It was enormously prosperous and, for the most part, content, except that there were other rich Greeks in the neighbourhood, and some of them weren't Achaeans. Ethnic problems were brewing.

The dig was taking place on a slight mound crowned by a disused, half-ruined brick building called Casa Ricotta. The archaeologists aren't allowed to go near this roofless wreck, as the owner has the right to make them build him a completely new stable if they touch it. There were five men with spades standing in the sun, and one with a large yellow bulldozer, complete with sabre-toothed bucket on the front. This roared enthusiastically and nose-dived into the earth like a terrier after rats, while the five men scraped. Observing them, without a great deal of excitement, was the archaeology superintendent of the area, who explained that as Mussolini's Riformia had put a pipeline through in the 1930s, most of the tombs had been robbed, so nothing sensational was likely to happen. 'We're looking at the skeletons,' he said, 'dating the burial; finding out their age, their sex, height and how they died.'

'What have you discovered?' I asked.

'Well, we know this part of the hill was a family graveyard – perhaps two families for several generations. The early graves are two or three metres down in big tombs; they must have been rich. Later on they buried people on top of each other in layers, some with just slabs over them, much poorer. The last ones are here just under the surface.'

The men were scraping at one, covered by less than an inch of earth, almost bonded to it and barely recognisable; first they were stone-shapes, then they became bone-shapes, squashed by time, tractors, tanks and stamping armies. There were fragments of brittle and rotting brown, a squashed skull too splintered to grin; the crushed stubble of someone; yellow-white wafer bits lying in the sun; paper-thin shapes of a 'who' that was; and once it was you, and soon you'll be that.

'How did they die?' I asked, and he shrugged.

'Heart failure, malaria, syphilis, other diseases – violence even. They didn't live long; fifty was old age.'

'They managed to build a few temples.'

'No, they didn't. Slaves did. They were too busy fighting: fighting among themselves for power; fighting other Greeks. They were greedy, like savages.'

I knew by now he didn't like them. Later I found out he was a Neolithic enthusiast and supported the indigenous tribes whom the Greeks had replaced.

'. . . you can forget your Greek gods here,' he went on, 'those statues of Hercules. They dreamed all that up; they invented it. Your average Greek here was only five feet tall and a complete thug.'

So much for Gissing's dream then!

In the afternoon he took me to see Metapontum's new museum. His museum. It's splendid. One of his specialities was on display: what the locals were wearing before the Greeks arrived. He likes the inland tribes best – the Peucetians, Daunians and Japygi – and says they taught the Greeks as much as the Greeks taught them, as there was lots of friendly intermingling and cross-fertilisation at first. They only started fighting later, when they got angry with each other over territory or slaves or whose gods were better. For the main part the Greeks thought they might be some distant pre-Homeric ancestors of theirs.

The whole of the ground floor was filled with transparent body-shapes of plastic, each draped in the fashions of more then thirty centuries ago: mini-skirts, brassières of beaten copper or silver, foot-long bracelets, giant earrings and moccasin shoes with ankle-thongs. There were bronze chokers intricately carved and long necklaces with fobs on.

The skirts were strings of beads or woven strands of leather, secured by belts of hide or reed, with ornate buckles or clasps that dipped to emphasise mystery. Some had bodices on like open waistcoats, and there were intricate head-bands. Their arms were mostly bare, with loops of cord wound round them, or a selection of bracelets made of silver, bronze, amber or coloured stones, and some wore elbow-guards. Age had darkened everything, but the detail was still there; the fineness of the engraving and the craftwork in the metal; the beauty was there too, as was the obvious pleasure they found in exhibitionism, self-decoration and the love of appearance. A *bella figura* fashion-show thirty centuries old.

I asked him about tomb-robbing, but again he shrugged as if it didn't interest him. 'They're everywhere,' he said. 'Nowadays they use detectors, or they prod the earth with long metal tubes that resonate when they hit a tomb. Then they dig it up: house-builders find stuff every day round here.'

'Do you try to catch them?'

'Pointless. They're professionals working in gangs. Tomb-robbing isn't a major offence anyway; they only get a fine. Car headlights might scare them off at night. I did that once, but it's not worth a fight. Anyway . . .' and he smiled, '. . . I've got more vases here than I know what to do with.'

That's probably true. It's been said more than once that there are more than 5,000 figured vases tucked away unseen in museum store-rooms in Puglia. You also hear official murmurs of support for these clandestine operators. Better to be privately loved and treasured than publicly unknown and ignored, some of them say. I don't think Bernalda is completely blameless, either. All the shops and offices have Greek *mortaria* being used as ashtrays, and amphorae for flowerpots. Would I like any?

We went back to end the day's digging as the sun weakened. Half a mile away, where the ground flattened towards the old Greek city, there were bent figures working in the fields, stooped over the soil like a school of barely moving beetles. They were harnessed to the present, and dibbed and hoed in the slowest of motions and refilled the ground with seed. Dark-clothed and silent, with shawls or handkerchief hats, they never looked up from their duty of renewing the cycle of life; while beside me the bulldozer sighed into silence from its search for the cycle of death.

'Have you heard of Isabella Morra?' asked Paola's father this morning. I said I hadn't. He then told me where to go and find out about her: in Valsinni.

Perched on Aldo's machine, I set off inland into the mountains and through miles of forests along a road that writhed as if it had been tortured, and never stopped going up and up. The wind came round every corner like an express train and at one point commandeered my sunhat. White as a giant rose petal, it floated into an anonymous Basilicatan valley and will doubtless land on a thorn bush until it's dined on by a goat. The road wound round itself like entrails in an abattoir or boiled-up rubber bands, and everywhere was steep and forested; a darkness of trees kept closing in; a shroud with a crack where a streak of sky was; and there were crags, rockfalls and dismal peaks. I went mile after moped mile through demonic dark green turning to blackness, where everything suggested fear and death. I felt thoroughly haunted.

Then suddenly on a clifftop I saw the castle. Almost eagle-like, it was perched on a pinnacle of rock where the walls on three sides fell away vertically into space. It was a triumph of unassailable loneliness. This was Valsinni, and I found my way to the entrance and read the plaque I'd been told about. 'This castle witnessed the birth, life and death of Isabella Morra, poetess. It was visited by Benedetto Croce in 1928.' That prolific Neapolitan man of letters – historian, critic and philosopher – stayed here for a single day. She lived here for twenty-five years until her brothers killed her.

The Morra family were Angevin supporters, but when Spain began to take over the southern kingdom in 1490, Isabella's father fled to France, promising that he would arrange for the family to follow. Some of his sons weren't unduly concerned; there was sport in the forests and amusement to be had among the village girls. But Isabella was different. She was the only daughter and she felt alone and trapped. The longer she waited for news from France, the sadder and more depressed she became, starting to fill notebooks about Valsinni's 'foul valleys of hell', the 'uncouth tribes of villagers' and her brothers' 'gross appetites and savage passions'. In captive isolation Isabella hated the forests full of ruined caves, rank rivers and bestial people, and she despised her brothers for being 'barbarous and wild because of the vileness of the surroundings'. As her anguish increased she began to express her feelings in verse, random lines to anyone: the Virgin Mary, Charles V, Fortune, Fate . . .

> Oh God, in your unjust hand the fates have lied;
> Your hate is this lonely and living hell . . .
>
> Oh Juno! You scorner of bodies and passion
> Pray find me one happy heart to love . . .

In desperation she would climb to the top of the hill behind the castle, Monte Coppola (where there are still some Greek remains), and look towards the sea, beyond vanished Erakleia and Siris, hoping for the sight of a sail that would bring news of her father and news of the French court, now complete with its polished symposium of fugitive Italian artists and poets:

> Swept with desolation and weary dread . . .

Metapontum

I mourn the dark storm of your long-gone going.

It isn't known how Isabella's poems began to circulate, but they came to the attention of a Spanish nobleman who lived nearby and who also wrote verses. Don Diego Sandeval De Castro was 'a sweet Petrarchan', according to Croce, and a handsome adventurer as well – 'Mars and Apollo rolled into one'. Whether the two of them ever met is pure conjecture. '*Di questo drama segreto non sappiamo nulla*' – of this secret drama we know nothing – growls Croce, but we know that one day in 1545 three of Isabella's brothers intercepted a letter from Don Diego being smuggled into the castle by her tutor. They killed the messenger on the spot, found Isabella and ran her through with their swords; and then that night they ambushed Don Diego in the forest and hacked him to death. It was something Isabella had already foretold – 'My life here steeped in blood and blind oblivion.' But this Websterian drama had a final act. A younger brother had escaped to France years earlier and had become a secretary to Queen Catherine de' Medici, and it was to him that the three murderers fled for forgiveness and protection. As soon as he had given it, they poisoned him.

None of this would be known at all, had not one of the three murderers confessed everything to his son on his deathbed: that a long-dead aunt of his had once lived in a castle in distant Basilicata, and had written poetry, and had had to die for being in love with a Spanish lord. So this nephew, Marcantonio Morra, wrote the whole story down in *Familiae Nobilissimae de Morra Historia*, published in Naples in 1629. But Isabella Morra had got there first; she had already become famous; her poems were published posthumously in 1550:

My dear father's promises weep inside my heart.

And:

> When from the east Aurora springs a crimson ray,
> Sounds the clarion bell of day,
> Salutes us; lifts our hearts again . . .
> Then can I smile . . .

I get woken by donkey-brays in the morning just as it's getting light. They are outside my window. Bernalda doesn't boast a hotel, only an old lady who offers rooms, and these are next to the market. After this strangled seesawing stentorian bellow, the sparrows that haven't been shot start, and then the market arrives. This is competitive selling at fever-pitch: a verbal punch-up of screeches, bawls and screams disappearing off the decibel range. They're Verdi-babes; full-throated *fortissimi* merchants. Centuries ago the rulers of Florence used to impose noise curfews. Today's Italians can't live without uproar; the louder, the better.

It was Saturday; invited to lunch by Paola's father, as Paola was back from Lecce, I took a bottle of spumante. I shouldn't have done. Paola is not a linguist, she likes the Beatles – but unfortunately 'Giallo Sommergibile' doesn't fit the music – and she is surprised I am not a personal friend of Meek Jegger and Medness. So we sit down to the *signora*'s helpings of *osso buco* with cold potatoes and bowls of salad, while Paola's father thumbs the spumante cork warily. It hit the ceiling and vanished, followed by a geyser that leaped six feet, turned into foam and settled back on the table in a cloud of wet dust. Not a word was spoken. The *signora* did a running tut for the kitchen to bale us out and deliquefy our plates, while we sat rigid in silence. I broke it.

'What about local folk songs?' I said. 'Shepherd songs?'

'*Non. Preferisco* Lee Sting,' offers Paola.

'Handel used Italian shepherd music. You know, *Messiah*.'

'Jesus Christ?' she nodded.

'Yes, kind of . . . like an opera . . . Monteverdi *Vespers* . . .'

'Si, I know. Superstar . . .'

'There's a group in Pisticci,' said her father weakly, 'they sing folk songs . . .'

Saved by the bell. The *signora* came back with cloths and we attacked our floating lunch.

In the south they still have the ritual *passeggiata*; it operates by some internal alarm clock. One moment the main street is scorched and empty, the next it is cool and heaving as if lemmings were answering a flood-call. It should be performed slowly and arm-in-arm, everyone harmoniously joined and burr-stuck, to farewell the fading day . . . and talk about it. It isn't easy. I sometimes wonder if they've ever seen each other before. I'm glued to Paola's father.

'Buona sera.'

'Do you think Andreotti was ever . . . ?'

'*Ciao, Professore.*'

'Do people know he . . . ?'

'*Ciao. Come stai?*'

'Why didn't the government . . . ?'

'*Buona sera . . . Va bene?*'

'Will Milan win the . . . ?'

'*Salve,* Dottore . . . *Si, sta bene.*'

'What about Bari then? Any chance . . . ?'

'*Professore . . . Auguri . . . Come stai?*'

'How many Albanians do you think are . . . ?'

'*Ciao, Dottore . . . Grazie . . . Si, grazie . . .*'

'That dig. Will they find any . . . ?'

'*Salve, amico . . . Ciao . . . A domani . . .*'

'Christ! What about drugs . . . ?'

'*Scusa . . . Professore . . . Buona sera . . . Momento . . .*'

'Jesus . . . !'

I know what's wrong with Italy now; nobody ever finishes a sentence – they don't actually say anything.

The young ones do it on wheels; they *autoggiata*, slightly faster speed.

Brmm . . . Brmm. . . Brmm . . .

'*Ciao*.' '*Ciao* . . . *Bella*,' . . . Wave . . .

Brmm . . . Wave again . . . Peep . . . peeeeeeep . . .

'*Ciao* . . . Peppino . . . *Salve* . . .'

Brake . . . Tyre squeal . . . Peep . . . Blow kisses . . .

'*Ciao*, Stronzo.'

Peep . . . peep . . . peep . . . peep . . .

'*Mamma mia* . . . *Che culo!*'

Brake . . . Peep.

Brmm . . . CRASH . . . TINKLE . . . Shit!

Tinkle . . . Tinkle . . .

Only a side light . . . Brmm . . . Brmm . . . Brmm . . .

A lot of this evening exercise is accompanied by gesticulations, provided you aren't glued to somebody and can find space to move. It used to be sign language once, using arms, hands or fingers, but now it's just octopoid waving and thrashing around; like live strings of spaghetti having hysterics. After a really thick *passeggiata* you can count your bruises. The men do it more than the women. They flail the air to assure you that what they are saying is really important, which it never is because they never finish saying it. It's quite amusing to watch two men having a conversation; even when they're quite old they have the gymnastic facility of excited squids.

I didn't know the Pisticci folk group performed in competitions all over Europe. Now I've seen them, I'm not surprised. I went over with Paola's father and found them rehearsing in a barn. It looked easy enough to get to – a couple of miles across the valley to a speckle of white houses sitting on the other side like a flock of roosting doves. It took us the best part of an hour by car, snaking down for ages, flattening out briefly, then snaking up again.

There were about thirty of them; all ages, fifteen to forty

and dressed in their work clothes, looking unconcerned. Greetings over, someone squeezed an accordion and it was as if they'd all had an electric shock; they bolted upright and started to dance, shuffling into formation. Their eyes had hardened into focus, bright with excitement, and their bodies went taut as catapults as their feet began to drum. They were remotely controlled; hypnotised; twisting, whirling, turning, stamping their feet and clapping their hands. Their heels went like castanets, getting faster and angrier. Don't touch us; don't interrupt. One dance broke into another without a pause; rivers of bodies flowed as formations changed for jigs, flings, reels and twists. They separated, partnered, turned and touched by fingertip – not ballet-sweet and slow, but vehement and determined, full of blood and vibrating energy. Sweat poured as they galloped, as if goaded by the tambourine beat, hip shaking at hip, breath meeting breath and eye challenging eye, as braced bodies asked and answered. It was urgent and unstoppable: a frenzy of shapes and movements possessed by music.

Afterwards one of the girls put on a proper festival costume. It started scarlet, with a wide-blown floor-length skirt edged in black, ballooning as she turned. The collar was a web of white lace and the sleeves puffed out into cuffs of black and gold. She put a waistcoat over it, black at first until she tightened it over her hips and I saw threads of gold and silver. Then, last of all, a winged wimple on her head; old-fashioned, nunnish, but this was just jet-black with edges of red and gold. She was out of time – a century old. You only see costumes like this nowadays in the paintings of some of the Grand Tour artists, Pietro Fabris, David Allan, Giovanni Lusieri and sometimes Jacob Hackert.

As the student said in Sternatia: they're anachronisms.

I've got to leave, and Paola's father's suggestion is to have a party first, and will I make a speech?

It's in a barn on the edge of town and nobody is dressed

up, casually putting jugs of wine on a thirty-foot-long table, while in a corner flames are leaping up from a brazier where something is being grilled. Musicians have been summoned; four of them gathered round a remarkable human shape spread in a chair – a Henry VIII figure, only older, clutching a Tweedledum belly, who croaks that he can't sing any more. 'Ah, you can hear him three kilometres away,' says a musician. He thrusts a weird piece of wood at him, with wire and bells on it plus a clapper, which the master pokes under his chin and starts to stroke with a stick. At the same time he draws breath and lets a sound come out of his mouth that starts like an intestinal escape, develops into a Gregorian wail, and gathers such force and intensity that it hits the ceiling, bounds off the walls, deafens the room and disappears through the barn door like a war-head. It's vast; throat, lungs and belly combined; a Minotaur roar in a cave, primitive and unmelodic; a noise that wants freedom. The other musicians start: two racing guitars and one with the *cupa-cupa*, which looks indecent, the nearest thing to musical wanking you've ever seen. The noise it makes sounds like a foghorn with gastritis. It's a primitive drum or tambourine; goatskin stretched tight over a hollow bowl, but instead of tapping it, they push a prick-sized stick through the middle and work it up and down at speed. It starts a double-bass howl; an accompaniment; a booming sound like thunder with indigestion on slightly different notes, if the operator is skilful.

Suddenly someone else joins in. A sleek young man with raven hair who looks like a Turkish pirate. Every time the old man stops to draw breath, the newcomer answers him, shouts him down. Some was traditional, some impromptu; a musical fight; the young one hip-twisting and dancing as he replied, contradicted and challenged. He had a young voice with power and a clever break in it, like a glottal yodelling note or a sobbing hiccough that changed the tone;

and I was told it was rare to find singers in the south who can still do this – it's like a vocal sob of sadness or remorse.

The dialect and speed made it incomprehensible. I could tell it wasn't polite – everyone was laughing; it went on and on like some Burnsian mating-epic until they'd both had enough; but how many wives and daughters were vocally ravished that night, God knows.

I tried to make the promised speech during supper, but only got one sentence out; ten words and they were clapping to shut me up. A stewpot on the table was being ladled into dishes called *ciaudedda*, a thick soup of onions, beans, oil and etceteras, with torn-off hunks of bread being passed and jugs of wine . . . Chin-chin, England . . . Chin-chin, London . . .

A bent figure started hammering something on the brazier, sending up sparks. It might have been a baby goat once – lumps of it were shovelled into dishes for finger-eating; goat-bone with meat on it, and fat dollops of polenta, which is a tasteless yellow porridge they ate to keep alive a hundred years ago. I didn't dare put my glass down; it kept brimming dark red; I kept drinking from it . . . Metapontum got twinned with Manchester United, Bernalda with Birmingham, Margaret Thatcher would win the World Cup . . . Cheeses like footballs were on the table . . .

I think the musicians left at some stage; slipped away into the night. And the fire must have died. I was thoroughly wine-soaked; crept back through darkness and silent Bernalda, where only imaginary shadows moved; or dogs and cats.

NINE

Gravina

I have deviated to Gravina to find some English archaeologists who were doing a dig here, but they've gone, which is a pity. Anyway, I now know they were actually Canadians looking for prehistory. The hotel proprietor is sad about it too as there were some girl students in the party, with the result that the bar was filled morning and night by local youth in search of hope and fruition. Being Canadian and brought up in a polar-bear climate, the archaeologists were totally unused to the Sahara-type sun of Puglia and dressed for the occasion. This not only filled the bar twice a day, but somewhat naturally brought most of Gravina to a standstill each morning and evening as they trudged along the main road to and from their dig. One man I met in the street asked if I was one of them. 'No,' I said.

'Good thing too,' he grunted, 'they were whores.'

'What whores?' I asked, bracing myself to be belligerent for the sake of Empire and a common language.

'*Donne nude*,' he said savagely, drawing an imaginary strip of something across his upper chest and then a codpiece-shape over his trousers.

I tried to explain that Canada was cold and they were used to snowdrifts, not ovens, but he wouldn't have it.

'Go to the beach to be naked,' he said. 'Here we're Christians . . .'

Christianity is not the first thing that strikes you about Gravina. I don't just mean the local youth, who thought that Canadian girls returning from an exhausting day's work in the sun, wearing shorts and with painful and electrically pink thighs, were inviting instant copulation, I mean death. Death is the first thing that strikes you here;

because Gravina is built on a series of deep ravines, and all
the ravines have caves in them, and all the caves are full of
skulls. They're white, ghoulish, battered, ugly, pathetic and
piled to the roof, complete with a spillikin shambles of
broken bones. The remains of mass murder. What a
country! Some students have just been marshalled to clear a
few out and they've already filled a thousand sacks.
Conjecture is useless: Romans, Byzantines, Saracens, Lombards, Normans, Angevins. And what the hell was there to
fight for anyway? Land, I suppose, because this is part of the
Tavogliere Plain, rich for grazing and growing cereals and an
important staging post on the road south from Rome into
the Mediterranean.

Now the archaeologists have left, the hotel doesn't serve
meals, so the proprietor advises me where to eat, rubbing
his nose with one finger and looking coy at the same time,
which is a semi-Masonic sign that he trusts me and is
letting me in on a secret. The secret is about two miles
away: an enormous mock-Georgian villa set in acres of
garden with fountains, lawns, tennis courts and a swimming pool with submerged lighting. 'It's a private club,' he
said, 'you eat well and can stay there for the night. You
know, private rooms,' his expression oiling its way into a
suggestive leer. It was obvious that someone, somewhere,
was doing very well.

The restaurant, a liveried flunky informed me at the main
door to this *palazzo*, was across the gardens. It looked like
the twin of the hothouses at Kew – a glass monstrosity the
size of an aircraft hanger – and I arrived in the middle of a
wedding party, or it could have been the dying throes. The
bride certainly looked like it; lying on a sofa in the entrance
foyer, red in the face, and giving hydraulic gasps as if she'd
just completed a marathon; vast bosoms heaving like
animated blubber and faint whispers of 'Pah! pah! O, *Dio*'
coming out of her mouth. She was being brought back to

life by two kneeling handmaidens fanning her like Furies and giving squeaks of consolation. Enormous! It could have been a body or it could have been wrapping. She looked like a badly travelled parcel arriving in a blizzard or as if the polar icecap was breaking up, except that octopus earrings with pink tips were hanging down from invisible ears. Which reminds me. There's a racket going on with this wedding-dress white-stuff. Apparently the Chinese are importing it illegally along the coast by the ton – all cheap and made back home by slave labour – and are flogging it off at a profit here that runs into thousands. But all the girls have to have it. If you see an opening, cash in; rather like this place I'm in.

I went through to the restaurant. It was massive; big enough to seat a hundred; all painted pale green and white to keep it cool, and with huge chandeliers hanging from the ceiling.

The waitress was Albanian, dark-haired, slim and pretty, speaking fluent Italian. I peeped through the double doors into the ballroom to see how the wedding party was getting on – nobody seemed to have missed the bride. Waiters kept popping through doors carrying trays of glasses; they gave Groucho smirks this side and metamorphosed into silky seriousness the other.

'Quite a party,' I said to the Albanian girl.

'Weddings are out of date,' she answered. 'A waste of money.'

'Aren't you Catholic? Don't you believe in marriage?'

'I'm Muslim. No, actually I'm atheist. All Albanians are atheists. We've grown out of religion. It's pointless. Italians don't think; they've got closed minds; they do what they're told. It's not like this in Durazzo. We're really advanced. Things like this are stupid.'

I went to investigate the party again. The ballroom was twice the size of the dining room, all neo-mock Adam-classical: white everywhere with ribbons of Pompeian creepers creeping and mirrored walls cased in swirls of gold plaster. Now it was lined with exhausted wedding wall-flowers, all heavily seated and numbed by the nuptial extravaganza. At one end some dehydrated musicians in paper hats were playing half-hearted solos to a shoal of children doing fifty-yard dashes up and down the ballroom floor, skidding, bumping and turning and throwing streamers. They kept just missing a man in dreamland, waltzing to himself with a baby on his chest. The waiters did Charlie Chaplin minces as they picked up glasses, half-bowing on tiptoe, and a girl started crooning love into a microphone.

'When did it start?' I asked the Albanian.

'Three o'clock,' she said. 'It's been going for nearly five hours. This place is a gold mine. It's like this every weekend. Two or three in the week as well, specially in summer.'

'Expensive, I should think?'

'Millions. They must be mad,' and she laughed.

'Don't you miss Albania and your family?'

'I go home every month. It's easy. I telephone them every day. They're fine.'

Her eyes showed how happy she was. Miss Albania was not only attractive and self-assured, but obviously content and doing very well. Lucky somebody, and lucky Miss Albania.

The kitchen doors opened and out came the wedding cake. Usually when the doors opened it was the chef popping out to keep his eye on the football match on the dining-room television, but this time it was the food finale. Nearly two yards high on a trolley, with four waiters in attendance, stood a silvery-white Pisan tower-block of four diminishing upward sections, each supported by pillars; it was a lavish sculpted colossus with minglings of green, pink and red, soaring to its summit of a spray of blush-roses; the base bedded in an ocean of white tulips and lilies. A hyperbole of happiness; towers, friezes, dripping garnish and wrought icing rolled forward to relight the matrimonial embers, greeted by saxophone screeches, drum rolls, scattered hand-claps and an avalanche of photographers.

'Do you speak Albanian?' I asked.

'Of course I do.'

'You know about Skanderberg, your great hero who came over here with his army?'

'Who?'

'Do you ever go and see the Albanians in the mountains? The old ones in the villages?'

'Not likely, they're horrible. Ancient. No one likes them.'

'I've been photographing them, recording folk songs.'

She looked at me as though I was mad. 'That's ridiculous,' she said, taking my plate. 'I like Jimi Hendrix.'

When the party was over, tired nuptial troopers drifted away into the night, turned pale by the floodlights. Fountains sparkled as they splashed into pools of sleepy fish, and paths led to the darkness of secret arbours. The black figures of trees grew tall as they watched in state, and moths beat at the lights to scorch and die. Darts of children flashed across lawns and disappeared as the growl of car engines started.

There would be more tomorrow.

Being built and rebuilt on a series of ravines, Gravina is uneven. Every street goes up or down and nothing looks level. You can walk round a cobbled corner, look over a wall and gaze down, bird-like, into a hundred feet of space. You can also walk down precipitous and twisting steps, past banked-up, white two-roomed houses glued to the landmass, one piled unevenly on the other, till you end up in scrub and debris; or you can walk the other way over a different chasm by a narrow stone footbridge that must have been there for hundreds of years. There are two tiny chapels the other side, both deserted, and one with some pre-Christian graffiti on the walls, and beyond that the

gloomy grey mountain called Botromagno, where the excavation was. Looking back, you can see Gravina's erratic
shapelessness; its discomfort; wars on wars and death on
death; an illogical and ragged outline against the sky; part of
the cracked and juiceless backbone of Italy. You can sense
the hopelessness of its history.

I have met a local historian who is going to explain it all to
me. (There are local historians in every town in Italy;
sometimes several. This one's speciality is infant mortality,
which is encouraging.) Point one is that Gravina is very old
and probably lies on the ancient Appian Way from Rome to
Brindisi; and that rather gruesome mountain about a mile
away, where the Canadians were digging, was once called
Silvium; and Silvium is the only staging post mentioned by
the geographer Antoninus in his Appian itinerary that has
yet to be identified. The historian knows the mountain was
Silvium, because he found an old coin up there with
Sidinon on it. Point two is that Gravina was once enormous, very rich and a thriving city twice the size of Bari
because of all the fertile land surrounding it, which was
perfect for grazing livestock. Furthermore, the largest agri-
cultural fair in Europe used to be held here, and this is
where the crusaders bought new horses before setting off for
Jerusalem. Point three: all was well with Gravina until a
certain duke called Bernaldo Orsini took over, who happened to be the son of Pope Clement XIII, and was so greedy
that he quadrupled – or thereabouts – all the local taxes,
behaved like a tyrant and in a few years reduced the
population to one-fifth of its original size. There was such
misery, the historian explains, that people were reduced to
eating rats, and mothers would drug their babies with wine,
smother them and throw their bodies into the ravines to be
eaten by dogs. And Gravina has never recovered.

Which may go some way to explaining the number of
skulls, though he did add that the Saracens devastated the

town in about 980 and held it until the Normans arrived to take it; they then did roughly the same, as bands of them were always fighting each other for ownership. In its fractured history Gravina has also belonged to the King of Hungary and to Skanderberg's sister. Also, there was a tornado in 1687 which actually blew houses down; and if that didn't kill people, the dust did; it choked some of them to death.

Gravina has an air of melancholy hanging over it. Hope has been defeated too often; like a hearse on its way to a funeral, wanting to end it all.

I went up to Botromagno today to see what all the fuss was about. On my way across an unkempt mile of sparse grass I saw an old man walking with his head down, who kept stopping in his tracks and diving at the ground, rather like a bird on a lawn pouncing on worms. He was collecting mushrooms, or to our minds toadstools, as they were saucer-sized and mucky brown. This curious, low-lying fungal object is apparently a delicacy hereabouts – called *muligno* – whose proper name I have discovered is *Agaricus olearius*. Apparently, in some parts of Puglia, collecting edible toadstools is a full-time occupation. They're sold to restaurants.

The climb up the hill was not amusing as the path didn't appear to have been used for hundreds of years. After stumbling over endless areas of broken rocks, I was at a very flat and windy summit, where a few pine trees whined in discomfort and the Canadians had obviously been busy. What they had found were the foundations of a considerable Roman villa with gardens, courtyards and stables, all signifying a certain wealth, and probably the residence of a local governor. The Roman historian Diodorus Siculus says the Romans took it over in 306 BC and had to kill at least 5,000 of the indigenous inhabitants there before they could command the hill. These weren't Greeks, but probably a tribe of Samnites or Peucetians. What these people left behind seems even more remarkable than the Roman villa: remains of fortification walls almost three miles in circumference and originally up to three yards high, made of giant rectangular blocks. The Canadians calculated they would have needed 40,000 of these to complete their defences, which suggests that they were both incredibly strong and knew a lot about weight-lifting and overcoming gravity.

The Gravinese very seldom come up here as they claim it is haunted. It is. Up here dwell the original spirits of Puglia, deep in a 3,000-year sleep, who before they vanished cast a curse that Gravina would always be as they were: possessed by death.

My historian friend is not at all happy. He feels isolated; something is missing from his existence. Like the artist in Brindisi, I would call this patriotism. He is not the first person I have met who hates Garibaldi and wishes Italy had never been united.

We were sitting in his tiny workroom-cum-office.

'The north raped us,' he said. 'It was an invasion. They came down here like a pack of wolves. They starved us, turned us into slaves.'

'I thought you wanted it; wanted to be one country; loved Garibaldi?'

'Some of us did, but we were all stupid. The idea of it was so marvellous – to get the Bourbons out and have a change. We even let off fireworks here and knocked down some of the town walls. We all danced in the streets, singing songs of freedom:

O Redenti; Sorgete, Sorgete,   (Redeem yourselves and rise up,
Del selvaggio piu figli non siete . . .   You are no longer sons of
                                     savages . . .)

'What happened then?'

'They overran us, as if we were the enemy; called us brutes, *"Caffoni"* – savages. They forced all our little farmers off the land, fenced off the grazing on the Tavogliere Plain, said we didn't know how to farm properly, then turned all the fields into huge estates owned by rich northerners and made us work for them. Anyone who didn't obey had to starve.'

'Couldn't you do anything?'

'How? They brought armies down with them; men with guns to patrol the fields. And officials from the north came down as well: judges from the north, police from the north, local governors from the north. It was hopeless. That's why so many people went to America; they fled. It was despotism. I've got letters, diaries, photographs to prove it. Estate foremen, the Massari, pointing guns at people to force them to work. There was unemployment too. If you wanted a job you had to bribe a northern official and, with no money, all you could do was offer him your wife or daughter for the night. Sometimes they just took them anyway.'

'Do people know about this?'

'Course they do; but it's so long ago nobody cares any more. We forget things too easily and have no sense of history. We're fickle. Only the present matters. It's shameful.'

'Why don't you write about it?'

'What's the point? Nobody would care. You can't turn the clock back. I've got a description here of a boy of ten working in a field, having to pull weeds out with his prick. The Massari tied string to him and made him walk up and down pulling weeds out. You know Lenormant, don't you? He called it *"Un despotisme sans limites et sans contrôles"*.'

'Surely people know this . . .'

'Of course they do, but it's not the official version. The official version is all joy and happiness; our gratitude at

being liberated; welcoming our Italian brothers. Nicola
Leoni told the truth in 1880. "The Risorgimento is a lie. We
live in hell. Religion, order and justice are dead. There are
murders every day. Priests take mistresses and girls are
raped. Italy is not noble; Italy is squalid, ignorant, foul and
miserable."'

I was silent, not knowing what to say as he looked at me.

'Here in Gravina we had "Milking Time" every evening,'
he went on. I waited. 'When the men came back from
working in the fields all day there wasn't any food, only a
communal kitchen in the square. The wives would all have
to line up, holding their bowls out at huge troughs that the
Massari had filled with food; filthy soup and bread made
with chalk. As the women came up for their ration, the
officials would fondle them, bare their breasts and feel up
their skirts. If they objected they went without . . .'

'Didn't anyone fight back?'

'How? We were disorganised; taken by surprise. How
could we fight against armed men? People who grumbled
were beaten or left to starve. There was one uprising here.
About a hundred labourers went to complain to the official
in charge; they were ambushed by some landlords on
horseback, who killed ten of them.'

'What about the Church? The priests?'

He looked at me, almost smiling.

'In Italy priests go where the power is; they were in league
with the landowners; by cooperating there was butter on
their bread. One whiff of real trouble, or of cholera or
disease, and they vanished.'

He gave a final sigh.

'So now you see why the south votes Communist. It may
be stupid, but it's the only escape they can see. They think
it will give them the power for a change.'

I'd had a history lesson, and thought it was time to leave
him. I was feeling uncomfortable, inside and out, thinking
of the Bourbons, the Carbonari, Byron, the revolutionary

Liberals, Nelson murdering them, and Dante Gabriel Rossetti, safe in England, singing 'In the balmy garden of Italy bondage is no more'. Giuseppe di Lampedusa had been right: the old lions had gone; hyenas and jackals had taken over.

Just as I left, he pushed a newspaper cutting at me, covering the date with his hand. 'Politics is confused with private interest and with greed and profit. The result is maladministration, neglect and waste.' Then he uncovered the date. The article had been written in 1890.

Charles de Brosse said it all in five words in his letters in 1799. 'Italy is a sad country.'

Gravina does have a small and rather charming museum concealed in a side street. It is not really a museum at all; it is a time capsule with some archaeological additions; the private house of the wealthy Baron Santomasi, who lived here just before unification and then left his home and estate to the town when he died. (After what the historian had said, I thought it might have been burned down.)

The first thing of interest was the visitors' book; more than 400 Germans had been in the last three years, seventy-one Swiss and five English. While the Hun is exploratory and predatory and the Swiss get tired of their snow, the English are totally incurious; just flockers and trippers. The upstairs living quarters were Bourbon elegance in miniature, small tidy rooms full of *ottocento* decoration and furnishings. Gilded mirrors lined the walls, swags of silk curtains shaded the windows, their yellow, blue and pink flower patterns slightly faded, their edges brocade-bobbled. Most of the furniture was dark, almost coffin-like, and one bed had a bell-shaped canopy over it and a small oak cot on rockers beside it on the floor. There were no carpets; blue and white Dutch tiles on all the floors; and the ceilings were all pale-blue skies where fairy-tale maidens danced or dabbled in streams or pursued suitably rustic pleasures.

Photography must have arrived. There were strained black-and-white family faces on almost every surface, slightly fuzzy as if held for a time exposure; uncomfortable old ladies stony-faced with swept-back hair and buns; old men in buttoned waistcoats wearing Al Capone hamburger hats; girls wearing bonnets and stiff-necked boys in Eton collars. Self-inflicted torture in the heat to gain immortality.

Downstairs was a collection of objects found in local caves; an amateur's assemblage of curiosities, probably brought in by peasants more than a hundred years ago; and some strange pieces of folk memorabilia. I wanted to know what a small concertina arrangement of wood was, and was told it was a 'love-arm'. Amorous swains would stand below balconies they couldn't reach, and by expanding this slender tong-like contraption could pass forbidden notes up to waiting young ladies.

Then there was a very ordinary piece of string hanging on a hook, but apparently an extremely important item as it was a virginity test, and in this respect totally unmedical. You proceeded with your enquiry as follows: place the string round the girl's neck once; remove it and double the length; join the two ends together so that it forms a loop and get the victim to hold the ends in her teeth; now try to pass the loop over her head. If it slides over easily she is *intacta*, and if it doesn't, she isn't. Ramage mentions something like this in his *Nooks and Byways* and thinks it might even be an ancient Greek custom. I suggested later to the historian that it would be interesting to try it out on a few girls, but he was against it.

The hotel proprietor has a piece of scandal to tell me. It is, of course, extremely secret, but as I am '*simpatico*' and '*una persona per bene*' he is prepared to share this very hush-hush and confidential matter with me. I ought to know anyway, he says, because after all nationality is important to all of us, and this was almost about a compatriot. One of the Canadian archaeologists went mad on Botromagno. Instead of digging or scraping at shards or measuring skeletons, she became severely overheated by the sun and ran round shouting, 'Let's go fuck.' This shocks him, or he makes a good pretence at it, being a total hypocrite, and he expects me to be similarly horrified; but I'm not. I have a certain sympathy. The heat of the sun here does remarkably strange things to one's constitution; unusual alarms start to ring in normally unresponsive places, and there are uncalled-for, irreverent and tumescent tingles kindled by the warmth of the air. Iceberg Jekyll turns easily into hothouse Hyde. No doubt the Peucetians ran round shouting the same kind of happy paean on occasions, and so did the Romans, and no one would have been surprised.

Events such as this aren't recorded in official archaeology journals or the reports of excavations. They ought to be. It would make them less dry, and would encourage more young people to take an interest in it as a profession. Burins, barrows, spalls and moulded rims are all very well in their place, but a little more news of personal triumphs and travails might widen the readership. They even make mottes unremarkable. I have heard that one young digger at Carthage went astray by steeping herself in henna, blackening her eyes with kohl and shacking up for a while with the Tuareg. Something curious also happened to an American excavator at Metapontum. After a lengthy night out, he climbed into the wrong window at his hotel and found himself in the bedroom used by the owner's wife, and apparently suffered considerable damage.

That kind of discovery makes the subject more interesting. Archaeologists should be made to keep diaries.

I desperately need some sea air again, so I left this evening: all downhill and back to Metapontum. Gravina looked sad as I left; I didn't; I was positively grateful. But when I looked back and saw its outline against the lowering sun I hesitated. Its ragged silhouette stood against the paling sky; steeples, chimneys, turrets and towers were spread among uneven roofs, all etched in black. The sun was bouncing golden balls of fire off windows and there were miles-away cries of children. For a moment it was a cut-out shape of fairyland; a dark stillness on a ridge of domes and arches. The darkness and stillness of ghosts and death.

TEN

Erakleia

I wasn't sad to leave Gravina. A bleak and unloved place. Scarred by two thousand years of war and greed. So Aldo's bike flew me down the mountain road to the plains again, past grey elephant boulders, through villages, misshapen fields the size of prairies, lines of whispering eucalyptus trees, bundles of sheep with crouched-down shepherds, a chaos of fitful land changes from shoulders of hills to parch-dry valleys where rocks seemed to grow. It's impossibly varied: bright and happy one minute, dull and sad the next.

The moped loved it. It was all downhill; the Pollino mountains were behind us now and there was flatness in front, hurtling past greens, greys and browns and rocks on hillsides blasted white. Plants tried to sprout out of broken walls – hellebores out of cracks, and spiraeas in patches and waving poppies. Freedom, I thought, freedom. Gravina had numbed me.

So I'm back in Basilicata, that middle bit of the south named after a Byzantine emperor called Basil who waged war everywhere here against the Saracens, insisting Christianity was better. Just to confuse matters, it is sometimes called Lucania, after the local tribe of that name who lived here before the Greeks started arriving. Erakleia is another of their misfortunes; it vanished like Metapontum, probably because it sided with Rome against Hannibal and got involved with Pyrrhus and his elephants. All you can see now is a patchwork of foundations sticking out of the earth like stumps of rotten teeth, but obviously organised and delineated into clear-cut squares and rectangles laid out on the grid system, disappearing up a slope where there are doubtless more remains to be uncovered. But at the moment it is used by local boys for motorcycle scrambles.

When Ramage was here in 1828 he spent his time looking for ancient Siris because 'there was no spot on earth so sweet, lovely or desirable', according to the poets; it was also fabled for its wealth and luxurious lifestyle, outdoing even Sybaris. But all he could do was struggle through swampy woods because it had totally disappeared. It was the usual problem of the Greeks being fiercely tribal: Ionian settlers wiping out Achaean settlers wiping out other settlers. Even those woods have gone today, making it easier for some German archaeologists to look for it. It was here that Ramage was nearly suffocated one night. He had been given a bed in an alcove in a baker's shop, just above the oven where the bread was cooking. Hardly able to breathe, he stumbled out in the dark shouting, '*Santo Diavolo, Bacco* and all the saints of the calendar,' until he woke the owner up.

Ramage is my favourite traveller down here; on a par with Norman Douglas, but completely different. If any young man today wandered off into the wilds of Borneo wearing a merino frock-coat, a large-brimmed straw hat and carrying an umbrella, you'd think he was mad. Craufurd Tait Ramage did a similar thing aged twenty-four when he wandered off into unknown and brigand-infested southern Italy at 4 a.m. on 29 April 1828, after attending a ball in Naples that had ended only an hour earlier. He was employed there as tutor to the children of the British Consul, Henry Lushington.

His book *The Nooks and Byways of Italy*, which he subtitled 'Wanderings in search of its ancient remains and modern superstitions', makes Henry Swinburne and Keppel Craven look leaden-footed. Instead of an armed escort, the only thing he had with him was a letter from a Neapolitan prince asking people to be nice to him.

After what Harold Acton, Norman Douglas, Edward

Chaney and Edith Clay (who edited the 1965 edition) have said about Ramage, it's impossible to comment. He was reckless, brave, determined, robust, perceptive, humorous, sympathetic and mildly eccentric. His account is full of personality. He doesn't mind being chased by dogs, falling downstairs in the dark, being bitten to pieces by fleas, being left in bed by his host during an earthquake, or sleeping over a bread-oven. 'Thank God I was neither robbed nor murdered last night,' he says at one point. But all the time he is in the south he wants to know things: how people here live and behave and what they think. He is quite prepared to be tempted by beautiful girls and quite prepared to tell interfering officials to mind their own business. At the same time as he finds a 'loveableness' in the southern nature, he finds 'mummeries' in their religious beliefs. He is also a classicist, so he has little trouble identifying ruins, battlefields, inscriptions and references made by Greek and Roman authors.

Ramage comes across as shrewd, tolerant, sympathetic and full of common sense. However much he likes or admires the southerners, he is prepared to say, 'I have as yet seen nothing to incline me to believe that the body of the people is fitted for a representative form of government.' And the overall impression one gets as he describes his day's adventures and discomforts is that he is enjoying everything, and to wander alone through southern Italy for sixty days was well worth all the trouble.

During its heyday, Erakleia was in the unenviable position of being nominated as the senior Greek state in Magna Graecia and was supposed to look after all their interests and settle their disputes. It didn't, of course; over a period of 500 years they all tore each other to pieces, and if that didn't decide matters, then Pyrrhus did, or Hannibal, or the Romans, or malaria.

The town must have been very extensive once. Most of it is probably still buried under the ramshackle village of

Policoro, which rises on a significant hump only yards away; and on an even more significant hump sits an imposing-looking building that doubtless covers even more remains. This one-time palace was turned into a farm by the Jesuits, where their possessions included 5,000 sheep, 400 buffaloes, numerous goats and horses and 300 servants. By the time Henry Swinburne got here in 1770, this avaricious and green-eyed order had just been dissolved.

The pride of Policoro is its museum. It shows how much of the past they have already found here, and suggests how much more there is to discover. It was opened in 1969; superbly arranged in chronological eras, from primitive Stone Age tools to Greek tombs and relatively recent suits of Roman armour. Everything is well lit in vast display cabinets and, for a change, is clearly labelled. One wishes that the National Museum in Naples could take the same trouble with its even greater collection. It houses the most confused, badly indicated, atrociously arranged and seriously uncared-for assemblage of past history; plus the surliest and least helpful or interested attendants I've ever come across. Here, there should be more visitors; you can move from 7,000 years BC through the jewellery, ornament and dress of the Lucanians, into the coins, mirrors and red-figure vases of the Greeks and thence to the swords, javelins and helmets of the Romans. It is quite superb.

Another object of pride here is the Erakleian Tablets, found by chance in a nearby river in 1753. On them are inscribed a series of planning regulations and by-laws stating how the countryside should be maintained and run, and how farmers should behave. Part of it reads like a script from the Society for the Preservation of Rural Magna Graecia. 'Tenants will pay the rent yearly, and will prosecute anyone entering or damaging property; they will not deepen ditches, drain or divert rivers, nor will they split, saw or cut any tree. Tenants will not make tombs on their land . . .' With such orderly organisation one wonders how it all came to fall to pieces.

Erakleia likes to boast about its famous artist Zeuxis; but this is debatable, as there is more than one ancient town called after this heroic demi-god. However, 'Zeuxis of Erakleia' they insist belongs here. He had the fortune to be commissioned to paint the picture of Venus to decorate the magnificent temple at Crotone further along the coast, an undertaking he accepted on condition that he could select the six most beautiful girls in the town and see them naked. By doing this, he insisted, he could combine all their finest attributes into one single figure and produce the perfect goddess. The Hugh Hefner of the ancient world; a Miss Magna Graecia contest, or the calliphygian playmate of the century.

If the museum is a place of studied silence, the town outside certainly isn't. The tiny room I am in faces onto the main street, a positioning that is most unwise. Conversations outside start soon after five, by six have become animated disagreements and by a half-past are vociferous arguments. Policorans don't talk, they shout. A point of view is meaningless unless it is delivered *fortissimo*. At times you would think there is about to be bloodshed. No such luck. The centre-half was offside; no, he wasn't . . . yes, he was . . . no, he wasn't . . . They have inherited a volcanic gene; they are self-ignited; without warning there is such deafening combustion and verbal ferocity, complete with war-like gesticulations, that the window rattles. After ten minutes these merciless eruptions vanish into thin air, but only for seconds. Because silence unnerves them, yet another low growl becomes a bombardment; a cauldron of Minotaur roars. Italians have the unique gift of being able to fight without actually hitting each other. It's a form of entertainment, a side show that relieves boredom and obviously results in a triumphal sense of personal achievement.

Erakleia

I'm beginning to think this decibel competition is a national disease.

There is a very seductive and challenging hilltop not far away with a church sitting on it. This windy and otherwise totally deserted spot is called Anglona, but was once called Pandosia until some hierophantic and zealous reformers got hold of it and considered that its name contained in-appropriately heathen concomitants. It did. Among what Robert Graves calls 'the disorganised corpus of Greek mythology' there is mention in one of the legends that Pan lived here. It was his kingdom, Pandosia; 'the giver of all good gifts'. This all started when Jupiter was on his way to visit Arcadia, having heard that King Lycaon was maltreat-ing some of his subjects by killing and eating them. During his journey, however, Jupiter was distracted by an attractive young nymph called Thyrsis (or Thymbris or Hybris); she might even have been one of Lycaon's daughters; the result of this brief affair was an ugly little beast with horns, beard, goat's feet and tail, who looked so repulsive and was obviously so oversexed that it had to be fostered out straight away as far from Arcadia as possible, preferably on a remote mountain top. Here it had a wonderful time, as the area was the source of numerous streams well populated by obliging water sprites. Meanwhile Jupiter, who had arrived in Arcadia disguised as a beggar, found Lycaon's behaviour such an abomination that he promptly turned him into a wolf – hence lycanthropy – and ordered up the Deucalion flood to blot out his kingdom. Miraculously, however, two of his sons managed to swim to the shores of Italy (it's reported that Lycaon had fifty-two children) and began sowing their seed. One was called Peucetios, who peopled the south-eastern quarter of Italy with tribes, henceforward called the Peucetians; Oenotrios, his brother, travelled further west to originate the Oenotrians.

Precisely when Pan's kingdom disappeared from this

hilltop isn't clear. Some say the Roman general Lucius Silla destroyed it in 81 BC during the Social Wars; others that the Goths overran it. But by the tenth century AD it was firmly Byzantine with a church on top of it, which was rather unfortunate as the Byzantines built an equally impressive church only three miles away in the valley below at Tursi, leading to endless rivalries and bloodshed as to which was more important.

The whole area down below had been even bloodier before that, as the entire plain is where Pyrrhus first let his elephants loose on the Romans. This wasn't entirely a success, for although he had dosed them on alcohol and had painted their faces red, white and blue, the Romans – initially terrified by what they thought were local buffaloes – soon learned to open ranks and let the thundering herds through, then prick their bottoms and send them charging back. Although Pyrrhus was victorious on that occasion, Lenormant has calculated that he lost 13,000 men, and the Romans 15,000. It was a victory, Pyrrhus is supposed to have said, that was equivalent to a defeat.

There is absolutely nothing on this windswept hilltop except for this large church – several times altered – and on knocking at the door to find the priest, I discover that he insists Anglona is only Anglona and was never anything else; that its name derives from being the source of two rivers, the Sinni and the Agri; that its first bishop was called Enghilberto; that it was visited by Pope Urban II in 1092; and that everything is vouched for in a document at Monte Cassino. He didn't mention that Emile Bertaux, the French art historian, found sheep and goats in the church in 1901. The idea that Pan had anything to do with it makes him laugh, though he does concede that the area is exceedingly fertile: '*Qui prodigiamo ogni bene per la fertilità*' – we have an abundant means of fertility here.

He was absolutely right. I was in the middle of consuming a warm-wine lunch outside, assisted by Anglonan flies, when a small car drove up and cautiously entered the church's small orchard of fruit trees to park itself discreetly in the shade. The heads of the two occupants were visible for a moment before sinking slowly out of sight and managing to remain unseen for nearly quarter of an hour. It's a bit embarrassing being an unintentional voyeur and trying not to look. When fifteen minutes was up, they got out, ran into the church holding hands, remained there for ten minutes and emerged together with the priest, showing a trio of smiles. It must have been lunch break in Tursi because three more cars came up during the next hour, went through exactly the same routine but under different trees, and all the occupants were blessed afterwards.

At two o'clock precisely the priest emerged on his own and gave me a wave, before climbing on his scooter and heading off downhill. He'd obviously had enough fertilisation for the time being.

I sat there for a few moments longer, surrounded by the swoop and turn of a hundred swallows circling and winding their invisible slipstreams into a joyful ballet, all uttering their appreciative and thrilling squeaks to the joys of nature, and to procreation and everlasting life. *Et in Arcadia . . . Et in Auto.*

I set off free-wheeling down the hill towards Tursi with wind assistance and stopped after 200 yards to stare at the inland mountains. They were like giant lumps of pale cheeses with dark mould on top floating towards the horizon in waves, all shouldering and pushing each other aside. There were hundreds of them; mammoth remains with surfaces boiled white or yellow in the sun, glaring as if they'd been furnaced, and they didn't look friendly. Then a fat jovial man drew up in a three-wheeler delivery scooter, thumped his chest with a gulp and said, '*Aria pura, un bacio di Dio.*'

'Yes,' I answered, thinking a kiss of God was about right

because it sums up the beauty of parts of Basilicata perfectly.

'Better than Rome,' he went on. 'My daughter is there. Hates it. Pollution. All paper pushers. Basilicata's better.'

'Much,' I agreed.

He looked at me. 'London?'

'Yes,' I lied.

'*Zuppa di piselli*,' he laughed.

'No pea-soupers . . . Clean Air Act,' I answered. 'No more fires.'

He looked dumb-struck, lost for words – 'What? Iron Lady finish pollution?' he managed.

'Sort of,' I said.

'Or Queen?' he added.

'That kind of thing,' I agreed.

He obviously couldn't understand a law actually operating and being obeyed. 'Taranto,' he said, pointing. It was too far away to see; only a grey foggy cloud hanging over it. '*Sporcissimo*' – filthy – he said bitterly, then smiled. 'Going to Rabatanna?'

'Where?' I asked.

'Down there,' he said, pointing closer. 'Go and see it.' So I did.

There are quite a number of Rabatannas in south Italy, but they don't appear in guide books. They're too small. They're old Arab settlements, probably founded by pirates who stayed on and settled, or more likely by leftovers from Frederick of Hohenstaufen's big army of mercenaries. He liked Arabs, thought they were good fighters, and he liked a lot of their ideas, a number of them being doctors, philosophers and poets, and they studied the stars. The Arabs admired him too, although one of the sultans said Frederick wouldn't fetch much in a slave market. A geographer called Idris drew a map of Italy for him; Capri was Qadra, Calabria was Qullawriah and Venice was Fanru.

It was rather like a moonscape in sepia slipping down and

round the curves to Rabatanna: precipices one side, gorges the other, and pale, pregnant mountains popping up between. Some of the rock faces had caves in them, old sockets of God-knows-when, with clumps of trees trying to hang on. Bubbles of mountains stretched everywhere; they were like the limbs of giant corpses going mouldy, some curves of brown, some rotting grey with cracks in between sprouting body-hair.

Then I found Rabatanna. Most of it had fallen down and there were only twelve people left living on a ledge with lots of cats and the last lines of washing flapping in the wind. One night they will creep away like desert nomads and disappear into the dark. Another corpse will be born.

ELEVEN

Trebisacce

This trunk road along the coast shakes with mammoth lorries, hurtling east to west and west to east. They are urgent; an urgency to which dogs and cats bear witness; mangled bodies lie in the roadside and, if I'm not careful, a moped may join them any moment as the power-draught that their passing causes is frightening. They like to give rattlesnake hisses too, just to test your nerves, and I'm not completely happy about Italian MOTs, and, on present performance, how they manage to pass driving tests. They're always a bit coy about statistics, but I don't want to join the other 6,000-odd who get written off on the roads every year. This isn't a great surprise as they consider that seatbelts and crash helmets are an infringement of personal liberty. The annual figure of a quarter of a million road accidents is quite impressive.

It would have been much more peaceful for the sandalled feet of the plodders along the dusty old road here, as mapped out by the ancient cartographers Antoninus and Theo-dosius. They both mention Tursi, which is now far behind me. Strange to think that thousands of Greeks, then thousands of Romans, then thousands of everybody else walked this way on war-business or love-business or god-business. The lorries echo it; they always have two coloured pictures stuck side-by-side on the inside of their wind-screens; there's the BVM looking melancholy and protec-tive, and then either Sophia Loren or La Cicciolina with nothing on, looking stunning. Body and soul, I suppose, like the ancients; different gods or goddesses being needed for different things, one being unable to cope with it all.

The sea was out of sight to the left somewhere, hidden

beyond uneven and borderless land masses, pock-marked with trees and scatterings of shanty houses. It was desolate and unloved; a tube of tarmac driving through an organic growth of chaos; rubble in the ditch, half-built houses, abandoned cars. The road shot through the seaside hamlet of Rocca Imperiale without stopping, till in the heat haze ahead I imagined a land-change. Mountains. A dark line of shapeless purple beckoned – the colour of a storm or dusty grapes, growing into a land barrier feathering down to the sea. It was the wall between two plains; two battlefields; two abandoned granaries of Magna Graecia; Erakleia behind and Sybaris ahead; all hatred and annihilation. Those mountains seem to encourage it; their darkness breeds suspicion, fear, hostility and violence, even death. The shapes of them threaten and their shadows terrify. Even when the sun shines they look brutal, their frowning surfaces split by crags. They must be the enemy.

The sea has come back again, gently lapping at the foot of a small hill with Amendolara at the summit; only a village now, but once a Greek outpost and later Roman. There are lots of bumps all over the hill that no one bothers to dig at. Further on and higher still, perched on a spur in the barrier of grey-green mountains, sits Trebisacce. The Byzantines called it Trapesakas, on a ledge, crouching there with turret-eyes, watching eastwards for friends or foes. It's a compact of alleyways coiled like a spring round the huge green-and-white dome of St Nicolas's church, bouncing the sun off like a beacon; a cluster of houses round it like a plague of snails. As if tempted by the sea, an offshoot of buildings has sprung up along the shore below, but it remains a little uncertain of itself and is remarkably unbusy. A sign says Hotel Paradise.

I went to look for the old one that I stayed in years ago. It was called Miramare and was right on the beach – a bunkhouse more than a hotel, like a barrack-room strung out along the sand, built out of breeze-blocks with a dozen bedrooms leading off a central passageway. Sand blew everywhere. Gritty grains of it hung in the air looking for something to settle on: mouth, hair, eyes, inside your clothes. A genial, hyperactive young man called Pepe ran it; he cooked, served, swept, cleaned up, with his permanently naked son of three, which he explained saved on clothes. I remember his unbounded excitement. 'We have another English,' he beamed. 'Come,' edging me down the passage and throwing a door open into what looked like a cell. Against one wall was an iron bedstead with a shapeless heap on it covered by a sheet. '*Ecco*,' he cried, whipping it away like some conjuring climax, and two owl-eyes blinked up at me somewhat unsurprised, the eyes of a well-tanned and rotund female with nothing on. 'English,' he exclaimed proudly, as if this was the real Stanley and Livingstone occasion he'd waited for all his life. 'Maltese,' grunted the brown body wearily, as if this kind of afternoon interruption was nothing unusual, and not bothering to pull the sheet up.

And that was the Malteser; the same shape and colour as the sweet, and as well as being gently educative, slowly rolling round the Mediterranean looking for home. Pepe's naked infant had a habit of removing cutlery from the table at mealtimes, just as we were about to eat, and hiding everything in the sand outside. I asked him once if his son had anything or any toys to play with. 'Only this,' he grinned, seizing the offender and half-pulling his willie off.

Yesterday I rather wished the old place was still there. In Paradise my shower water disappeared briefly down the escape, then seeped up again through the gaps in the floor tiles. It didn't look the same colour. There was also a group of earnestly amorous cats outside my window, giving long imitations of Florence Foster Jenkins, sometimes an octave or two lower. The object of their passionate serenading was lean and ginger, bedded firmly down on a wall to keep things out of harm's way till the chorus was over and someone got a piece of the action.

I fled to the dining room where the obsequious *padrone* bowed, asked if everything was to my satisfaction, and said how lucky I was to have won the war. His wife would cook anything I wanted, he assured me: *licurda*, a soup of onions and eggs with hot peppers, or *gliommarilli*, which is goat's giblets and stomach lining; or how about horse, he suggested, any way I liked – boiled, baked, stewed, roast or fried? The only decent thing was the wine; it was from Amendolara.

The lone diner, apart from me, was in a suit at another table reading a coloured comic. Probably about forty. I could just see bubble-speak coming out of people's mouths and it took him rather a long time to turn a page over after studying it. Italians don't read very much. There's certainly plenty of paperwork around, as there's a whole industry employed to create it; they're called bureaucrats. They specialise in inventing forms in quadruplicate, which nobody ever reads, or understands, or completes, but still they keep producing more of them. Try sending a parcel from here back to England; try travelling on a train without a ticket; try asking for a work permit. *Dylan Dog* is one of the most popular reads: it appeals to all age groups. If the literary diet is not strip-cartoons, then it's usually puzzle-books or people doing things with no clothes on. Statistics here are notoriously unreliable – they're usually 'surveys' – but it is thought that about half the population finds reading difficult; which probably accounts for the popularity of television; and which confirms that ancient papal edict that 'pictures are for the ignorant'. Today they can zap away through fifty channels and on Sunday find the Pope saying Mass in St Peter's on one, and Madonna taking her clothes off on the next. They do have a literary tradition – somewhere – from Dante onwards, but you wouldn't think it. There's little status attached to being able to read.

*

Today I went into the mountains.

Trebisacce is terrible. Apart from the Malteser, the only thing it's remotely famous for is the lighthouse keeper whom Ramage got drunk, but that was nearly 200 years ago. Apparently the man had been a slave in Algiers and rather wished he was back there, as the food was better.

The sign in front of me said CIFTI in large bold letters, which I found out meant eagle's nest. Underneath it said *Cifti Mir Se Na Erthtit Civit*, which means 'We welcome you to the Eagle's Nest'. The Albanian language, according to Henry Swinburne who dabbled in it here in the 1770s, was a 'jargon' compounded of Tartar, Macedonian, eighth-century Greek, early German, some Italian and crusader-speak. He also said they had no alphabet and their vocabulary contained such useful English words as mushroom, grumble, mud and tickle. Norman Douglas, more than a century and a half later, down here on his search for satyrs rather than sylphs, declared that the Albanians possessed 'more than thirty different alphabets, each of them with nearly fifty letters'. If this philological mélange is true, one wonders how their great leader Skanderberg managed to unite enough of them in 1450 to rush as one body into Italy to help Pope Pius II get rid of the Angevins. But he did. And the Albanians were so successful they were allowed to settle and make new homes here; moreover, as the precipitous peaks of Basilicata and Calabria reminded them of their eyries at home, they promptly scaled the most unassailable heights they could see to claim as settlements. This didn't prove wise. A naturally war-like breed, they thought anything moving below them must be an enemy, or at least worth attacking and looting, which didn't make them popular; and because in the south memories die hard, this eastern mud has stuck. Furthermore, as time marched on and they did become more integrated and eventually raised a corporate voice for some sort of recognition, and for more liberal treatment and tolerance of the Greek rites they wished to practise, the Bourbons suppressed them. The Albanians have not had a happy time here.

They look happier now. '*Mirtet . . . mirtet*,' they nodded as I wandered along the street, the only pleasantly flat part before it began a rapid climb. Somehow I had to reach the houses I could see banked up, one on the other, like a pyramid of vegetables on a grocer's counter and ending up smaller than dolls' houses against the sky. I wished I hadn't started. Aldo's bike refused; it died after twenty yards. A Fiat 500 ground its way up in bottom gear and disappeared. I plodded on . . . concrete, then stone, then cobbles, then earth; wild roses growing out of broken stone walls; endless and pointless zigzags quadrupling the distance and not achieving anything. 'Madness!' I thought. Why do it? What corporate idiocy could keep them here? It was like walking up a ski-slope. Roofs below started to look as if they were brown mushroom-tops tumbling over each other; up above they were waiting to crush me. I stopped by a ledge to recover. 'Express Water Station,' croaked an old man sidling up, which I thought might be an Albanian crossword clue. It wasn't. He had been a prisoner of war and worked for Express Dairies at Waterloo Station.

People actually lived here. Flights of steps fell out of house fronts onto the path, and bony grey-haired women sat on them saying '*Mirtet*' and sparrow-chatting as they sifted beans or fiddled with embroidery. Did they know there is a life elsewhere? I asked one why there were five chimneys on her roof and she cackled. 'Because we never know where the wind will come from,' she said. A waddling shape went past uphill, too quickly for me to photograph her; a long, black flowing skirt with white trim, and a waistcoat embroidered in gold ribbing and flecks of green and silver; the last signs of a dying tribal uniform they've worn since before the Renaissance. Every village had its own coded insignia, like regiments in an army; so did the women – virgins, wives and widows. It had its point. Douglas said that in full dress on feast days they looked like 'animated tropical flowers'.

Word gets around quickly and invisibly here. When I'd climbed for half an hour a young man ran up panting. 'I'll show you our museum,' he said. It must have been on the twentieth corner; two rooms, one above the other, and all Albanian memories inside: maps, drawings, pictures, documents, newspaper cuttings, photographs, farm implements, a bagpipe, items of clothing, an old wedding dress. 'We get a grant from Brussels,' he told me, 'to pay the electricity; but we're a minority language now. The children here won't speak Albanian, only Italian. In thirty years it will be dead.' I tried to make him say something, but he was too shy. 'Write it down,' I said . . . and this is what appeared on my scrap of paper: *Nole Parrajsit e iligri, lum e lum kush vet'e rri bashk me Zonjen Sher Meri*, which he said was part of a children's prayer – 'In Paradise there is happiness; happy is the person who goes to stay with the Virgin Mary.' He said the language used was Tosco, which is modern Albanian, whereas some people still used Geygo, the old language.

He took some flints off a shelf and banged them together. 'They'd take these into the fields to work,' he said, 'and they'd knock them together to make sparks. It was to frighten off evil spirits.' I asked him why there was a stick nailed to a wall. 'It's a time-stick', he answered, 'they'd push it into the ground when they started work and, by watching the shadow made by the sun, they could tell how long they'd worked for.'

As I walked downhill later I remembered something I'd seen written on a wall somewhere – 'If Greece has lost its marbles, Italy has lost its memory.'

Then a woman came out of a dark doorway and said, '*Miru pavshin*' – which I hope meant goodbye. She handed me a cheese the size of a football and as hard as rock, and we professed everlasting thanks to each other. It weighed like lead. When I was safely out of sight I'm afraid I pitched it over a wall into the undergrowth for time's chariot to look after.

I was hot and I think I must have been angry. The unfriendliness of the mountains had taken over. So had man's ingratitude to man.

It was most unexpected, his voice coming out of nowhere. '*Sono Borbone, io,*' he announced loudly, standing by me and watching as I crouched, trying to adjust the moped's brakes, which seemed to be in danger of giving up after the descent. 'Can I help you?' He was large, with a red, wrinkled face and well into his sixties, dressed untidily, but with his hands on his hips as if used to authority, and an interested expression on his face.

'Brakes,' I answered. 'Too many hills.'

'Ah, tourist?' he suggested.

'Traveller,' I corrected him emphatically.

'Ah. Like Jissing,' he beamed, 'Jissing and Dooglas.'

'Gissing,' I said, 'G ... G ... G ...' but he wasn't listening.

'Come along in,' pointing behind him down a lane. A gate led into an abandoned orchard. It hadn't seen a scythe or a mower for years. Where the grass was knee-high it was speckled by various flowerheads fighting their way through for light. Morose-looking, unkempt fruit trees lurched sagging with fruit. 'My farm,' he announced proudly, pointing to the open end of a barn leaning precariously against a dilapidated *contadino*'s house, the barn stuffed with straw and sacks, with two broken ladders propped against it. 'A paradise garden,' he explained, thrusting his way with difficulty towards an outside wooden staircase and then tearing twines of clematis off the handrail as we began to go up. It was a loft we were in, bare save for three beds against a wall, a rickety table and three old chairs, but from somewhere he produced a bottle of black wine and two grimy glasses. '*Salute,*' he said as I gulped at it thirstily and unwisely, most of it going downwards, but some percolating upwards behind my eyes.

'Definitely,' I answered when he said how peaceful it was and not like Castrovillari, where his wife and family lived.

'I hate towns,' he added. 'I used to be in charge of the hospital there.'

'Do you live here now?' I asked, eyeing the beds.

'My Albanian,' he answered, 'she loves me like a dog. And her family. Have some more . . . I saved her. She looks after me, works here, looks after the animals. It's my farm . . . Except they stole my tractor . . .'

'Who did? The Albanians?'

'No. The farm down the road. I see it quite often.'

'Can't you get it back?'

'Why? It doesn't matter. They use it every day. I never did. It would only cause trouble; they'd burn this place down.'

His philanthropy seemed admirable, yet defeated me. What would I say if I saw a neighbour using my mower without permission? It all seems a bit of a help-yourself place; the undergrowth certainly thinks so – have a tractor; have an Albanian; have a cheese; have another glass of wine. The froth was dark purple bubbles as I held my glass out.

I almost fell down the steps when he wanted to show me round; at the bottom, white trumpet lilies were growing out of the foundations of the walls, and he kicked them aside. 'Fruit,' he said, swatting at a jungle of close-knit branches as he passed, each obligingly releasing a cascade of multi-coloured offerings. It was almost obscene; a luxuriant floral and fruital fantasy; an Horatian garden out of control; pregnant, womb bursting, prolific as rats, fertility oozed without effort and ragged trees sagged with the weight of offspring. I lost count as I pushed at branches that clung to each other: oranges, bergamots, avocados, olives, tangerines, apricots, lemons – sweet and sour – he kept pulling them off the trees and pushing them at me, long grass clasping my thighs; a tangle of unweeded garden, interlocked, haywire and happy. A Gordian mêlée; nectarines and curious peaches; marrows bulging in the grass – or were they courgettes? – among overgrown mint bushes with oregano and fennel. A tabletop of scarlet peppers boiled in the sun, as we kicked at an angry army of ducks and geese running into a dark undergrowth of purple scabious; jasmine drooped everywhere, clinging to fruit trees.

'GGGissing,' he kept muttering to himself and chuckling as he shook his head. 'GGGissing . . . GGGissing . . . Did you know him?' Time seems irrelevant to some people; here they live so completely in the present.

'He died twenty years before I was born,' I said, which caused no reaction. Centuries can merge here and concertina into a week. They live each day with the evidence of 3,000 years all round them, and draw it in with each breath, and touch it with their hands. Antiquity has become meaningless.

Suddenly he is talking about Lenormant, still pushing bits of fruit at me, unaware I am hugging a load to my chest and trying to drop some into the long grass discreetly. '*Si* . . . Lenormant . . . *un poeta* . . .' he exclaims, which I could almost agree with, had it not been for his invasive passion for numismatics. Then it is Ulysses. He stands firmly in his forest of grass and denounces tradition . . . 'They're all wrong,' he says. 'Ulysses sailed up the Adriatic. Circe was at Gargano, Calypso is Venice, Scylla and Charybdis are the Krotorska Fjord, and the Sirens were at Paxos.'

'Oh,' I said, 'and the Pillars of Hercules?'

'They are the Bosphorus,' he announces, 'and Penelope slept with all the suitors.'

At some stage we weren't alone any more; dark-clothed swarthy people were in his front orchard shaking the trees, and unknown things were cascading like raindrops. His Albanian had arrived, plus bits of family; his lady of the

Hesperides; a fierce-looking long-skirted mother with broad shoulders, jet-black hair swept back and fierce eyes scolding ragged children as they heaved at the branches. Her dark clothes were pure Ena Sharples. Nets were spread on the ground and everything was tumbling into them: twigs, leaves and nut-like berries. *'Gelso,'* he says – which are white mulberries; they were coming down like hailstones. 'I'll get a bag,' he goes on. 'You must have some . . .'

The mad doctor has just asked if I want to see another Albanian village and I couldn't very well say no. Last night I decanted most of his worse-for-wear fruit with the hotel owner, who was neither impressed nor complimentary, assuming it implied some kind of criticism.

So he rattled me up in his car – as unkempt as his garden – for what seemed like hundreds of miles into the mountains. They're so big they make you feel helpless; a nothing; giants of brown, green, purple and grey hanging in space, and looking a bit sleepy, but you know they're watching you. He was talking all the time about when he was Chief Medical Officer for the whole area – God help them. Actually I think he's rather nice; very generous; gives away his tractor; gives away fruit. He hasn't yet offered me an Albanian. I think I'd refuse. The old ones look a bit rugged.

Up and up again, right into the wind-stinging heights, while he said Sybaris wasn't where it was at all, but ten miles inland at Francavilla because the Greeks wouldn't have built in a marsh. He's in danger of rewriting ancient history. 'Lungro,' he announced magnificently, parking his car in a tiny square so that it blocked access and escape, beside a plinth with a bronze head on it. 'Communists,' he said, 'the most Communist town in Italy. Look at them,' as if he was showing me a cage in a zoo. And they did look a bit off-putting. Men sitting around in the square wearing dark, untidy clothes, with dark cloth caps on their heads and dark surly expressions. They began muttering among themselves. Creepy. 'Come and see the Chief,' he said, pulling me across the cobbles towards some kind of shop.

The Chief was a publisher of Albanian literature; stacks of it stood on the shelves; poems, novels, translations – God knows what. One glance and the contents were meaningless. He made an equally unintelligible noise. *'Kush di nje gjuhe me shume eshte me I turte.'*

'Oh,' I answered.

'A wise man speaks more than one language,' he said, promptly changing the subject to Gissing. 'Did you know he was homosexual?'

'No,' I answered.

'Had a friend in Paola . . . There are letters . . .'

'Oh,' I said. 'Where?' And he just looked at me as if I was an insect.

'You know Altomonte?' he went on.

'Who?' I asked, stupidly.

'The salt mines,' he muttered. 'No employment here now, but they all worked in the mines fifteen years ago digging salt out. A man got paid by the amount he got out each day, and there were fifteen hundred steps down and fifteen hundred steps back up again.' I must have stared at him blankly; those kinds of numbers defeat imagination. 'And in the dark,' he went on, 'the candles kept going out.'

I can't remember how the exchange ended; only the salient facts, as I suspected hideous notes of woe were about to start, so I went outside and stared at the bronze bust of George Castriota, the Albanians' great national hero whom they like to call Skanderberg – from Iskander Bey, the name he was given as a fearsome Turkish warlord and army commander fighting the Christians. But in fact George Castriota was a Christian himself, who had been kidnapped by the Turks as a child. When he discovered this, he turned against his original captors and became such a famous warrior for the Christian cause that Pope Pius II, the poet, invited him over to Italy to help drive out the Angevins. So

Iskander Bey sailed over with a force of furious Albanians who loved a fight, and Lungro is one of the results, stuck up a mountain and thoroughly discontented.

He looks very menacing in hard, dull bronze; big bushy eyebrows and steely eyes full of cruelty and determination, and a small pointed beard doesn't soften things. His helmet has swept-back hawk's wings on each side, suggesting speed and savagery.

The Chief came out and patted the bronze head fondly. 'No work,' he said. 'No religion. The Pope doesn't like us; he's shut our seminary; says priests shouldn't marry. Our religion isn't religion at all. We can obey our bishop, but he has to obey the Pope. There's tolerance for you; Christian mercy,' and he spat.

When I eventually got back to Paradise it was nearly dark, so I left the doctor to his home-brew of Albanians at the farm and went for a walk along the beach. I've got to go, I thought; this is awful, it's all so sad. As I stood there little white ribbons of sea came licking at the pebbles and I kicked at them. Everything is sad here, I thought; sad, stupid and pointless. Waves are pointless too. Where does it get them, doing the same thing for years? Where does anything get anywhere in this country, everlastingly caught up in a torpor of defeat and idleness? Then I saw the moon in the sky and felt better. It wasn't Sappho's 'rose-fingered' one; though sometimes it is. It was a cool, white silent moon-globe watching me calmly, just as it watched exactly the same thing hundreds and thousands of years ago. Confused, muttering people. Blue was turning into black everywhere; shadows of inland hills one minute, darkness the next. Moths started flitting around street lamps and a night-breeze wandered in. I thought I saw fireflies, or it could have been distant lights.

TWELVE

Sybaris

You can't write about something that isn't there; only miles of emptiness. Vanished! Sybaris doesn't exist. It was wiped out – obliterated – by its neighbour Crotone in 510 BC, the same year that the Tarquins were expelled from Rome. Apocalyptic times. Now there is nothing but green flatness in a perfect arc; acres of it, disappearing into endless space; a semi-circle of smiling and sunny innocence, one boundary lapped at by the sea, the other bordered by a gentle curve of grey mountains. Lenormant gazed at this empty plain and said it was the most beautiful sight he had ever seen. Sybaris shone in his imagination. Temples, statues, the glint of golds and purples, columns and arches rising to the sky; hedonism. He lamented the injustice of its annihilation. And so did Swinburne: what had 'the golden city of voluptuaries' done to deserve such total extinction? How to compare the culpability of wealthy citizens revelling in love and wine with the guilt of an exterminating conqueror bathing his hands in the blood of slumbering debauchees? But Telys, the Sybarite tyrant, had offended; he had offered an impetuous and ill-judged insult to his neighbour, and the Greeks were a jealous, aggressive and vindictive race. Sybaris had to be punished; she had committed a capital offence and had to be exterminated; and so she was. Sybaris suffered the final solution.

It wasn't easy getting there; trying to scramble round the barrier of the mountains after Trebisacce, uneven and threatening; ledge on ledge, roughly patterned in grey and green, broken by ribs of dark rock and jagged outcrops, where streaks of yellow sunlight tried to settle. A solid wall of dry bones. I found a rough, unused pathway down to the sea – it was yards away, murmuring through a curtain of bamboo and bulrushes tickling each other's leaves where sparrows hid in the darkness. The ragged hills behind me sank into dismal scrubland alongside, severed by dried-up stream beds and littered with debris; old fridges, cookers, bed springs and car corpses, wheels in the air like upturned woodlice. Don't they have a better way of disposing of them? In efforts of recompense, little shrubs sprang up in random patches, pink oleanders and yellow broom, a bit shamefaced.

I could see it stretching out ahead of me; hazy and huge, a green half-circle of nothingness was disappearing out of sight; the shadowy ring of mountains, the blue uncaring sea. No temples, no trumpets, no dancing horses and no 'carpet of bright flowers' that Rose Macaulay saw; no white buffaloes descended from Sybarite herds. Just an open sweep of savannah, unloved, unused, hiding its secret.

The extinction of Sybaris was really brought about by the Etruscans; and by Pythagoras; and by the Sybarites themselves; all coincidentally, and indirectly, connected. The body of southern Greeks knew about the once-primitive people in the centre of Italy called Etruscans, whose lifestyle had become so eye-catching and luxurious; and who had artists, craftsmen, inventors, engineers and manufacturers of useful and beautiful things among their population. They were obviously clever and they needed to be explored and traded with; particularly as the Etruscans themselves were glad to have in exchange some of the goods the Greeks produced. But it was a perilous journey to carry valuable merchandise to and fro along the ragged coast of south Italy, all round Sicily or between Scylla and Charybdis, and up the Tyrrhenian Sea towards Rome, risking storms and pirates and probably shipwreck. Even if a journey was successful, it could take three weeks. The Sybarites had a better idea. Once established on their plain, they found a way to reach these curious northerners through the mountains – a journey that only took three days. So, in a very short time, Sybaris monopolised the entire import and export trade between the Mediterranean and that colourful, decadent and productive civilisation in the north. Caravans made their way through the mountains; wine, oil, jewellery, animal skins, silks, amber, gold, ivory, lapis lazuli, slaves, metals, bronze ornaments, glass, decorated vases and dildos from Miletus. It was a flourishing business charging import tax, transport tax and delivery tax. Greetings were exchanged as well; thoughts, ideas and influences spread between north and south, and Sybaris became fabulously rich and pleased with herself. She owned vast territories up into the mountains, befriended neighbouring tribes, controlled twenty-five other cities; established important trading outposts such as Paestum on the Tyrrhenian coast; and with all her wealth built herself the most splendid capital she could conceive beside the sea. And that all happened in the space of a hundred years; but in another hundred Sybaris had vanished.

Sybaris now had money to spend and was determined to enjoy it. Why not? Believing in the good things in life, the inhabitants wanted ease, comfort, amusement, pleasure and beauty; they needed to gratify their senses; high on the agenda for such everlasting contentment were good company, good food and good sex. In the fabulously prosperous city they had created for themselves – steeped in luxury – with temples, villas, baths, gymnasia and banqueting halls, they constructed wide, canopied streets to protect them from the sun, and they built proper drainage systems; they made certain they had hot water and central heating. So they could sleep undisturbed, there was to be no morning cockcrow; such nuisances were banned from the city; and so they could eat well, prizes were given for the best banquets and the best individual dishes served; and so they could show off and be admired, they competed with each other in appearance, inventing elaborate hairstyles and having ostentatious clothes made of purple silk embroidered with gold. And the matter of sex education was left to the womenfolk; it was their job to teach the young all about it from their own experiences; and if any of them had trouble with their own husbands, they were allowed to take young boys as lovers. The Sybarites believed in equality of the sexes.

But this Utopian existence began to go too far. The other Greeks, who had once marvelled at their brilliance, grew more wary and critical as their pride and vainglory became excessive. The Sybarites insulted the Delphic Oracle. They also boycotted the Olympic Games and started their own; not just of athletic content, but to include the Arts and Poetry. There was one occasion when a Sybarite youth, who was a contender in marriage to a Greek princess, took a thousand slaves with him to the selection ceremony and was dismissed as an effeminate ponce. The Sybarites were in danger of overreaching themselves; their own power and pride were corrupting them. They thought they could do no wrong.

But in 510 BC, when Telys was their leader, they did. Some of his more democratically minded subjects objected to his authoritarian rule and fled to nearby Crotone to ask for asylum, which Crotone – then thriving under the peaceful and democratic guidance of Pythagoras – granted. But Telys insisted they were revolutionaries and demanded their return. In a bad fit of diplomatic misjudgement, Pythagoras sent a deputation of senior ambassadors to plead the refugees' cause, but the Sybarites wouldn't even open their gates. Instead they hacked the ambassadors to pieces and fed their remains to the dogs.

It is said that, on hearing this news, the sacred statue of Juno in Crotone's temple at Capo Colonna stepped from her pedestal with her mouth foaming blood, as she shrieked for revenge at such an impious insult. Pythagoras unwisely agreed and called 10,000 Crotoniates to arms; and, led by

Milo, their six-time Olympic champion, they marched on
Sybaris for war; but the Sybarites only laughed, because
their army numbered 300,000.

Which is all legend and highly fanciful, as nobody really
knows exactly what happened; even the tale about the
horses of the Sybarite cavalry starting to dance instead of
charging, when they heard the approaching army's martial
music. All that is certain is that after seventy days of war,
Crotone was victorious and, in true biblical fashion, they
Sodom and Gomorrahed it; they set upon Sybaris to destroy
it; devastate it; tear it to pieces . . . which they systemati-
cally achieved. And when their rage had finally subsided,
they decided that to sow salt on the remains wasn't good
enough; to direct a river over it would be a good deal better
as Sybaris would then probably disappear for ever. So deep
under the muddy waters of the River Crathis lies what is
left of Sybaris, and all that is left of the Utopia of the
ancient world.

And that, says Swinburne, was an 'irreparable catas-
trophe', and Lenormant and Douglas agree. Had it not been
for that 'pious puritan' believing that Greek man was
basically good and reasonable, Sybaris might have endured
and there might have been a new Greek world in Italy. But
instead the old Bruttii tribes in the mountains watched all
the senseless battles on the plains and knew that these
strange newcomers who built fabulous cities were divided
among themselves; and that their time would come. And
200 years later, with Rome to help them, it did.

I have been to look at the guilty river; the one that knows
all the secrets; the sleepy and silent Crathis, which in those
days was navigable for up to ten miles inland. It's now a
sluggish, slow-motion stream of brown mud-water, wandering between overgrown banks ten yards apart, and it doesn't
even flow – it seeps. You can't believe that this rust-
coloured sludge could once have turned dark hair to 'an

amber and golden hue', as Ovid says it did. The only sign of life was an extremely mangy dog paddling in the shallows, hoping that the water might cure its eczema and put a little hair back to cover its patches of blue-blotched skin.

The origin of the river's name is curious and slightly indecent. There was once a young and comely shepherd tending his flocks in the nearby meadows, and his name was Crathis. Being short of company for days on end in these idyllic surroundings that nature had so kindly provided, and bored by hours of flute playing, he found himself starting to take a fancy to a pretty young she-goat. She, being not averse to this unusual compliment and pleased to be singled out, was happy to return the sentiment. Unfortunately, however, their amorous encounters were noticed by a keen-eyed and jealous billy, who didn't approve, and he decided to butt poor Crathis to death for bestiality. The young shepherd's blood is said to have flowed into the nearby river, thus giving it its name and its magical qualities.

The Greeks, who were fully understanding of the errant ways of Eros, and a great deal more tolerant than we are, decided to immortalise this spirited union in marble, and both participants can be seen in full congressional enjoyment in the cellars of the National Museum at Naples. They are part of the considerable 'secret collection' that is usually kept there, together with numerous similar bedtime diversions of which the Greeks approved, but which we aren't supposed to know about.*

The eclipse of Sybaris wasn't quite as easy as all that. While some of the remaining inhabitants fled to Paestum, Laos or Scidros on the Tyrrhenian coast, others stayed behind to try to rebuild. We don't know how far they got, but in 476 BC Crotone ransacked it again, and then again twenty years later. This wasn't only due to their inherent vindictiveness,

---

* This is now on view in the Museum but it is a satyr, not Crathis.

it was also because they'd got rid of Pythagoras by now and had absorbed all the Sybaritic finesse at being thoroughly decadent, dissolute and fun-loving, and they didn't want any competition. They had caught the luxury disease and had sunk into a stupor of lascivious inebriation. Left alone at last, the Sybarites managed to call in some new settlers and succeeded in building a new town on the ruins, which they called Thurioi. Unfortunately history hadn't taught them very much and, although the town had some success, when it came to deciding matters of citizenship they declared that the new settlers weren't Sybarites at all and couldn't vote, which promptly led to a revolution. By this time the Bruttian tribesmen in the hills were so bored with watching the fiasco that they walked down and took Thurioi over. This was all too much for the few remaining Greeks; they were exhausted, so they asked Rome for help, and Rome came down and built a completely new town called Copia, on what was left of Thurioi.

But the 'whirlwind of war' wasn't over yet, because there were Pyrrhus and Hannibal to cope with; and if that wasn't enough, Spartacus arrived in Copia in 71 BC and ransacked it.

So the unimpressive little sign by the roadside saying 'SCAVI DI SIBARI' isn't Sybaris at all; the remains they periodically dig at are those of Copia. Sybaris the first, second and third are somewhere yards underneath; so is Thurioi. The few workers here seem to know it; they are resigned to the great untruth; my guide has little interest and would rather talk about the Mafia and the government, and the terrible pay he gets for looking after the nation's treasures. In his case this is a half-mile stretch of recently excavated Roman road, some miscellaneous stumps of *opus reticulatum* brickwork, and a field full of barely visible house foundations. This area is called Parco Del Cavallo.

These guides aren't guides at all really; they're 'friends'; the parasites involved in Italy's 'clientilismo'; part of the nod-and-wink favouritism and cronyism arrangement, and the importance of knowing the right people. He says I can't take photographs, but doesn't care when I do. He is so utterly bored that when a shining coach full of Germans draws up at a quarter to twelve, he waves it away saying Sybaris is closed. All he wants is to be relieved of having to parrot Baedeker or Murray at me and to be allowed to retire to his shed with a comic.

The museum has the same air of *ennui* about it. It is a depressing-looking building on a corner, two miles from the excavations – though there is talk of it being moved to more sumptuous premises soon. It is another 'jobs for the boys' arrangement. There are only ten small rooms, but there is a total of seventeen staff divided into units of three, each working an eight-hour shift. I couldn't work out the mathematics of this and nor could they, but they said it worked perfectly. It certainly wasn't foolproof, as a necklace was removed from a cabinet two months ago by a visitor.

One of the seventeen followed me round all the time, halting two yards behind me every time I stopped, in case I was going to remove a small inscription to Kleombrotos for winning an Olympic medal, or a scarab supposedly belonging to Rameses II. Having a minder with me was so unnerving that I couldn't wait to get out, just managing to pause by a collection of ancient musical instruments and wondering what kind of noise they made. There were cymbals, gongs, rattles, trumpet-like tubes and a cross between a xylophone and a harp.

I can't help disliking guides. They're self-important, autocratic, ill-mannered and usually illiterate. They can't read the 'open' and 'shut' times, and if there are seats anywhere they sit on them. They scrutinise your every movement as soon as you arrive and they hurry you on if you pause to admire anything. Signs that say 'Chiuso, in restauro' invariably mean that someone has taken a day off, or as they are strongly unionised it means they have gone on strike because of a grievance. This is usually about money; but as the government knows most of them supplement their income from time to time by disposing of the odd knick-knack from among the hundreds of unrecorded items in the store-rooms, increasing their wages wouldn't change anything. And as it is generally acknowledged here that at least 50 per cent of disappearances from museums, art galleries and excavations are attributable to employees, it could be well worth making friends with the right guide if you are thinking of taking a piece of old Italy home with you.

It is just possible that there could be one tiny bit of the real Sybaris left, if it weren't for the barbed-wire fencing. But as this is extraordinarily old and rusty, and already well abused in places . . .

It's in an overgrown field and looks like an extremely large bomb-crater, about twenty feet deep and lined with water at the bottom. Sticking out of it and just discernible are what appear to be the stumps of buildings. Most definitely of Greek construction, I was told, though that could just as easily make them part of Thurioi and not of Sybaris; moreover, they were not buildings of any importance, as the rooms were obviously small and mean, probably the dwellings of artisans who lived outside the city walls.

So that seems to be that, as far as Sybaris is concerned. Reflecting on what was and what might have been was rather sad, as I sat in the garden of a small *trattoria* being cooked by the sun and drinking too much Lagarian wine to cool it, with ducks waddling round my feet sniping at blades of grass. It must have been quite pleasant here in Utopia. Home of the long morning lie-in, the good-food guide, the noise-abatement society, women's rights, nice bedrooms (rose petals for mattresses, or sponges if too hard), the sauna, deodorants, *haute couture* fashion-shows, lap-dogs, circuses, social etiquette, proper drains, constant hot water and a thousand ways to enjoy oneself. And the weather, of course. I think I'd have made quite a good Sybarite, contemplating such pleasures in this garden of tranquillity, and drifting into pagan images, while sitting under a canopy of clematis and orange branches full of fat bosoms of fruit, and woven so tightly that only keyholes of sun peep through. It really is vicious sometimes; the sky a violent and naked blue; midday and merciless, dribbling out sweat. It is quite combustible, prompting thoughts of false gods and deadly sins. I can just see green lizards on rocks, tail-squirting and vanishing; and there's an orchestra of sparrows buried in the dark of a bay tree giving piccolo shrieks, and the geraniums look like big bubbles of blood. I'm having a Trimalchian feast of buttered spaghetti, in this garden of memories where there's too much good in everything. And I'm on my own dreaming of a world elsewhere, sitting among myrtle shrubs, pink hydrangeas, jasmines, clematis the size of purple saucers, and riots of white hibiscus looking like virgins sticking their tongues out.

Most definitely, yes. I'd have slept on rose petals and got up late, and I'd have had oysters for breakfast with anchovy sauce. Then a leisurely warm bath in scented water and a friendly toy with nubile slaves. They'd have dressed me spectacularly in embroidered silk with lots of purple and gold, and they'd have combed my beard and made me smell nice. After wondering what to spend my money on, I'd have instructed my household in their daily duties – all exquisite slaves carefully chosen for their beauty, ability and charm – and I'd have answered a score of invitations to parties and feasts. And then lunch. I think a large succulent lobster would have been appropriate, simmered in wine perhaps, and a few oysters again from Taranto to lubricate the libido for later, with some leeks and raisins and olives. Finally a bowl of grapes, each dipped in honey and nibbled off naked flesh; to be followed by a contented siesta fanned by my parade of ebony ephebes and their sisters. On waking I'd have taken my pet dwarf and lapdog for a walk to the sea, along a marble-smooth road carefully canopied to protect me from the sun, and I'd have gossiped with other exquisite millionaires about the prevention of boredom and what new pleasures we could invent to pass the time. And after an hour of delicious idleness and contented self-indulgence, I'd have retired to bed early as the sun went down, in order to escape the malaria mosquito, to an evening pantomime of promiscuous promise. And I'd have loved every moment of it and known life was perfect, and I'd have helped invent civilisation.

It is strange to think that after all this Paestum was just an afterthought; that those huge and almost complete Greek temples standing in the wilderness a few miles south of Naples were a relatively minor satellite of the mother-city; only a trifling but useful trading post. The legend about the amazing 'discovery of Paestum' started in the eighteenth century when the English traveller Patrick Brydone wrote that he saw magnificent temples 'peeping over the tops of the woods' in 1770. This was fairy-tale stuff as their existence had been known about for years, but since Greek temples weren't fashionable, nobody was interested. In 1740 King Charles's architect, San Felice, had even had the idea of pulling them down and taking some of the columns to Naples to decorate the new royal palace at Capodimonte. It was only the insoluble problem of arranging transport that prevented him doing to Paestum what Crotone had done to Sybaris 2,000 years earlier.

In fact 'the old ruined buildings of Peste, called Poseidon by the Greeks' had been described by Scipio Mazzella in 1597, and even before that had been mentioned in a letter by Pietro Summonte in 1524. Early in the eighteenth century a plan of them was drawn by Constantino Gatta, who described them as being a lair for sheep – '*un covile di pecore*'. When the English traveller John Breval sailed past them down the coast in 1728 he didn't even bother to mention them. That all changed suddenly twenty years later, following the discoveries of Pompeii and Herculaneum, instantly causing a rush of interest in the ancient world, and the temples of Paestum to suffer an invasion of what Byron called 'parcels of staring boobies'. Today they're in everybody's photograph album. Spike Milligan hung his smalls up in the columns when he helped to win the war, and every summer they are surrounded by charabancs full of trippers and flockers.

So if Paestum is fairly remarkable, it makes you wonder what the mother-city must have been like. 'If there is any single excavation in the world worth pursuing regardless of expense,' wrote Lenormant, 'it must be Sybaris.' And he said that in 1880.

THIRTEEN

Rossano

At the western edge of what was Sybaris the mountains start again – real ones. This is the beginning of Calabria proper; the old brigand land; where people get kidnapped and murdered or have their ears cut off. Dark and sinister, where the wind howls at night like wolves and the ghosts of the vanished walk. Or you can have a holiday: ski in the mountains and swim in the sea on the same day.

AB (Aldo's bike) is being temperamental; coughing a lot and taking absolutely no notice when I accelerate. I would like to beat it and beat it, like that awful song in Aldo's bar. It just ambles along regardless of all instructions; and then suddenly, after diving into a pothole, it will perform a sprinter's leap out of the starting blocks from ten to twenty-five miles an hour and almost leave me behind. It is obviously Italian; an 'al' improviso' machine, spontaneous and self-willed. One could say ungovernable.

Having arrived in Rossano, it has refused point-blank, as Rossano is perpendicular. An ancient and rugged town made for eagles, it perches out of reach over chasms and awesome precipices; not just balancing on one peak but on several contiguous ones, which must be uncomfortable; plenty of hills up, lots of slopes down, hundreds of sudden steps. As a result the inhabitants are robust and sturdy. I'd like grappling irons. Everything is off-balance. A labyrinth started by the Romans (Antoninus recorded it in the third century and so did Peutinger in the sixteenth century), and then helped on by Totila the Ostrogoth, and by Lombards, Normans, Byzantines – lots of energy to change things. Nice and safe for monks. St Nilus was one of them, an energetic and determined Basilian who founded the monastery at

Grottaferrata near Rome. A good place for penitents, cenobites and new messiahs, with plenty of holes in the cliffs in which to muse and think; work out the secret of life among the rocks, ravens and jackdaws. Perfect for bandits later too. They had more fun. Pino Orioli, who was in the south with Norman Douglas sometimes, heard about the famous ones when he stayed here in the 1930s: Palma, Romanello, Catalano, De Simone; and you can read all about their bloodthirsty deeds in his account *Moving Along*. Faccione had a harem of girls living with him in the caves; one of Palma's ransoms got him 20,000 gold francs.

I can only just see the sea, miles away downhill like toytown; tiny ribbons of foam moving. You can understand why cats rush up trees to get away from dogs – it's safer higher up. The fisher-folk did just the same when they saw the Turks and the pirates coming. The path is so tortuous and erratic that I have set off in a straight line and ended up where I started. This is snakes-and-ladders-ville; endless surprises and exasperation. Totally lopsided roofs on one side of me, foundations on the other. Some of the alleyways are only shoulder-wide and then they can split into two or three even narrower ones; useful for hiding in and getting lost. Useful for other things too, sometimes; the really tight ones are still called cunt-alleys.

The road down makes a corkscrew look straight. I've travelled it twice now in the local bus as Aldo's bike is in the hands of a mechanic for a health check; and as upper Rossano has no hotel, I am temporarily bedded down at the Marina, Rossano's beach village. I've never swayed so much; like a tug in a force-nine gale; everyone standing, then keeling over en masse like rhythmic pendulums; then we all have to tack back at the next corner and get intimate. It's worse when we pass the cemetery: males trying to kiss their fingers, cross themselves and raise old hats while poised on one leg. Lots of impromptu body contact, which Italians like; it makes them laugh. My co-flounderer, in a

brief moment of equilibrium, expresses interest in my visit
to such an out-of-the-way mountainous habitation that's
been ignored by every one of some fifty governments since
the war and has the highest proportion of unemployed in
Calabria. As this perennial monologue of woe no longer
interests me, I inform him that I'm in search of food and
then of miracles. The first he is anxious to help with, as he
professes to know every tavern for miles, but the second –
with raised eyebrows – he is less sure of. 'If you believe
there are miracles in Rossano,' he says 'you'll believe
anything.'

But a lot of Italians do. There's an image here of the
Madonna and Child that wasn't painted by human hand.
They call it Madonna Achiropita, meaning no human
involved, believing some heavenly gust of divine colours to
be responsible, fanned by Gabriel's wings. It's a wonder
therefore that the restorer who touched it up in 1929 wasn't
struck by a thunderbolt. I persuaded an urchin who was just
closing the cathedral door to do a little more sweeping
inside while I photographed it – which is forbidden. It is a
circular image kept behind glass, sitting in the main aisle
and internally illuminated, like a lighted oyster shell, and
embedded in a flamboyant baroque reredos topped by an
ornate baldaquin. Quite a holy showpiece. A tabernacle in
fact, thought up by Archbishop Adeodati in 1700. The
thick, dark hair of the infant seemed unusual; about five
years old, I would have thought, with big worried black
eyes. As Rossano was one of the principal Byzantine
religious centres in south Italy, it doubtless arrived with
them, particularly as some 50,000 priests are reported to
have fled to Calabria around AD 700 after an edict had been
passed forbidding the showing of human images in the
Eastern Church. The cathedral observed the Greek rite well
into the fifteenth century.

The next miracle probably arrived the same way. It is so
jealously guarded that the priest had to use seven different

keys to unlock seven doors before I could see it. He said the Pope wanted it in the Vatican, but Rossano wouldn't part with it, and if it ever went on exhibition it had to have an armed guard all the time. This is the Purple Codex, part of a sixth-century manuscript of the Gospels according to St Matthew and St Mark, beautifully lettered on 188 leaves of purple vellum. Some pages are illuminated in silver, a few in gold, and there are twelve full-page miniature illustrations of incidents in the life of Christ: Lazarus, the Wise Virgins, the Healing of the Blind Man and the Last Supper. I rather liked it, but I was even more struck by a startlingly bright Madonna in silver standing on a shelf with the dead Christ in her arms. This time her face hadn't been sentimentally overdone; it was just agonised. The priest said the statue had been stolen once and taken to Naples, but the city gates had refused to open and so the thieves had had to cart it all the way back. That kind of thing ought to happen today; a few auctioneers' doors refusing to open. The priest was very excited by the last English visitor who had been to see the Codex a few months before. Apparently he knelt down in front of it – actually it's in a big green safe with a large viewing panel – and he said that the thrill of seeing it was better than winning the football pools.

There's plenty of disagreement about who first found this little 'miracle' tucked away in south Italy; rather like who first discovered Paestum. French, Germans and Italians all say they did, and the guide book says the Italian traveller Cesare Malpica first noted it in 1864. They tend to be rather nationalistic about this kind of thing. But they've overlooked Ramage. He was here on a mule in 1828 and he not only managed to sleep through an earthquake ('no one felt any particular interest in my safety, and I was allowed to sleep undisturbed'), but he also saw these illuminated leaves in the possession of a local canon, but couldn't find out where the reverend gentleman had got them from.

*

A trial run on Aldo's mended moped. I pottered down the coast and got lost. I ended up thirsty in a village no one has ever heard of, made up of ten small white houses on the shingle only yards from the sea. I've now found out it's called Fossa. Lines of washing flapped in the wind and a wooden shed had a rusty Coca-Cola sign on it and a locked door. I waited for a drink in case it opened. I went on sweating and waiting. Then the local juvenile Mafia turned up: six of them looking bullish, with half-broken voices. Football first. 'Do you like Manchester United?' 'Probably, I've heard of it.' 'Are they good?' 'I think so.' 'Milan are better.' 'Yes, if you say so.' Sex second. 'What does fuck off mean?'

This tiny village is right at the end of the plain of Sybaris, and the mountains are steep and serious. They make you feel a dwarf. It's the start of the Sila, and in the sunshine the scenery is miraculous; everywhere you look, blue mountains, green ones, grey ones with blotches of forest on them among jagged peaks, as if split by an axe. They're huge, sky-touching. Geologists say it's the oldest part of Italy; the bit that rose up first out of the original convulsion; reared up like a colossus with monster spikes on its back; and with shelves, chasms, gorges, escarpments, crevices, gullies, caves and grottoes. Their looks change every minute as the sun moves, as if they want to speak; they welcome, they threaten; they want to kill. Avalanche edges tip towards the sea and bellies of rock burst open to make way for fields of wild grass to wave with yellow sweeps of giant buttercups. Colours are everywhere, like rainbows – azaleas, clematis, sags of wisteria and splashes of jasmine . . . No one wants them, they just grow; so do camellias, oleanders, magnolias, bougainvillea and great bundles of tamarisk. None of them can help it.

Someone told me once that the Garden of Eden was in south Italy.

*

I'm rather wondering why this Marina hotel is full of women. They must be the wives of the developers. There are bulldozers everywhere outside, and the cars have number-plates from Pisa, Milan, Bologna and Genoa. They've been busy chopping down forty olive trees to make a football stadium. An olive tree is supposed to mark a grave, according to some. It's going to be the grave of Italy, I kept thinking, if they go on putting signs up saying Rocky Tavern and Dallas Ranch.

The hotel isn't bad, but dinner is gruesome. The men are all out making money or chasing Rossano tail, so it's girls' night. There are two tables full of them, partying. They smoke like volcanoes and keep slapping each other on the back, with screams of delighted laughter as if they've just won huge divorce settlements. They all talk, but never listen; voices clattering like plates of jelly falling off a rack; picking their teeth at the same time, one hand foraging, the other cupping, and still trying to talk. They're in kitsch Versace, hoisting straps up as they roll about, pawing each other and letting off shrieks as if they've been goosed and like it. I can't understand a word; they never finish a sentence; it just drowns.

There's also the 'Tesoro' table. Tesoro is a boy of about six and is odious. He's got eight women admirers and doesn't half know it – he milks them. He is so oozing with wolf-litter charm that he lets them feed him, push pasta into his mouth like a baby cuckoo, and when he spits it out they clean it up. Bored with that, he starts singing in a wavering trill that would send any sparrow apoplectic, and as they keep clapping he starts again. I wish I had a gun. I got him to shut up eventually by putting my tongue out at him. It unnerved him so much he started covering his eyes up, which made him look better. One of his harem of adoring aged mutton saw what I was doing, so I had to stop.

I have just had a sloping lunch. The *trattoria* was halfway up a steep hill and one side of the door was a foot higher than the other. I shouldn't have told the *padrone* I was meant to be writing a book. He wanted to write one too, he said, about this 'rotten place'. He wouldn't stop; it was real venom, and my lunch could wait. The mayor was a thief; every official was a thief; the mayor should be in prison; they should all be in prison; the mayor charged him water tax for no water and dustbin tax for no dustbin; IVA (VAT) inspectors checked his books; the mayor was *'un cap' u cazz'*, which means a 'dick-head'. He, the guileless *padrone* meanwhile, paid floor tax, chair tax, refrigerator tax, television tax, light tax, window tax, telephone tax and gas tax, and if his payments weren't made on time, they'd close him.

On top of all this Rossano was a designated *'Centro Storico'* with valuable monuments, but the roads weren't made up, buildings were falling down, and when it rained water poured into his kitchen. With an expressive wave of his hand he then declared himself bankrupt, and said Rossano was like an old people's home as all the young ones had left to go north, and what money the mayor didn't keep for himself was spent on developing the Marina because he had a financial interest in it.

Although I believed most of it, I knew he was lying at the same time. There's a very curious characteristic the Italians have, called 'honest dissimulation'. It is how to lie yet be truthful all in one. Their politicians specialise in it. It's a verbal art form. Tommasso Accetto wrote a book called *Della Dissimulazione Onesta* as long ago as 1500, saying how by sheer rhetoric one could bamboozle the listener, purple-passage lies into reality, dress untruths up as truths, exaggerate, make something worthless look good, and use powers of persuasion rather than facts. It is ritualised lying; a façade. Castiglione advised 'abundance' and 'copiousness' in speech; be grandiloquent; call everyone *'Eminenza'* or *'Illustrissimo'*, but don't mean it. It is the baroque habit; appearance and reality. Grand Tourists did it when they had their swagger-portraits painted by Batoni in Rome; they were fake, but they created the theatrical illusion of spontaneity; 'impression management'. Italian men do it when they go to the hairdresser. In a painting by Berruguete, Duke Ferdinand of Urbino is reading a book while wearing a suit of armour, being learned and valiant; but I'm told that to do both at the same time is physically impossible.

And now I've met someone else who is angry. She looks after the Byzantine church of St Mark's, which is up a small hill beyond the town, and she is seething. It could be that the mountains breed this fury in people; perhaps they give off some indiscernible odour that shortens temper. How about the Scots and the Welsh and the Albanians? Has anyone ever done a study of the effect of landscape on human nature – the placid plain-dwellers and the hot-blooded hill men?

Peter Gunn, in his *Companion Guide to Southern Italy*, calls St Mark's 'one of the two finest examples of Byzantine architecture in Calabria'. (The other one is La Cattolica in Stilo.) It sits squat and square, right on the edge of a jagged, shapeless and rambling valley full of little sloping plantations, stray clumps of trees and the sockets of old caves. It must have been a focus of worship for the anchorites, but it's only used once a year now, on St Mark's Day. What she is angry about are the restorers. 'Ruined,' she says explosively, with her hands on her hips. 'They've completely wrecked it. Once the inside was full of beautiful frescoes, but they've covered them all in whitewash. They've ruined it. They're worse than barbarians.'

St Mark's is on a small plateau surrounded by palm trees, which give it a romantic flavour of the East; and there are three symmetrical bulges to show the line of the apses, and the roof is made up of five small cupolas. One gets the impression that Byzantium found more favour among the wild hills of Calabria and Basilicata than it did on the plains, probably because the Byzantines were persecuted so badly and could find places among the peaks that were out of reach.

It's evening, almost night, and I shall leave in the morning. I've been packing the saddlebag and hope AB will cooperate. Day slides into night with no warning here; you can watch it move. There's one pale streak left touching the sea as the grey shape of thunder comes, darkening to purple-black, and the waves dance to a breeze creeping in from the sea. Walkers glance at each other, gather cardigans round shoulders and shrink two inches as they hurry towards home. Up on top, the old town sits like a grey ghost in a milk mist, one or two slopes still spotted with fading oranges, then pinpricks of light come on slowly, staggered in broken rows. Glow-worms, Faustus-time . . . *currite, currite* . . . The black greyhound of night comes; it gulps up the day and runs on.

FOURTEEN

Ciro

Edward Hutton, the traveller who didn't like Gallipoli, didn't like Ciro either. He said it was 'not worth a visit'. I think he missed a lot. There's something about his writing that makes me think of a buttoned-up old uncle. He's enormously scholarly, but coy at the same time; repressed. There's a part of him inside waiting to burst out, but he won't let it. When you've read him you don't know anything about him, except that he's scared. He must have been here in about 1920, checking up on what Norman Douglas was up to, which would explain why he missed the remains of the vast temple to Apollo here, as it wasn't discovered until 1925 by the great Italian archaeologist Paolo Orsi.

Ramage enjoyed Ciro considerably more than Hutton, as he was more inquisitive and responsive. He does admit that he was 'put rather out of countenance' by some peasant girls he was chatting to in the fields, when they started telling him the facts of life; and were delighted to discuss things 'not usually introduced by us in the presence of ladies'. He wouldn't have mentioned it, if he hadn't appreciated it; finding out that boys married at fourteen and girls at twelve; and that men were fined for committing adultery, but women were sent to prison. As Ramage was used to life in Naples – that cosmopolitan beehive of copulation and cuckoldry, where balls ended only at dawn and you eventually woke up wondering whose bed you were in – I can't imagine that these 'damsels of Ciro' told him anything he didn't already know, though they were probably more demonstrative and explicit than he was used to.

Being a staunch Scottish Presbyterian, their directness might have surprised him.

Ciro is rather the reverse of Rossano; very little left at the top of the hill and a great deal down by the beach, where I am now sitting in a bar having a drink. There is a Polish girl serving who speaks very good English. She has already had eleven proposals of marriage since she arrived a month ago, all of which she has refused. Apparently she took a bus from Warsaw straight to Rome, where she spent a day looking round, then took a more local one to Cosenza, and then another one here. She said it was all remarkably simple, as there are plenty of Italian agencies with a clandestine department that can do wonders with travel documents and work permits, particularly if you're female with fair hair. She said she can't stand the dirt in Italy as they throw their rubbish round anywhere, and as for marrying one of them – who would want to slave in the kitchen surrounded by kids while he goes off screwing every day? Which for directness has a vague echo of Ramage's 'damsels'; and one wonders where she learned about the habits of Italian men. Their reputation must be worldwide.

She now earns, £175 per month, with free living, and she sends most of this home to pay for her intended course at Warsaw University to study botany.

There are two passable hotels in Ciro, if one takes Mrs Moens' advice in *English Travellers and Italian Brigands*, published in 1866, and establishes the price of a room before committing oneself. Having bargained to the bone the owner of the Atena, thus gaining his grudging respect, I was unwise enough to ask what he knew of Ciro's history. His grunt of non-interest was like hitting concrete. 'See Enzo,' he said. Having noticed his Mercedes outside with a Swiss number-plate and an Audi from Milan, I should have known better. Hotel owners concentrate on money and food.

But who on earth was Enzo? Enzo was invisible and mercurial; he was Ciro's pimpernel. Nobody knew where Enzo was. He had that kind of leper or Gadarene swine reputation; unhinged, ungodly, unstable, uncontrollable and probably untouchable. When I asked people where he lived, they didn't know; they shied away and walked on quickly. When I eventually found him I thought I'd met Moses. He didn't have lightning coming out of his hair, but he did have a beard reaching nearly to his shorts, which was all he was wearing. He had a bovine body as bristly as a doormat, fierce dark eyes, and his handshake was a pressing introduction to torture. He wasn't a time-waster, either – more like a hairy whirlwind. I'd hardly said who, why or what I was before he grabbed me by the elbow and took me to see the mayor. This unlucky young gentleman was sitting in his office in shirt-sleeves attended by a couple of sycophants, and he greeted Enzo like a long-lost friend or saviour and immediately asked him if he'd like to be mayor, as he himself was heartily sick of the job; always hearing about car crashes, infidelities, tax fiddles, power cuts, late buses, truancies and inept football referees. Enzo waved the offer away, slapped the mayor on the back, and introduced me as a reincarnation of Henry Swinburne who had come to write the history of Ciro.

It then transpired that the local inspector of antiquities might be arriving later that morning, information that caused the mayor to laugh, and Enzo to snort and ask for the key to the antiquities office. This room had a dusty metal desk in the middle of it, three fold-away wooden chairs and all the walls lined with makeshift shelving crammed with 2,000-year-old bits of Ciro's past. 'Mine,' announced Enzo, carrying out a quick inspection. 'I don't bother to hand things in any more when I find them. A couple of years ago I gave them two beautiful gold coins and that bloody inspector took them off and sold them. Now when I find anything important I tell the director of the museum in Reggio. He's okay.'

Enzo, therefore, is among other things a 'tombarolo' and says he knows the whereabouts of every Greek tomb within miles, has emptied most of them, keeps detailed records of his finds, which he passes on to Reggio, and says that the anticipated inspector is a complete ignoramus and *'una fica della Madonna'* – for which kind of blasphemous utterance one could have had one's head cut off in years gone by. Curiously enough, female anatomy doesn't figure a great deal in Italian swearing; it's very much a male preserve. You can hear 'cock' used in almost every conversation – 'You're talking cock', 'Stop being a cock', 'The referee was a cock', 'I don't care a cock', 'Where the cock is it?' – and they even give God a cock when things get heated.

While imparting all this information about tomb-robbing, and even more about gentlemen who drive down from Switzerland and Germany with suitcases full of money to see what priceless treasures they can pick up, Enzo has been dismantling the telephone on the inspector's desk and has removed a small metallic disc, which I am to put in one of my pockets as Enzo's shorts don't have any. This, he explains, is because the inspector's tour of duty will consist of nothing but sitting at the desk for one hour and telephoning all his girlfriends at the *comune*'s expense.

Which is exactly what happens. The inspector, obviously pleased with himself for being on £1,000 per month plus antiquarian perks, and nattily dressed in a lightweight suit, sits straight down at the desk and reaches for the telephone to make an urgent call. He can't. This annoys him. His persistent *'prontos'* go unanswered and there is a strange absence of dialling tone. So there is a baffled panic performance of slapping the receiver, rattling the pop-up button, tracing the wires, shaking the entire contraption like a rat, muttering curses and looking sulky. 'It's broken,' he announces rather petulantly.

'So are the things on these shelves,' says Enzo. 'Isn't it time we got them mended?'

I have had an extremely serious discussion with the hotel proprietor at dinner tonight as we are the only two people in the dining room. Being at separate tables, this makes for a loud discussion, getting on towards a shout. It is to do with women: their role, their function, their usefulness. He is very old-fashioned; decidedly against any feminist movement.

'So what do you think about women?' he asks from fifteen yards away.

'I never stop thinking about women,' I want to answer, as I'm already halfway through a bottle of Ciro's white wine, which is called Oenotria and is among the best in Italy; and I am therefore a little unclear about anything serious at the moment. It is beautiful, smooth, delicate, easy to drink and deceitfully over-powerful. Might even be called feminine. So I'm not really fit for any kind of discussion at all; certainly not about Italian women.

'What do you think?' he asks again. 'This Female Liberation?'

'Good,' I answer emphatically and loudly, without thinking; which is treason, sacrilege, anti-Pope, anti-God, anti-Italy, and obviously anti-him. His reply is to 'huff' because he doesn't like it, and I'm obviously in for trouble; I'm also having confused and spasmodic fantasies about the Polish girl, La Cicciolina's bottom, and his very fat and silent wife who is cooking our dinner in the kitchen and serving it to us at the two tables.

'Woman should be a mother,' he announces, putting his knife and fork down, 'she should be a wife and a mother.'

'She usually is,' I answer.

'Wife first, then a mother,' he emphasises. 'The Church says so. And God.'

I am not sure what he means by this. I don't recall the

Bible being so dogmatic; enmity between seeds, yes; women not being willing, and woman learning in silence, and silly women laden with sin – I can understand all that, because it was written by an ancient bunch of warp-minded misogynists anyway; but putting the domestic duties of looking after a husband and bearing his children first must be sheer papal invention. Anyway, this discussion is pointless, because I'm drunk and he's an Italian male whose views are set in stone; but I hear myself saying something; 'Suppose a woman doesn't want to be a wife and a mother . . .'

'It's wrong. They must be. They're women . . .'

This is getting nowhere. I wish he'd come out and say it: that they're for fucking, cooking, washing your clothes and having your children. I think he's stupid.

'Yes. Biologically that is true,' I tell him, 'and the body is important, but it isn't everything; there is also the brain and the power to think and feel.'

'But marriage is a duty.'

'Suppose she would rather get a job; go to university?'

'She should stay at home, show respect. There's no respect now. They disobey; go dancing and drive cars. It's all that television . . .'

'You can't stop women having brains and thinking for themselves.'

'They never used to. It's all wrong. A father used to rule like a king – tell everyone what to do . . .'

What he means is that, besides being a tyrant at home, he could do as he liked outside. Having surrendered his virility in marriage, he could go off and prove it elsewhere. 'Flames for a year and ashes for thirty,' as Lampedusa said.

'So you don't like women today then?' I ask, becoming placatory.

'Yes. No. Yes, if they're obedient and do what is expected; but they don't.'

It's no use going on. Have to let the old bull elephant die. He can't understand that free will has arrived to challenge obligation, and that history and time move on. His Church gave power to the males (unlike the Greeks who gave a lot to the females) and his Church is disintegrating; it tells yesterday's truth, not today's. He nearly choked when I mentioned female priests. And all this time his wife is a few feet away in the kitchen cooking our food – prawns on a bed of rice – and bringing it to us at the table in complete silence, which is what he likes because it shows subservience. A touch of the Islamites; she might as well be wearing a veil.

He's old and frightened because social disobedience has set in and he's not in control any more. Was he ever? he starts to wonder. He knows he has been unfaithful, but might she have been too? Is his daughter still a virgin? He can't trust anyone or anything because deceit is no longer his prerogative, so who can he talk to about it? To his *nonna*, because the family grandmother is not an ordinary woman any more; she's too old and wise; she's an oracle and knows everything. And he'll cry when he talks to her and put his arms round her, because this is the only real love he knows, and he won't realise he's come full circle. Italy is really a crypto-matriarchy, their own commentator, Luigi Barzini, said; but Italian men don't know that and nor does the hotel proprietor, eating his prawns as his wife waits to take his plate away. He never was king really; he only thought he was.

Enzo, I have decided, must be pagan, a Pythagorean reincarnation. He denies this, but does admit to being non-Christian, as he says Christianity was started as a political movement – something it still is – and has more to do with power than it has had to do with faith or religion. It's an autocratic empire, centralised in Rome, he insists; the world's biggest secret society; furthermore, while it professes to be original and unifying, it is in fact imitative and separatist. He dislikes doctrinaire brainwashing and says that if you repeat the words San Paolo (St Paul) ten times quickly enough, you end up saying Apollo; anyway, the bread-and-wine business was started by Demeter and Dionysius.

When pressed, he likes to consider himself Oenotrian; a throwback to those early settlers who arrived from somewhere in the Balkans or the Dodecanese thousands of years ago and settled in the western part of south Italy. When the Greeks landed later, they thought these strange uncouth men of the mountains might be their forefathers, enormously ancient Greeks who were pre-Homer and might have come from Arcadia. Any mention of God and Enzo says he is an Isis and Osirian, with a touch of Confucius, Zoroaster, Buddha and Tantra added, and that he would have liked to have been an Egyptian.

He thinks popes are craftily manipulated usurpers, and his comments on Eugenio Pacelli – i.e. Pius XII, famous during the Nazi era – are completely unprintable. As for the sad state of Italy, Enzo's theory is that the south of the country has more affinities with Africa than it does with Europe, and to have a Mediterranean union of countries would be far more sensible than Brussels trying to legislate for peoples and lands that are more equatorial than arctic.

I'm discovering all this sitting on a sofa in his small apartment, sipping wine and munching *sardedda*, an *amuse-bouche* of crisp toast fingers covered with minced fish and peppers that tingle on the tongue, being besieged by his two young daughters – Nefer (Arabic for beautiful) aged five, and Titi (Arabic for something I've forgotten) aged four. As he adores them, they disregard all his protestations and empty jars full of ancient coins onto the floor to play tiddlywinks, and climb onto shelves, making several Greek redfigured vases hop around drunkenly. Most of the available wall space is covered in drawings, and these are Enzo's. He is certainly no mean artist, which may explain his eccentricity and why people cross the road to avoid him in case he's a *mago* or has got the evil eye. The huge drawings he has done of the Riace bronzes that hang in the mayor's office are as lifelike as the statues themselves, and now he is working on a calendar of Calabrian Graces: January – chestnuts, February – fir cones, March – cheese, April – bannock, May – swordfish, June – cherries, July – figs, August – muscatel raisins, September – pears, October – fruit, November – nuts, and December – oranges and roses.

He has promised to take me to a church he is working in tomorrow; nativity scenes, he says wryly, and lots of Jesus and Mary. 'They won't pay me anything,' he adds, 'they never do. They always want something for nothing. They call it charity.'

Somewhere in Old Calabria Douglas counted fifty-two bugs in his bed. Last night I had the same number of mosquitoes drinking my blood. Vampires! With the light on I could see the cloud of them dancing round the naked bulb in gleeful anticipation. With it off they were onto me in seconds, their evil appetites screaming for my blood an octave higher than a Formula One engine, then dipping their neat little stiletto noses in and working their stomachs like suction pumps. I got one or two of the slower ones, but the rest didn't care; it was a kamikaze sacrifice. Even when I was sobbing with fury under the sheet, it didn't make any difference; I could hear them whining in, followed by a terrible silence as they sharpened their armour-piercing equipment and went on gorging on my corpuscles.

Enzo's church-painting day. He borrowed a car from some-one, which I had to drive along the coast to a village called Melissa and on the way we stopped at a house somewhere to call for the Virgin Mary, because Enzo likes to draw roughly what he can see. I nearly died. Mary was last year's Miss Calabria and a runner-up in Miss Italy, with the looks and body-shape you don't try to describe, only wish for, or dream about. I can't remember what she was wearing at that visionary point, but when she sat beside me in the car I was aware of two very long legs disappearing somewhere, and of smoke rings appearing from further up.

The church we arrived at was ghastly. It was modern and close to the beach and had a green tiled roof with 'Dio e Qui' in flashing lights over the doorway. The vestibule was semi-circular like an apse, with preparatory sketches on the wall tracing the Annunciation story through to the flight into Egypt; there were holy births, angels, shepherds, donkeys, visiting kings; and Enzo was supposed to put paint onto and life into them. While he got ready, Miss Almost Italy disappeared to change into something shy and virginal and came out in a black habit looking like a *Playboy* nun, with her mind obviously fixed on a large lighted altar candle. She already had matches and Marlboros ready, and was puffing away under her hood and hitching her long black skirt up to air her legs. Enzo started a commentary on what he believed life must really have been like in Palestine 2,000 years ago, and please would she try to look happy, as if she'd just been impregnated by an angel, to which she muttered something I couldn't quite catch about seraphic orgasms. He was doing his best with her, and things were certainly happening on the wall as she was obviously his daily muse, but she didn't enjoy having to cuddle a doll later and be reminded how pleased and pure she ought to feel, or that Mary probably didn't keep crossing and uncrossing her legs; nor did she blow smoke into Jesus' face all the time. I suppose there might have been occasional moments of levity up ladders in the Sistine Chapel.

It was when the art was over that the crunch came. We went outside onto the beach for a breather, and the BVM began to walk down towards the sea, slowly discarding her bits of nunnery with a pause to light up, until she'd lost everything except a very small pink bikini and was paddling happily into the shallows. It was as if Mary had done a strip for Herod instead of legging it into Egypt. The few people on the beach went electric. Some boys began to whistle and shout; a number of women crossed themselves and got up to leave; men sat up and waited for her to come back; and two children who ran after her clapping were almost concussed by their mother on their return.

Once Enzo starts on something he won't stop. Did I know how often Turkish pirates had sacked Ciro? No, I didn't. Well, certainly on more than fifty occasions: in 1569, 1582, 1587, 1590, 1594, 1595, 1596 . . . then in 1618 and 1624 . . . and 1711 and 1712. Small wonder then that there's very little left of Apollo's Temple: a rectangle of barely discernible foundations in the grass that we are standing in the middle of, being watched by seven cows. Enzo has mapped it all out in detail and drawn a complete reconstruction. He says it was Doric, with an inner sanctuary that was aligned with mathematical precision to face the daily sunrise and contained a statue of Apollo. It was nearly 160 feet long and 60 wide, supported by fifteen pillars on each side and eight across the ends. That would make it slightly smaller than the Temple of Neptune at Paestum. Enzo has his plan and his notebooks with him, carefully marked with all his discoveries, nearly a hundred of them: tombs, buildings, small tabernacles, a Roman villa, a cache of coins . . . He's angry that they have just concreted over a school playground with six tombs underneath it, which he won't be able to get at.

We go and sit on the deserted wide sweep of shingle at Punta Alice, with the temple 200 yards behind us, hidden by a tangle of scrub and bushes, and I listen to the relentless growls of the sea while Enzo dreams. 'There's a Roman ship fifty yards out there,' he says pointing. 'One day I'll go out there and excavate it; but I don't know how to swim.'

Punta Alice is really Punta Aleous, named after Apollo Aleous or Helios, the doubly powerful deity who was God of the Sun and God of Life. He was also god of other things sometimes: art, medicine, poetry, music; and he might have been born in Arcadia or in Crete, and he might even have loved Hyacinthus. The Greeks were endlessly inventive about their deities and happy to give them different origins, life stories and attributes, even though they all ended up meaning the Great Creator and Supreme Power, just as Baptists, Methodists, Lutherans, Presbyterians, Nonconformists and Hot Gospellers have invented their own systems to say the same thing.

There's a lighthouse just behind us surrounded by trees. Swinburne said that a lighthouse keeper at Ciro was also a keen bee-keeper, and once he fought off a Turkish attack single-handed by emptying one of his hives all over them as they landed.

I watch Enzo in the semi-silence, leafing through photographs of his illegal excavations, all carefully annotated, and his drawings of the Farnese bull, Hercules, Perseus and Andromeda, and scenes of gladiators, nymphs, satyrs and a hundred different demi-gods, and I listen to the persistent sea that always speaks without telling you what it is saying. And the everlasting warmth of the wind as it rolls the waves in and bends the withered grass behind us, scattered with the red and yellow heads of blown-over poppies. What do they know, I wonder, of white bones underwater and grinning skulls from the haunts of history, and of a temple as big as Concord in Sicily that once stood behind them? Nothing. They belong to a vanished world.

I have had it out with Enzo and the answer is 'Yes'. His best piece is now – or was – in a museum in Malibu, valued at about £10,000. He didn't deny it. It was a glass figure of Venus, beautifully carved and about eight inches high, and he got £500 for it. 'Why not?' he says. 'It's not so much the money, as getting it out of Italy so it can be seen and appreciated.' He doesn't want to know any details; he leaves all those to the middle-man who is a wealthy landowner living not far away in a house as impregnable as Fort Knox, where the inside is like Aladdin's cave. Enzo showed me some photographs. A death-mask of a Bruttian tribesman, probably the only known example of an ugly, round-faced individual with squashed nose and thick Negroid lips and fuzzy hair like a Hottentot; nightmarishly unattractive. A brooch he bought from a shepherd for £5 and passed on for £100. Plenty of figured vases that he thinks are probably in Switzerland now. An amazing painted cockerel on a stand, designed as a drinking vessel with jewels round its neck.

It was spectacular, almost frightening. 'It's our own fault,' he said without rancour. 'We've had a museum promised in Ciro for over ten years. The money is available, and I could fill it in six months. But there are too many committees involved, all arguing. The architect has done the plans, but people don't like them. But he's a government appointment and he won't change them, so it's stalemate.' Then he smiled. 'Why should I hang around for a bunch of imbeciles? If Ciro doesn't want the stuff, somebody else can have it.'

FIFTEEN

Crotone

There is an intriguing mystery not far from Ciro, where the single-track railway line crosses the River Lipuda. Once, at dead of night, Lenormant came across *'deux vieilles Anglaises'* calling for help. There had been an accident. A storm had washed away the bridge over the river, and the passengers had been forced to leave the train and find their way over the ravine and the swollen torrent to some carriages waiting for them on the other side. It was then that he heard the unmistakable voices: 'I'm afraid, I'm afraid.' Where on earth does one not meet old English ladies, he pondered as he helped them – *'où ne rencontre-t'on pas de vieilles Anglaises?'* Where indeed? Unfortunately he says no more about this intrepid pair, braving brigands and mosquitoes in the 1870s. Where are their journals and notebooks today? Their annotated Murrays and Baedekers with scribbles about Ruvo and Trani cathedrals and Metapontum's temple; their pressed flowers and faded photographs? The postcards they had sent – probably to Hastings or Eastbourne – and the impedimenta collected from hotels and shops? Such will-o'-the-wisps of travel, which appear like fireflies and suddenly vanish, tantalise the imagination – their clothes, their thoughts, their uncomfortable adventures. They are the *fata Morganas* of ancient travel, glimpsed for a moment, then invisible.

Likewise Mary, though she was a hundred years earlier. Charles MacFarlane, who wrote a book about the customs of south Italy, came across her in the Abruzzi mountains. A slip of a girl from a village near Manchester, she had fallen in love with an itinerant Italian travelling with his dancing bear. Although she was only fifteen or sixteen they had married (Protestant) and then travelled back across Europe together, through countless vicissitudes to his mountain village, and then been married again (Catholic). That had all happened around 1790 at the time of the French Revolution and Napoleon's invasion of Italy. When MacFarlane came across her in 1840 she only had a few English words left – bread, meat, money; and of her two remaining children, one girl was in service in Sulmona and a son was a shepherd. When he asked if she would like to see her own country again, she shook her head as it was many a year too late, she explained, and nobody would know her.

This would certainly not have been the case for another girl who came to Italy at roughly the same time and from the same part of England; and who made herself famous by hobnobbing with a queen, sleeping with an admiral, prancing about in diaphanous negligées, and singing an aria about the Battle of the Nile that was specially composed for her by Haydn. Whether or not Miss Emily Hart had, or had not, danced naked on the dining table, aged fifteen, to amuse male guests at Uppark before she landed in the arms of the British Ambassador to Naples is immaterial, but she doubtless had more fun out of life than Mary in the Abruzzi, though she almost certainly died a more wretched death, penniless and ignored in a Calais boarding house.

I enjoy these mysteries. That strange worshipper at Rossano, who knelt in front of the Purple Codex – the priest said he was on his knees for three days. And the English sailor whom Berkeley saw prize-fighting in Brindisi; and the fat, sweaty Englishman observed by Lady Blessington as he attempted to climb Vesuvius, but was 'in danger from an attack of apoplexy' and kept falling over.

There must be hundreds of travel phantoms like these who leave no traces; all sucked up into the world's vast womb without a whisper.

I have now arrived in Crotone, which nobody has ever heard of, which is a pity as it is famous. It is famous for

Pythagoras, Milo, Alcmaeon, Democedes, outrageously beautiful women, Capo Colonna, the Montecatini chemical plant, Bishop Lucifer, for liquidating Sybaris and for being briefly taken by the British in 1806. It is also Norman Douglas territory, and is where George Gissing caught malaria and had hallucinations. In addition it has an extremely large and splendid hotel with about a hundred rooms, and I am the only echoing occupant.

Gissing is the one south-Italian travel writer I cannot get on with, which is my fault, not his. *By the Ionian Sea* is lifeless and it annoys me. He is old-maidish and constipated, and the whole tone of the book is self-conscious and lugubrious. He doesn't seem to have been happy in the south; perhaps he was disappointed at finding so few ancient remains to muse over. He was certainly upset that he never got to see what was left of the Greek temple at Capo Colonna down the road. Strangely enough, most southerners love him. They all call him Jissing, and obviously enjoy his gooey romanticism and his maudlin meanderings about the beauty of the place and the marvellous memories it holds. They don't seem to notice that he calls them a 'flaccid race' and thinks most of their inns are ghastly.

It was here that he spent a wretched feverish ten days bedridden in the Concordia, which incidentally is still here just round the corner (another favourite haunt of Douglas), where he was attended by 'friendly' Dr Sculco and badgered by the 'stout slatternly' hostess. He records the remarkable visionary dream he had during his illness: a Pythagorean transportation back in time into vivid 'scenes of ancient life, thronged streets, processions triumphal or religious, halls of feasting, fields of battle', when he saw 'great vases rich with ornament and figures'. He even saw Hannibal slaughtering his Italian mercenaries on the beach here because they refused to go to Africa with him.

The chapters about Crotone are the only ones that come to life as they touch on Gissing personally. It's as if he's had an enema. Everywhere else his writing is listless and heavy; totally humourless. Things are either reposing his mind or quickening his pulse. He's a misanthrope. Perhaps the conditions he found in the south a hundred years ago made him melancholic. The faces he saw in Crotone were 'coarse and bumpkinish', and when describing the Concordia he says any normal traveller would think the staff 'little short of savages, filthy in person and in habits, utterly uncouth . . .'

At least he has one claim to fame. The name of the next landlord he met on his travels after Crotone was Signor Paparazzo, a word that has entered the English language, but in a less distinguished context. I suspect Gissing's inner feelings about the south had to spill out in the end when he said there was need for 'an honest capable government in this heavily burdened country', as if little had happened since unification. I'm afraid *By the Ionian Sea* sends me to sleep.

Pythagoras is a little more interesting. Having won an Olympic medal for wrestling and then travelled all round the known world in search of wisdom, he came to Crotone to preach peace, democracy and self-denial. This was around 550 BC, the same time that Cleisthenes was inventing democracy in Athens, Ezekiel was helping write the Old Testament, and Nebuchadnezzar was throwing enemies into a fiery furnace. Pythagoras also had views about mathematics, music, ascetic menus, sin, reincarnation and the earth revolving round the sun.

Dr Walter Leszl, in an article in the periodical *Magna Graecia*, says Pythagoras could remember events from his previous life on earth, could hear the music of the spheres and once had a conversation with an eagle. Dr R. W. Bernard, in his book *Pythagoras, Immortal Sage*, says that he was a vegetarian and his diet consisted of poppy and

sesame seeds, the skin of sea-onions, daffodil flowers,
mallow leaves and a paste of barley and peas, all to be mixed
together with wild honey, because this had been Hercules'
diet 'while wandering in the Libyan desert'. Bernard also
notes that Pythagoras advised against making love in hot
weather, and among the titles for further reading that are
suggested in his remarkable book are: *Nutritional Sex
Control and Rejuvenation* and *Flying Saucers from the
Earth's Interior*.

In fact very little is known about Pythagoras, though it is
generally agreed that he was extremely learned, and on
arriving in Crotone gathered a band of followers around him
who, by abstaining from all temptation and the nice things
in life, were destined for a perfect existence in this world
and the next. This theory of asceticism, limitless goodwill
and universal brotherly love so impressed the Crotoniate
dignitaries that they invited him to apply his system of
endless content, everlasting purity, total understanding and
permanent uncarnal love to government, which he did. The
destruction of Sybaris was one of the results. Another was
that two young Crotoniates who had been refused entry to
his 'lodge' of self-denial started to denounce Pythagoras
publicly for prohibitionism, dabbling in witchcraft and
wanting to start a revolution, with the result that our 'sweet
and noble figure moving as a dim radiance through legendary Hellas', as Gissing calls him, was banished to Metapontum, where he died soon afterwards and where Cicero
looked for his house years later but couldn't find it.

The fact that the oracle at Delphi is supposed to have
foretold Pythagoras' birth, and that he reputedly performed
certain miracles such as knowing the number of fishes in a
net before it was pulled ashore, and casting evil spirits out
of animals, have suggested to some that he was a Christ
figure. There is also a letter from Pope Nicholas V's
secretary, written in 1474, saying that Pythagoras' teaching
'differs in little or nothing from the Christian religion'.

If ever there was any reliable record about him and his theories of monotheism and the immortality of the soul, it was probably in Ptolemy's Library at Alexandria, which ended up in cinders, much to the delight of the Christians who by then had their own man in place ready to save the world and make us love each other. But, judging from the history of this area, I don't think His plea for peace on earth and goodwill towards men had any more success than Pythagoras'.

Gissing didn't have a good time at Crotone; as well as spending most of it in bed suffering, it rained much of the time and he was only allowed a brief visit to an orchard, as long as he didn't touch anything. Also, he dined off a bird that tasted like boiled gloves. None of this sounds too auspicious. Nor does the Honourable Keppel Craven's description of Crotone as pestilential and tedious and 'the ugliest tract of land in all Calabria'. Augustus Hare, among his handbooks and guides, went further and said it was God-forsaken and entirely wretched, and the German traveller Baron Johann von Riedesel went completely hysterical and said it was *'la plus affreuse'* town in Italy, and perhaps in the whole world.

So why on earth am I here? Because I like it. It vibrates with something. They were all writing when the population was way below 6,000, whereas today it is nearly 60,000. Being charitable, I wouldn't like to think this boom is entirely due to the import of asylum-seekers or to the drugs trade, as Crotone is well known for being a port of easy access for clandestine traffic; but then if Pythagoras and his clan dined on poppy seeds every day . . . it probably runs in the family.

I have a hundred beds at my disposal up two flights of marble stairs, as this was once a palace belonging to the Berlinghieri family; but there is no restaurant, which doesn't matter as the town is full of them. At the reception desk I have discovered a German gentleman in place during certain hours who has lived in Crotone for twenty years, because, he says, he has renounced the 'poisonous over-civilisation' of the north – with its cold, capitalist values and meanness of spirit – for surroundings where, he says, 'life is spontaneous and natural'. I will not probe further. Though I do remember reading an extremely well-known columnist in *The Times* taking the same line and asking, 'What makes a place civilised?' He then opted for Italy because it was beautiful, content, good-hearted, sensible, proud of its past and had every right to call itself civilised. I would like him to live here for a couple of years and see if it changes his mind.

His thesis was probably based on a visit to Florence, where things may look beautiful and the people appear good-hearted and proud of their past, when in fact they're arrogant, bisexual, don't know how much art they've got and couldn't care less when it gets flooded, as long as somebody else pays to repair the damage.

I like Crotone because of its variety; it is also exciting, particularly at the centre where the fish market is, most of the shops, the cathedral and my hotel. There are constant gatherings of people with a lot to say. It is also unpretentious, as if it knows it is famous, and you can take it or leave it. Outside the hotel there are small public gardens where people sit and chat; a hundred yards away is the cathedral square where people stand and chat; all along the sea-front there are boats moored where people fish and chat; in all the tiny alleys leading up to the castle children run and chat; and at the castle itself the squatters who have been about to be evicted for the past three years complain and chat. There is also an extremely long road leading to the railway station, lined on both sides with garages and repair shops where mechanics mend cars and try to chat over the noise of blowlamps. Less than a mile beyond the town to the east there are vast sand-dunes higher than houses, which is where a large part of Greek Crotone lies but has never been excavated, and here there is no chat at all; there is silence.

Once upon a time there was an unhappy Greek hunch-back called Myskellos, who was told by an oracle to go and found a city. This order rather perplexed him, though the instruction became clearer when the oracle added that it was to be where rain and fair weather met. He eventually found two possible sites that fulfilled these conditions: the plain of Sybaris and the plain of Crotone; and, being undecided, he returned to the oracle for further guidance. The oracle, presumably getting angry by this time, told Myskellos to go away and make up his own mind; and on his return visit he met a beautiful woman in tears on the plains of Crotone, which, symbolically speaking, fulfilled the conditions even more, so that is where he settled. His name now appears in the local dialect: if you are 'misched-dhu', it means you can't make your mind up; you hesitate or dither.

It is equally possible that Hercules founded Crotone. He got involved in an argument here while shepherding the oxen of Geryon around, and he accidentally killed the son of his host called Croton, and promised he would found a city here in recompense. It is just as likely that some Trojans landed here and, joining up with a small tribe of local Coni (sometimes known as Cheoni), they established it together. What isn't very likely is that it's called after the noise that storks make as they fly overhead on their way to warmer lands each year, crying 'crot . . . crot . . . crot . . .'

Does it really matter how it started? It flattened Sybaris and in its turn was flattened by its next-door neighbour Locri; and on account of its climate of both sunshine and rain it bred in its heyday such a host of healthy, beautiful, well-proportioned, energetic and consummately lovely peo-ple that it won so many Olympic medals it was said that the puniest of the Crotoniates could beat the best of all other Greeks. Milo was their main medal-winner and was reputed to be so strong that he once carried a young ox round the Olympic arena on his shoulders, felled it with one blow and then proceeded to eat it at one sitting; which Lenormant says is a nonsense legend, as is the story of Milo tying a rope round his head and bursting it by swelling his veins. One wonders why they needed medical assistance if they were that fit, but they did. Alcmaeon is supposed to have been the first doctor who carried out a successful amputation not in anger, and Democedes was so famous for his medical skills that he was kidnapped on the orders of the King of Persia, who had a very sick wife; having restored her to health, he then overcame all the king's efforts to keep him as part of the royal household and managed to escape back to Crotone.

Then there is always the kind Dr Sculco, who attended Gissing when he was bedridden in the Hotel Concordia, which I have now visited, but I think I will stay in the Berlinghieri Palace as it doesn't look as though the Concordia has changed much in a hundred years. Of the thirty rooms (cost £10 per night), only one had a washbasin in it, and that was in a corner and made of stone with only one tap. Two old sisters showed me round and pointed out where Gissing's and Douglas' bedrooms were, which may be convenient fantasy. And now another phantom traveller has arisen. One of the sisters said that someone was there from England earlier this year and that he was seen stroking and kissing some of the walls.

I simply had to talk to somebody, and luckily I met someone in the museum – he was a numismatist. The girls here are absolutely outrageous. They just hang around in the square outside the cathedral most of the day, trying to give men erections without touching them or taking their clothes off. Zeuxis must have had one hell of a time choosing the six best. I try to analyse how they do it. The eyes have it, first. They just fix you, deep as an ocean; unflinching, friendly and inquisitive, not quite challenging but very knowing; black as midnight and soft at the same time, with long lashes and a liquid expression that says: what are you thinking about, because I might be considering it too? That could be male imagination of course. Then it's the hair, which is also black, but it is sleek and shiny and so well groomed and velvety it makes you want to stroke it. Then the mouth; they just have incredible lips that look soft and relaxed, not tight and not loose – but tender and expectant, almost vulnerable. Where heaven seems to lurk, as Marlowe would say.

Their whole face combines into something so ridiculously attractive you can't stop looking at it. And they are provocatively body-conscious too, as they posture carelessly; they send shockwaves out through their clothes like a radiator giving out heat, and this is not just the boring dryness of looking at Page Three; because this is hidden; but it is concentrated, deliberate and magnetic. It may look casual, but it expects recognition and response. They want to control you. They dress well too; showpieces; everything clean and immaculate, and worn proudly to suggest a tantalising shape inside, and when they turn round the skirt or the jeans over their bums is as tight as a sausage-skin. Furthermore, should they be wearing a jumper, they wouldn't consider pulling it down over their bottoms as a nice English girl would, for fear of appearing unseemly; they ceremoniously haul it up to make you think harder.

The boys hanging around them in the square are shy, confused and uncertain at this display of wanton teasing; most of them are on Vespas, and they have to wriggle on their saddles and hold their crotches in discomfort. Which is not an unusual male occupation in Italy anyway, as a lot of them keep having to feel it to see if it's still there.

My friend of recent acquaintance in the museum, and a

well-known expert on Greek coins, came straight to the point.

'You must remember this is Crotone,' he said. 'Our women have had this reputation for over two thousand years, that they are the most beautiful in Italy. In fact, some of them are so beautiful they blow your balls off . . .'

I agreed. We were sitting in the garden outside the hotel.

'In fact,' he went on, 'I have to give talks and lectures sometimes in schools about ancient Crotone. In summer, quite honestly, I have to talk to them with my eyes shut . . . And what's worse,' he added, 'is that they are very *"compiacente"* – compliant.'

I sympathised, but I wasn't going to let it rest.

'Well, why,' I asked, 'with the greatest respect and with all these beautiful girls in abundance, do Italian men, instead of valuing them and honouring them for life, have the reputation for just wanting to stick it in as quickly as possible and then move on . . . ?'

He looked at me patiently. 'We are southerners and you are northerners; there is a temperamental difference. You strive for calm and a steady equilibrium; you like to be settled, organised, and know where you are. We are very different; we are excitable and restless, always wanting change . . .'

'Is that the real reason?' I asked, and he smiled.

'Well, there are historical precedents,' he said. 'Remember we are part-oriental, and Easterners very often have more than one wife . . . And don't forget Pope Alexander VI and those prostitutes kneeling on the Vatican floor completely naked, having to pick up chestnuts in their teeth, and what was said to the watching courtiers . . .'

'What?' I asked.

'That there'd be prizes for the men who could fuck the greatest number of them in the shortest time; prizes of shoes, hats and clothes.'

I didn't say anything. I couldn't.

'It's quite simple really,' he concluded. 'You see, in sex, speed is very important, and we also love variety and enjoy conquest. An Italian would rather win fifty women than win one war. We all love all our women so much we can't wait to get on to the next one.'

I hadn't thought of that, and I'm not sure I'm convinced anyway, but it sounded all right at the time.

He added another point before he left. 'You must realise that original sin has nothing to do with the genitals. Original sin was stealing the apple.' Which made me think of what Lawrence Durrell once said about Greece: that there's so much sex around, one gets heartily sick of it.

Later on I found myself wondering if this sexual exuberance might not have some advantages. I was wandering in an alley towards the castle and saw a little girl of about ten elbowing off an old man at least five times her age.

'Piss off,' she said. 'You're an animal. You're all cock and no brain.'

I've now been to both the museum and the castle. What is left of the latter is hardly impressive, though it must have been stupendous once; only the remains of a moat and some vast unassailable walls on one side that slope down towards the sea. It was built by, or on the orders of, the Spanish Viceroy Pedro di Toledo, who was the only constructive – though thoroughly hated – Aragonese overlord. It is easy to see that this peak must have been the Greek citadel, though there is absolutely no sign of it now; their pinnacle of perfection that gazed out over the sea on one side and over a city with walls nearly seven miles in circumference on the other. The iron gate says 'No Entry', which doesn't stop one wandering in to find some wooden huts and one or two of breeze-block among the rubble, and an old woman wanting to know if I'm from the ministry of something come to evict her. She's been being evicted for three years, she says, but it never actually happens.

Crotone

The museum is a few yards away; it's small, but trying hard and has a reasonable display of things Greek, but not nearly as much as one would expect. There are lamps, vases, coins and two striking red-figure *kantharos* and Egyptian-looking ladies with hair rising off their heads like beehives. Crotone's decadence was in evidence: a cabinet full of grotesquely leering Silenus faces with their tongues out. I wrote in the suggestion book that a small printed explanation or guide book would be useful, and then saw that exactly the same thing had been written in by somebody else five years earlier.

'That's S—— for you,' said the numismatist when I next met him. 'He's our local inspector. Useless. We've actually got another museum here, much bigger, but it's always closed. It only opened last year; a huge ceremony and lots of speeches; then it closed the next day. He couldn't get any attendants to man it, and we've got twenty per cent unemployment here.'

The numismatist has given me some coins, very nice ones; a silver stater from Metapontum showing the famous ear of wheat that advertised its prosperity, and one from Crotone that shows the tripos with a stork standing beside it. He looked them up in a Spinks auction catalogue to show me how much they were worth. I now know what 'incuse' means: hammered through, so that the design pops up clear on one side and is just an indented shape on the reverse. Apparently Crotone was the first Greek city to mint coins this way.

Then he asked if I was going to stay for the Madonna festival, when they carry her effigy all the way from the cathedral to the old temple at Capo Colonna. Crotone's Madonna is black. She is at the end of the right-hand aisle in the cathedral in a large silver frame. She is only slightly less than life-size and is taken extremely seriously. So seriously that when the cathedral is open, there is hardly a moment when there is not someone kneeling in front of her or lighting a candle and muttering a prayer. She is Crotone's miracle, and my booklet says she was painted by St Luke and brought here by St Dionysius, adding – as a footnote, as if doubting itself – that there was an artist working in Messina called Luke around AD 1000 and there was also an Archbishop Luke of Capo Rizzuto down the road at the same time. So her genesis is lost in a mist, as is the hidden hand that conveyed her here, though it is most likely that at some stage she usurped the position of Hera (Juno) on the point at Capo Colonna, and became a source of equal wonder and worship, though not quite so frenzied; a Pythagorean transmogrification in fact. Though the minuscule remains of what might have been her Christian chapel on the Cape suggest that the builders decided that to compete with Hera and her nearby temple would be pointless.

The first we hear of the Madonna with any certainty is that Turkish raiders captured her in 1519 and tried to burn her, but she was like the trio in the fiery furnace and lay in the bonfire untoasted and smiling for three hours; she even exuded luminous rays – 'raggi luminosi'. When the cinders were cool enough, the thwarted and unspeakable Turks tried tearing her to pieces, but again she proved indestructible, so as a last resort they took her out to sea to drown her. But alas! She could swim and, being happily buoyant, she eventually ended up on the beach exactly where she had come from, at Capo Colonna, where she was found by a fisherman called Morello who thought she was so beautiful that he decided to keep her to himself in his cave. It was only when he confessed to her whereabouts on his deathbed that Crotone's years of mourning ceased and wild celebrations broke out at her successful return; and instead of being taken back to the chapel on the Cape, she was enshrined in the cathedral with full honours. This move proved highly successful, for when the Turks next raided Crotone they were so horror-struck to see smiling at them in the cathedral the person they had recently drowned that they turned tail and fled.

Her day is in the middle of May, when there is a week of spectacular celebrations culminating in an eight-mile procession from the cathedral to the Cape. This starts at one-thirty in the morning, and is to be done on foot, and if all goes well you will reach the remains of the tiny Christian chapel there just as the sun rises. There will be a brief service of thanksgiving followed by a more light-hearted return journey. The programme of *'Manifestazioni'* arranged for the days preceding this climax includes special church services, film shows of past processions, public lectures about her in Resistance Square, a schools' athletic competition, a boy-scout jamboree, firework displays, daily piano recitals and evening performances by the Verdi band.

This week-long overture will ensure that the right degree of exhilaration and fever-pitch has been reached by the final night, so as the cathedral bells ring, the Madonna will be borne out in triumph to start her candlelit pilgrimage to the Cape; just as another image was carried along the same route 2,500 years ago for much the same reason.

In the days when Gissing was hoping to reach Capo Colonna, the only way to get there from Crotone was by boat. Now there is a passable country road that wanders round hillocks and along the cliffs before breasting a final rise; and there in front, incongruous and sudden among all the miles of grumbling mountains, is a vast plain – a whole sheet of green that vanishes ahead as far as the eye can blink and to the left towards a distant point touching the sea. Surprise is the reaction; a moment's shock of incredulity after the sweat and grind of climbing into the wind with dark shoulders of mountains at one's side. Miles of unbroken flatness at last; the goddess's sacred plain and her sacred wood, where her sacred herds were allowed to roam, and where one day archaeologists and antiquarians are hoping to re-establish a site that might conjure up some tiny memories of an ancient magnificence.

But the past has powerful enemies. There are three or four large houses near the point; houses of the wealthy who have owned the land for more centuries now than the Greeks, and to whom tales of bygone history are of no interest. Archaeology is the weakness of dreamers; Hera's temple is a myth already crumbling; there can be no past here, only fantasy.

And it does look rather like it. Only one column remains standing now, not forty-eight, and around it desolation; a graveyard of piled-up foundations, part-Greek, part-Roman; shapeless and scattered growing out of the earth, scrambled over by laughing Sunday picnickers whose cans and torn plastic bags trickle in decoration. One column only, and one of the most sacred places in Magna Graecia: a Vatican of the ancient world for pilgrims, worshippers, devotees. It contained vast amounts of gold and silver – gold that Hannibal tried to steal in order to pay his troops, but was warned off by Hera who appeared to him in a dream; the fabulous painting of Helen done by Zeuxis of Erakleia using six different models so that he could at last see feminine perfection; the marble tiles on the roof that were stolen by a Roman general to decorate his own home, but had to be returned on the orders of the Senate. (No craftsman knew how to put them back on the roof again, and they were still lying in the sand here just over a hundred years ago.)

The numismatist is with me. For security reasons I had better call him 'A'. He is not the first person I've met here who despairs of his own race sometimes and says what a marvellous country this could be, if it wasn't for the people who live in it, who throw their litter everywhere without a care, who ridicule their past history, and who think of nothing but self-gratification and money and sex. He was so depressed he even started calling Italy a brothel run by thieves and assassins.

'It's not that bad,' I corrected.

'What? Eaten up by corrupt politicians . . . ? Rubbish everywhere . . . ? Crotone the dirtiest town in Italy . . . ? The river Esauro like a sewer . . . Montecatini closing . . . *Siamo in crisi* – it's a crisis here. It's like Petronius said: you either cheat your way through life or get cheated . . . The south is paralysed. We have to be anarchists to survive.'

He was angry too about Capo Colonna, so angry it made him laugh. He took a coin out of his pocket and slipped it into one of the joints of the remaining pillar as it moved slightly in the wind. 'They've been promising to make it safe for years,' he said. 'It won't last long.'

It was tall and tapering; yellow in the sun, and desolate; almost pathetic. It looked so lonely and unloved that it was hard to imagine the past; the whole site was too sad. No one knows very much about it. None of the local families with wealthy or vaguely aristocratic pretentions – Lucifero, Barroco, Berlinghieri, Gallucci, De Mayda – will let anyone see their archives; they guard them jealously in case there are past illegalities; family secrets about land, money, murder and children born out of wedlock. What is worse, says Lenormant, is that so many 'false histories' have been written about the south. Medieval priests and scribes would vaunt the importance of their towns or villages by inventing things that happened. It was done to give the local lord a sense of grandeur; battles, miracles, tempests or visions, even a visit by St Paul; any spectacular lie would do to make the place famous. These *'fausses chroniques'* and *'histoires forgées'*, he says, have already taken hold in some places and have made the story of Magna Graecia indecipherable, even up to a hundred years ago. It is said by some that there was another column here in 1638, but it fell during an earthquake. Others would have it that all forty-eight were standing in 1500, until Bishop Lucifero of Crotone wanted some for a cathedral and for his palace in about 1530; or it could have been that the Spanish Viceroy,

Pedro di Toledo, thought they'd be useful for improving the harbour.

So nobody knows and probably never will know, and it doesn't really matter. The last pillar doesn't look as if it cares much, either. It looks lost and miserable; almost unwanted; probably wishing it could join the others.

I must have been mad today; I'm still aching. There's quite a tall hill sticking up behind Crotone and you can just see what looks like a village at the top. It's called Santa Severina. It looked easy enough. The moped went on strike; total refusal after 200 yards. The first four or five miles were simple, across a wriggly plain with a fresh breeze blowing, and pottering past goats and cows and crouched-down shepherds, and even a level crossing to show that I wasn't lost, and the occasional house with a barking dog. It was fun. Till the climb started. AB took one look at what was above, gave a whimper of horror and collapsed. That produced a quandary: leave it in the ditch and get it nicked, or a reversal of roles and I'd do the work for a change. So I pushed, and it wasn't funny. The Italians don't provide incline indications, but this was horrendous and it went on a very, very long way, and the top didn't get any closer. My knees ached, I puffed, I cursed, I gulped for oxygen, sweat went everywhere it shouldn't and ended up in my shoes. I was bodily incontinent and damp all over, and gripping wobbling handlebars that I loathed and detested. I did five yards at a time, hating every car that rattled down and every silly little house that I began to pass. Why live here – for God's sake? Go somewhere else more sensible. My knees became agony, as if the bones were rubbing together and all the flesh had gone; the backs of my thighs were painful jelly starting to go solid.

It was all the fault of Robert Guiscard, one of those land-grabbing Normans; one of the same tribe that invaded England at about the same time. He and his brothers swept down into south Italy to make themselves rich, and he was the most ruthless of them all. He always built castles at the top of hills, and I was Sysiphus dragging a moped up to see one of them. Madness! Think of all the slaves heaving the stones up. Incredible! He wanted to clear all the Lombards and Byzantines out of the south so that he could have it to himself, and by defeating all the other Norman warlords who were trying to do the same thing he almost succeeded. He'd already been blessed by the Pope, built Salerno Cathedral and Latinised most of the southern Church when he died of typhoid in 1085. He had a remarkable wife called Sichelgaita who always went into battle with him. John Julius Norwich says that she was an Amazonian lady of enormous proportions, who must have looked a terrifying sight in full armour. Apparently she gave piercing Wagnerian battle-cries as she charged at the enemy. I felt like letting out a cry too, but one of despair; Robert's castle wasn't getting any closer.

I was resting and heard a donkey clip-clopping up, so I got out the camera, but he rattled on past, shouting 'That'll be five thousand lire' before I could release the shutter. All I got was the donkey's bottom.

Somewhere up the hill a woman came out to watch me, so I asked her where the castle was and she came out with the meaningless Italian distance of '*due passi*' or two paces, which can mean anything between 500 yards and three miles (for example, from my hotel in Crotone to the station is '*due passi*', which I decided to try out, and it's just 2,000 yards). When I asked her in breathless gulps if I could leave AB with her, she nodded and gave me a glass of wine as black as squid's ink, and I sat on a wall feeling like a punctured tyre and waiting for my knees to re-joint as I drank it.

I felt slightly less encumbered after that, almost springy, going round a spaghetti of corners until I was right at the foot of the castle walls, and they stretched up yards and yards and yards into somewhere above, into the sky even, always sloping, so the people at the top could just laugh at the no-hopers at the bottom. What carnage! Was there ever a time in south Italy when somebody wasn't fighting somebody else? Kill or be killed, for greed or God. Lie there and rot in silent heaps; let your white bones wither.

I trudged round it looking for a way up and in, under arches and along corridors, till I found some steps. I ended up right in the middle of Robert's castle, which was as big as a full-sized cricket field with towers at the corners. It was like a little village, with shops at one end selling groceries, sweets and drinks. There was a post office (God help the postman!), the town hall, a bar, more offices, a schoolroom full of noisy children, a playground, several gateways leading to houses further up the hill, and a small car park. It was breezy and cool, and as I'd arrived I didn't care any more, so I walked straight into school and photographed the children, which caused pandemonium and more cries of 'Manchester United'. For some reason the lady of the wine, who was supposed to be guarding AB, had followed me up and wanted me to see the cathedral, which she obviously considered more significant than a Norman castle. It was lower down the slope and I was surprised to find a large wooden model of a dragon inside the entrance. It must have been quite old because when I patted it the entire tail fell off, followed by a shower of woodworm dust. I managed to replace it eventually by commandeering some notices about forthcoming services, which I stuffed into the dragon's open fundament followed by the tail.

It was obviously time to go, so I began to walk down again, satisfied that I'd 'done' Santa Severina, which the guide book says is 326 yards above sea-level and which to me felt more like 3,000. As soon as I saw AB again my knees began to ache as if I'd got the Neapolitan pox. The lady of the wine gave me a whole bottle of her brew this time to take away with me, and said her daughter had once stayed in London for two weeks at a place called Oxford.

As AB started to drift me downhill without me bothering to start the motor, the wind began racing through my hair. We were friends again, shooting past all the colours of Calabria; jasmines, eucalyptus, oranges and figs. They sprawled over walls; they bulged and jumped. Brown-and-white goats tinkled without looking up, and cracked creamy cottages deadened by time and roofless gleamed in the fields, and wild cocktails of washing flapped, and dogs ran – as big as Shetland ponies; and the roadsides were yellow with sprays of aconites and red with poppies; and broken dry walls wore cloaks of clematis, tamarisk, japonica, broom and hydra hydrangeas, and silver wisteria climbing up trees.

I hadn't noticed any of it on the way up.

This evening I'm spoiling myself and sitting with A, the numismatist, in an extremely elegant fish restaurant beside the sea. One wall of the dining room is a huge sheet of glass, so you can see exactly what is going on in the kitchen: four white-hatted chefs throwing pans around among sheets of flames. Swordfish tastes very like veal.

'Will they ever bother to excavate?' I said. 'All those mounds beyond the river where old Crotone is?'

He grunted. 'Don't suppose so. They can't be bothered.' And he gave a slight smile. 'So we sit on a gold mine,' he said, 'and nobody cares if the odd thing turns up . . . if I buy something for a hundred pounds and sell it for a thousand.'

'Do you?'

He took a long time to answer. 'It happens . . . builders turn up things on the new estates. But you mustn't think of it as stealing. I like to say it's discovering; bringing something back to life. It's creation, not destruction, the way some of our old buildings are falling down, or Florence is being flooded and paintings destroyed. Italians don't care that nearly two thousand art treasures are stolen from museums, churches, galleries every year, or that Venice is sinking, that Urbino's walls are falling down or that the Leaning Tower is going to collapse. There's no such word as "heritage" here in spite of what the government says. They're even talking about driving a motorway through Pompeii. Look at that museum we've got, the sooner these things leave Italy, the better. Nobody here wants them . . .'

'Do you do a lot?' I asked bluntly, and he shook his head.

'Too dangerous . . . I've a job and a family. But there are channels . . . The Mafia and 'Ndrangheta get interested if you're not careful. But they're happy with drugs at the moment and illegal immigrants. Coins and vases are a bit specialised and they're not worth enough; they don't mind the odd Greek or Roman statue, because that could be valuable, but even they can be difficult sometimes. There's a lovely Sicilian Venus behind some sacks in a garage near the station; it was on its way to the US, but something went wrong . . .'

I had to smile. It all seemed so ridiculous; and nobody cared or did anything; except Enzo in Ciro and A in Crotone, who augmented their living occasionally because of a country's stupidity, and would go on doing so till they died.

It was a strange note on which to leave Crotone: the private liberation of an ancient Greek city bit-by-bit. I'd liked to have helped. Then I remembered something he'd told me about the Madonna in the cathedral, and the silver frame round her studded with jewels. They were all fake. The real ones were stolen on 13 October 1983.

He said something else too: that if you locked up every dishonest person in Italy there'd be nobody left on the streets.

I meant to leave Crotone but didn't. It may be dirty but it's friendly, and this hotel is quite ridiculous – an entrance hall you could get four double-decker buses into, and then a marble staircase sweeping up right and left. I'm lord of a hundred rooms, admittedly with the paint peeling a bit, except for a rather stout soprano from Bari, who gave a concert in the cathedral last night and sang a lot of Ave Marias and some Schubert songs. It was after the evening service, which didn't seem to be a service at all; there was a guitar-led choir of children swinging their hips and singing pop-songs or spirituals, presumably with a theological connection. They were as happy as a school of sparrows jubilating over a cat corpse. I didn't notice if the confessionals were full, but one young priest was sitting in a chair at the back with a female penitent's head in his lap, listening to her intently. Checking up on the Madonna, I noticed that if you put money in her meter she lit up for a minute. I did think briefly of Jesus chucking people out of the temple, though as everyone seemed to be enjoying themselves immensely one assumes that God was as well.

It was still light outside, so I went back up the alleys towards the castle, past the tight compress of houses on either side, glued to each other on a tilt, with sub-alleys darting between them and shrieks of children as they streak in and out like squirts of lizards. This is the old part; the safe part, where you can fall into unevenly cobbled sloping squares, and there are set back, slightly larger untidy houses with faded writing on saying Palazzo Grimaldi, Albano or Gallucci. At the very top you can see the evening sea heading out to Africa, where Hannibal came from, and you can remember his Italian helpers who wouldn't go with him, so he murdered them on the beach. Here, Lenormant says, was the last sight of one of those fabulously splendid Sybarite cloaks that the Carthaginians had bought from a Crotoniate for 120 talents; a long flowing robe embroidered with animals and the figures of gods: Zeus, Athene, Aphrodite and Hera.

Down the hill and just past the cathedral, where Crotone

has exploded since Gissing and Douglas were here, is Pythagoras Square with a five-point star of wide roads disappearing seawards or inland. One of them, the Via Veneto, is closed off by the police every evening between 5 p.m. and 8 p.m. so that the entire population can come out and take ritual slow-motion exercise; not a traffic jam, but a man-and-woman-jam of impenetrable thickness and crawling coagulation and leisured contentment.

I was sad to leave eventually. The town has a curiously magnetic quality, like Gallipoli. I kept thinking of two things as I left: 'Reposeful and orderly,' Douglas had said nearly a century ago. 'Anarchic,' the numismatist had said yesterday.

SIXTEEN

Catanzaro

The road has gone inland now to avoid the ragged contours of the coast, but I wanted to get to Capo Rizzuto and see the Aragonese castle, so I trundled down some narrow lanes towards the sea. Most of it was through acres of deserted scrubland broken by an occasional cultivated field where groups of labourers bent over their work. There was a crowd of them in one field, pygmy-people in the distance. They were Albanians, all with scarves on their heads to honour their faith rather than protect them from the sun. Soon after midday an old bus rattled down to collect them and take them back to their refugee camp. There were signs along the lanes in German pointing towards 'Health and Happiness' and these finally ended when I arrived at the gates of Italy's only official nudist colony. It seems strange that when you can get humans nearly nude, quasi-nude, pseudo-nude and as good as nude on any beach in the country, you can't get totality. Perhaps Italians don't want to exhibit themselves in full in case the result is a disappointment, but they don't mind other people doing it. Inside the chain-link fence two fully clad gardeners were raking gravel and watering beds of geraniums, and inside a wooden hut two fully clad receptionists regretted that single males weren't allowed to join in, and then handed me a coloured leaflet showing a number of discreetly unclad figures, such as might have been photographed by Harrison Marks or John Everard in the 1950s. As I left one of the receptionists followed me out through the gate onto a field of rough stubble outside and pointed towards the sea.

'Calypso,' he said, 'you know Calypso?'

'Vaguely,' I answered.

'Out there on an island,' he went on.

'I think it has disappeared,' I said.

He began shaking his head sadly. 'Ulysses stayed with her, didn't he? Just think of that. Seven years on an island with a girl.' Then he pointed across the downtrodden expanse of no-man's land in front of us, indicating what might have been a path. 'You can walk down there to get to the nudist beach, if you like,' he said. 'It only takes two minutes.'

Later I sat at a table in a small restaurant in Capo Rizzuto perched on the edge of a precipice, staring down at a green-blue see-through sea fifty yards below. It was as still as glass. Half a mile away the bulk of the castle glowed dark orange in the sun as it sat in the shallows like a stranded battleship. Down below I could count every rock and watch every dark-shaped idling fish, and I wondered at their secrets: sea battles, shipwrecks, storms, invasions, triumphs and despair; and at Calypso's exhausting seven years. Henry Swinburne went out to look for her island 200 years ago, but only found bits of rock sticking out of the waves that wouldn't have been big enough for a sheep to live on.

The ex-mayor of Catanzaro leaned over the balcony of the Belvedere, with me beside him, and said, 'Marmalade.' He then repeated it angrily several times. Catanzaro is very high up on a peak not far from the sea, and we were looking at what lay below us. Frankly, a mess. He is another anti-Italian Italian.

I'd left AB down at the railway station in a lock-up, out of kindness. Even the train that tried to get up here found it difficult and petered out after a while, leaving passengers to the mercy of taxis that went up and up and up, round hairpin corners as the temperature kept dropping. My driver knew just what I wanted – a really poor man's hotel. It was. 'You must be lost,' said the owner as I put my bag of pyjamas and toothbrush down. 'People only come here by accident.'

Gissing again. He said the tract of land between Catanzaro and the sea was the fabled Garden of Hesperides. A fairy-tale orchard guarded by nymphs, and full of all the fruits in the world, from which Hercules had to steal three golden apples. Still feeble after his illness in Crotone and glad to breathe some fresh mountain air at last, Gissing described the plain below as strewn with myrtle, cactus, agave and patterns of olive and orange groves. We stood there studying it. I'd given up hope by now; I was used to it; find a pretty piece of land somewhere, with services and a sea-view, and build on it quickly before somebody else does. But the ex-mayor was angry; he had fought against it, but he wasn't moneyed enough or Masonic enough or Mafia. As a result there was a rambling measle of misshapen buildings, mostly half-built factories or cement works, creeping along the corridor towards us from the sea, and clouds of dust where lorries were helping build new roads. There wasn't a great deal of countryside left. Catanzaro has caught this development epidemic as well. There is a huge hotel in the centre (actually Catanzaro is so rambling is doesn't have a centre) called Hotel William, which demands £90 a night.

Mine, on the other hand, may be spartan but it is informal and intimate; it is also friendly enough to let a deaf-and-dumb old man sit in the entrance hall all day watching television, which is deliberately left on for him. He is not part of the family; the staff have adopted him. I admire that kind of kindness and wish I had it. The owner extends it to me as well by lending me money when I tell him I don't know my PIN number and can't work Bancomat machines. There is no food available and he has no knowledge of a restaurant that was once owned by Signor Paparazzo – Gissing's landlord. While I was wondering how to start my tour of Catanzaro, four of the owner's young friends arrived and asked whether I would advise them to go to London or Amsterdam for one of those 'you know' holidays – a question asked with so much tinkering of hands in trouser pockets that I could hardly fail to know. Remembering the numismatist's theory that speed is of the essence, I am afraid I lost Soho some tourist trade.

Catanzaro is high, and the views – with the exception of the marmalade and measles – are spectacular. There are mountains round seven-eighths of it, close enough to touch; all jagged and misshapen, of awesome ugliness yet frightening beauty. Parts of them are bare, stripped to brutal shades of grey or black, white, green, brown or silver. They sleep and threaten at the same time; silent, but holding a muscular power that terrifies. They've been waiting for thousands of years. Here and there they've let trees alight on them: shrubs on ledges for suicidal goats, or groups of pine trees clinging by their toenails and fixed in fear. Others have somehow crawled to the top and hug the peaks like terrified black toupees, uncomfortable and uncertain.

This is the start of the Sila again, the cruel unforgiving land of unknown tracts of dark forest and the haunts of brigands. When Emily Lowe was here 150 years ago, that delightful young traveller with the enthusiasm of an Angela Brazil schoolgirl ('we boundingly dress and spring on the mules with palpitating pleasure'), the heads of any brigands caught were put on stakes along the sides of the pathways. It's not that bad today; family grievances and feuds are settled by a single bullet, the occasional kidnap or the odd disappearance; and nobody is ever caught; the 'omertà' of silence.

Calabria's Mafia – the 'Ndrangheta – are less well known than their Sicilian seniors, but can be just as vicious over extorting money and drug-dealing. The word comes from the Greek *andragadia*, meaning personal valour, which might have been appropriate a few hundred years ago in their constant fights against tyranny, repression and invasion, but seems a little overstated today. Once, I suppose, it was the hoplite's Victoria Cross.

Catanzaro

Catanzaro is Arthur Strutt country. He and his friends were captured by brigands not far from here in May 1841 when they were all on a peaceful sketching tour. They heard curious whistling sounds in the woods around them, followed by shouts, and moments later found themselves surrounded by a gang of ruffians, who relieved them of all their valuables including their sketchbooks and paints. Fortunately there were some 'urban guards' in the area, part of a local volunteer police force, who heard the commotion and came to the rescue; 'without whose generous and prompt assistance we all should, inevitably, have been murdered,' Strutt says.

I find *A Pedestrian Tour in Calabria and Sicily*, written in 1841, more fun that Gissing's account. Strutt was an artist and he wanted to sketch and enjoy himself; he was in holiday mood with his friends and wasn't going to let unusual circumstances spoil it, even having 'great difficulty in ejecting the pigs from our dormitory'. One suspects he was more prepared for conditions in the south than most other travellers, so found that 'one bed is to suffice for five of us' and 'the fowls that share our apartment are gone up a ladder to bed' nothing remarkable. I think there is more of a sympathetic and engaging personality in this account than there is in most of the others, apart from Ramage. It is easy to see where Strutt's interests lie; there are long descriptions of different dresses and costumes he comes across, and obviously whenever he can he sketches them: 'heavy blue dresses . . . looped up with a crimson cord' or 'a dress turned up behind discovers a yellow lining . . . and allows a scarlet petticoat to shine forth'. The second edition of *A Pedestrian Tour* has sixty-five etchings, at least half of them of local people in traditional costume.

I like the artistic nonchalance about him; his amused and carefree attitude. Murders, Strutt says, 'are too frequent in Cosenza (the regional capital) to excite any sensation', and he enjoys hearing from Calabrian men that they value their guns more than their wives, because a woman can be replaced but a good gun can't. On another occasion shepherds are convinced he is sketching them in order to know how to make sheep's cheese.

The aftermath of the arrest of the brigands whom he encountered has a touch of farce about it. During the trial any girls involved, who were waiting to be questioned, spent their time dancing the tarantella. Strutt is particularly taken with Petronilla Jaccia, the wife of the leader and an important member of the gang, who was 'tall, dark, with regular features, black eyes and no inconsiderable portion of sullen beauty', and obviously no newcomer to banditry as she was 'eminently indebted to her personal attractions for delivery from more than one well-deserved judicial chastisement'. One can't help feeling towards the end of the trial that he was beginning to admire her, particularly as she'd once been under sentence of death for her crimes, when he says, 'it would have gone hard for her, had not a private interview with the judge softened his obdurate sense of duty and induced him to exert himself in procuring her a reprieve'. Strutt had lived in Italy for a long time and he obviously knew the people and the system well, and considering the way some of the corruption and Mafia trials end nowadays, it doesn't appear that judges have changed much.

I found rather a sad postscript to the Strutt story in a booklet in the library here, written by a native of Catanzaro called Guido Puccio who was a journalist in Rome during the 1930s and 1940s. It seems he was intrigued by another member of the Press Club there, a rather shabby and frail old man who was often short of money and usually accompanied by a dog. This was Edward Strutt, one of Arthur's sons, earning a meagre living by doing the occasional translation or sending the odd story back to Fleet Street. Puccio befriended him and was amazed at his knowledge of ancient history and the classics and at his obvious love of Rome, but a little concerned that most of his earnings seemed to disappear into the taverns of Trastevere. When Mussolini's war broke out, Edward Strutt was sixty-seven and unfortunately – perhaps due to inherited artistic oversight – it seems he was not registered as being either English or Italian and as a result had no identity papers and no documentation to prove any kind of citizenship. As the British Consulate had no record of his existence, he was interned as an alien and for the next three years, always in deteriorating health and suffering from pleurisy, was shuffled from one camp to another until the Ministry of Culture freed him in 1942. He died in Rome a year later on 16 November.

Puccio had a very clear memory of meeting him the day before he was interned, when Strutt gave him a small parcel as a gift 'in gratitude for his help and friendship'. Inside it was Arthur Strutt's own copy of *A Pedestrian Tour*, together with two of his drawings, a 'View of Rome from the Pincio' and a 'Sicilian Olive Tree', which, says Puccio, was so lifelike 'it could almost speak'. I hoped I might be able to see them, but unfortunately the Puccio family left Catanzaro years ago. However, it is nice to know that one of Arthur Strutt's most famous paintings, 'A Meet of the Roman Foxhounds at the Tomb of Cecilia Metella – Via Appia', is hanging in a private house in Oxfordshire. A member of that family had been their Master of Foxhounds in Rome and had hunted with them regularly.

The local library is just inside the entrance to the gardens, and so is Catanzaro's museum, which the ex-mayor says hasn't changed in a hundred years. It really is a store-house of memorabilia; small and crammed; not as overflowing as Gallipoli's, and it probably hasn't been dusted for ages, either. Two old ladies look after it; actually they live in it, and they only open it for two hours on Sundays. However, this is negotiable. I could hardly move. One large endearing item to walk round on entering was a guillotine; not as large as the one used in Paris, but it looked equally effective, with a shining sloping blade held in position by a rope. It was a Bourbon implement for removing the heads of Liberal agitators, which were then hung up in cages over one of the town gates. It seems to be in the Italian nature not to mess around when they dislike someone. The museum catalogue, only obtainable in bookshops elsewhere, lists 183 paintings, but the museum is small, so there must be about 160 somewhere else. Those remaining are mainly by Andrea Cefaly, obviously a Victorian delighter in Garibaldi's exploits and syrupy interpretations of Bible stories. Four paintings by Salvator Rosa were listed in the catalogue, but I could only find two, and these were casually hanging on nails just by the entrance. No doubt the collection will be reduced still further very soon.

When I asked the ex-mayor about the collection of coins that Lenormant mentions as being in the museum – nearly 4,000 of them and mainly Byzantine – he shrugged. 'Some professor took them away years ago to catalogue them. Better that than having them rotting away in that place,' he said. 'It hasn't been touched since it was opened in 1880. The roof is going to fall in soon.'

The contradictions you can find in this country and in its people are bewildering. They are as likely to kiss the effigy of a saint when things are going well as they are to hang it upside-down and kick it to pieces when they aren't. The sublime art of Giotto and Fra Angelico rubs shoulders with contemporary accounts of murders, tortures and ritual disembowellings, with intestines falling out 'like fatlings into the fire'. They are not just unpredictable, they are oxymoronic, endlessly inconsistent and contradictory, and this either thrills you or drives you mad.

Catanzaro is generally dilapidated; unlooked-after; except for the communal Trieste Gardens, which are a showpiece and always have three old men with besoms sweeping at the leaves and the cigarette ends. Perhaps it's a leftover fraction of one of those formal establishments that Georgina Masson describes in her book on Italian gardens. Smooth walkways and box-hedges round every section; well-trimmed grass borders round all the beds; clumps of bright colours; small rose bushes, anemones, gladioli, peonies, mountain pansies, bell-shaped blue scillas and ubiquitous geraniums, all extravagantly neat and prosperous. In some places palm trees fan their canopies over them in protection; somewhere else there's an avenue of umbrella pines; and there is a little lake with saucers of lilies floating and two very possessive black swans. This is where Catanzaro's senior citizens like to sit all day to talk about the hopelessness of politics or to watch their grandchildren toddle away down the paths, amazed at this new world of unencumbered freedom.

The gardens look over a ravine, and to me the ravines here look Himalayan. There's no sign of any bottom, just endless depth and a few trees clinging onto the sides for dear life. In this limitless space swifts wheel and race, shrieking with happiness, and stately ravens flap past on leisured wings, probably waiting for the next thermal.

The ex-mayor's name, I have discovered, is Cesare Mulè, which suggests Albanian provenance. He used to love Catanzaro and even Calabria, but he is less certain now. He doesn't like Norman Douglas at all; says he was a snobbish and pretentious Puritan, but he quite likes Gissing; his real favourites, however, are both French – Saint-Non and Paul Louis Courier – and this is because they both loved Calabria. He quotes bits of them to me as we walk along: 'The most beautiful country that nature could offer . . . a vision of the golden age and of heaven on earth'; and then Courier: 'We are in the boot of Italy, in the most beautiful country in the world.'

I hope he has read some of the other letters that this young French officer wrote home in 1806 when he was part of Joseph Bonaparte's army occupying the south:

> It's just eat, drink and be merry here. There's everything for all tastes ... rough or smooth, meat or fish, wine everlasting. They're dark-skinned on the plains, pale in the mountains; passionate everywhere. Making love is fabulous as there's nothing else to do. [*Si fa solo questo.*] That's war for you; chasing women; having the young ones, stealing from the old ones ... Priests control everything here. Their vows of poverty make them rich and their chastity gets them the best women.

At the moment I am being taken on a short tour of the places Gissing visited, but not to the hotel where he stayed as it has been demolished. First to the Farmacista Leone, which seems hardly to have changed in a hundred years; it is still 'a museum of art', a Victorian apothecary's shop with dark wood-lined walls to provide its necessary sense of seriousness and worry; and deep shelves with rows of coloured bottles, and drawers underneath all carefully labelled with names of correctives, remedies, panaceas, purgatives, herbs, emetics and restoratives. Dickens has come to life. There are sets of brass balances for weighing powders, hinged tins for carrying curative capsules, and there is no till; only a wooden desk as high as a lectern, where you only pay cash to an elderly bespectacled gentleman in a dark suit looking down at you.

Signor Mulè has no fear of traffic. He once intended to pedestrianise the road outside, but was outvoted; however, he still thinks he succeeded and walks fearlessly in front of motor cars without giving them a glance. A real miracle in Italy is to see a 30 mph Fiat stop dead in two feet.

Exactly opposite Leone is the Bar Imperiale, probably enlarged since Gissing's day and with more chrome, glass and rococo decoration on the walls, but still the central venue for a business chat. He listened to deep philosophical conversations here a century ago and admired their intensity and seriousness, much preferable to English tavern talk, he said. It must have been more of a tea-room in those days than just a bar, as he mentions having to endure the sounds made by a pianist of great pretensions and small achievement providing 'painful music'.

Close by, Signor Mulè led me through an entrance into the Fazzari Palace, one of those initially undistinguished buildings you find here that turn out within yards to be vast, echoing and splendid. 'Gissing may not have seen this,' he growls. 'If he did, he didn't mention it . . . Fazzari was Garibaldi's pimp; he got him women all the time.'

It is enormous; now used as a gentleman's club by the ancient dignitaries of Catanzaro. Wide marble staircases and large rooms, all with chandeliers; the walls hung with mirrors and grand oil paintings, or sometimes Pompeian-style frescoes; gilded eighteenth-century furniture and deep leather chairs for the old-world philosophers to muse in. A haven of comfort and silence for the remembrance of times past.

'Oh?' I said.

'Yes. He was only a poor tailor here, but he joined Garibaldi's thousand on their march north, and made himself useful by finding women for him. It's said he even saved Garibaldi's life once, by throwing himself in front of him in an ambush and taking a bullet in his chest. He must have found him some pretty good women to be given this palace as a reward.'

When one is in this area it is obligatory to visit Tiriolo, because Tiriolo is unique. Not only is it high up, blustery and sun-baked, but it is central. When rain falls on the village, half of it drains down towards the Ionian Sea and the other half towards the Tyrrhenian. This does not mean the distances are equal, as they aren't; it is just a curiosity. Tiriolo, unlike Catanzaro, is extremely old, though there are few signs of it today; however, proof of this antiquity exists in a museum in Vienna. It is the edict issued by Rome in 186 BC telling the inhabitants to stop having orgies. This reprimand appears to have been made on political grounds rather than moral ones, as bands of dissolute revellers could be a subversive element and threaten the fragility of the intended empire with its recently introduced religious practices. So the Senate outlawed all Bacchic rites, though nobody really knows what these Bacchanalias actually consisted of; nor are we likely to know until the library, still buried at Herculaneum, is excavated properly. They might well have been a gesture by the last of the ancient Greeks in their final years of existence, deciding to leave the world in a celebratory frenzy of dissolute enjoyment with plenty of drink, quantities of opium and lots of sex. They always liked to get near their gods, so hours of stupefied hallucinations filled with nightmares of heaven and hell might have been a way of entering the kingdom of Pluto and Proserpine for a few moments. Whoever wrote the Book of Revelation must have been on a very similar high.

I arrived here by bus and the views are breathtaking. I can clearly see the two seas into which the rainwater flows, and a susurration of uneven mountain-tops, some clustered round, others in the distance; and I can just manage a tiny spot in the distance that must be the Lipari islands. And if I decided to roll down the slope in front of me for a few miles I would come to rest at the narrow stretch of land that Dionysius of Sicily thought he might build a wall across in 380 BC in order to cut off the toes from the rest of the foot and consolidate his empire.

One of Tiriolo's sons was also guilty of inappropriate behaviour, apparently. Called Cicala and brought up as a God-fearing Christian, he soon realised that whenever

Turkish pirates landed along the coast they had a great deal
more fun than he did stuck up his mountain, so he decided
to join them. Distinguishing himself by his bravery during
various raids on the coast of North Africa, he eventually
arrived in Constantinople, took the Islamic oath, caught the
eye of the Sultan and became such a royal favourite that he
was allowed to marry one of the princesses. Cicala was then
put in charge of a large Turkish army, led successful
campaigns against Baghdad and into Hungary, and even
involved himself in occasional raids on his native Calabria.
However, suffering from pangs of conscience in his old age,
he decided to visit his mother again in Tiriolo so that he
could tell her how rich he was and what a successful career
he had had, and then present her with lots of gold and
jewellery as proof. She refused to see him, of course,
informing him in true biblical fashion that treasure in
heaven was worth more to her than anything he could
supply.

'So you see the power of true faith,' announced the owner
of the restaurant where I was having lunch, appropriately
called '*Due mari*', as he finished the story.

'Yes,' I had to answer, looking out of the window and over
the treetops towards the Tyrrhenian. 'What's that?' pointing
to a very large mound about half a mile below us that
looked like an enormous bubble of cheese that had exploded
out of the earth. A considerable part of it had been sliced
away, leaving the remaining three-quarters with a skin of
dark trees on it, looking like a bad case of mould.

'They've cut it away to make a football pitch,' he
answered.

'No, the other bit with the trees,' I said.

'Oh. People are buried in there. It's full of old tombs,' he
replied. 'Why don't you go and see the bagpipe shop?' As if
tombs didn't matter.

It was down the hill in a little square and I remembered
how Arthur Strutt had called the sound of these strange

instruments 'detestable'. Perhaps he heard too much of it. I like it. A hundred years ago the south used to be full of their plaintive, warbling cry as shepherds played to themselves while they looked after their flocks. Nowadays you seldom hear them except at Christmas time, when the bagpipe players come into the towns from the hills and play tunes about the nativity. The sound they make is usually at a higher pitch than their Scottish cousins and is more reedy and nasal, and the melodies they play are sadder; soft, warbling notes as if hanging on to a melancholic past. The owner of the shop had nineteen different types of *zampogna* on display from different regions; one was tiny, the size of a small paper bag, while the air-sac of the largest reached down to the floor. He told me the sacs always had to be made of goatskin and there was a wide variety of pipes or flutes that could be used, some as small as penny whistles, others larger than oboes. He talked about the skill required to play one properly, and how an accomplished *zampognaro* could manage two mouthpieces at the same time, allowing him to play the melody on one and the accompaniment on the other.

As well as supervising a bagpipe workshop and museum, he was busy reconstructing old costumes of the area, particularly those that used to be worn by women. These apparently were very idiosyncratic and regional, every village dress having something about it that was slightly different from its neighbours', thus giving you pride in your surroundings. The difference was usually in the colour of the outer or more visible garments, or sometimes in the head-dress. These could be red, blue, green, gold ... anything.

It all looked very complicated, as in most cases there were nine different items of clothing to be worn – silk in summer and wool in winter – and a lot of the dresses had long 'tails', which had to be lifted and tied round the body in different ways. There were pictures of some on the walls;

the only freedom in design that a woman seemed to have
was in the patterns of embroidery she was allowed on some
of the undergarments. The dress code had signs attached to
it; all women had to keep their heads covered – perhaps a
Muslim memory – and anyone who removed her hood was
considered 'loose'. In some villages she had to marry the
first man who saw her with her head uncovered; in other
cases it would be deliberately removed to attract a lover. It
all seems to have involved tradition and certain recognition
codes, rather like uniforms in the armed services.

The males, although not dressed quite so gaudily, also
had certain rituals to follow. For a start, they all wore long
earrings, and having a moustache or a beard normally
carried certain significance. When there was a death in the
family they weren't permitted to shave or to change their
clothes for a year. (This was something Ramage found most
objectionable, as they went on wearing things till 'their
clothes were worn away by filth'.) And during this period of
mourning they weren't allowed a fire in the house or to
cook food, but had to be fed by neighbours.

When I asked if any old dresses still existed, he said
exactly what I'd been told before. 'No. Their best clothes are
buried with them.'

Most people in Catanzaro must eat at home because there is
a remarkable shortage of restaurants. At the bottom end of
the market, for a taste of Old Calabria, you drop in at
Pasquales. To feel comfortable here, which is not easy as it
is standing room only, you should be at least seventy and
have lost half your teeth. It is one of the few *cantinas* left in
south Italy (roughly equivalent to our fish and chip shop
but with a wine licence), where you eat what you are given
out of newspaper, which in this case, is a popular delicacy
called *murseddu* – i.e. pig tripe. My advice is not to think
about it, but to wash it down with tumblers full of wine –
which tonight everyone is anxious to buy for me. They are

incredibly generous, though it only costs about sixpence a glass for something either throat-tearing and nearly black or a gullet-clutching dark-orange cloud. They watch my efforts with amusement. Am I married? Of course. It makes them laugh. Happy for a day then, but kill a pig and you're happy for a year. I can't help liking them in spite of it: earth-bound and ancient hill-men with bright spider-leg eyes in walnut faces cracked in pieces by the sun, and skin as rough as oak-bark. They can't have changed much in centuries and don't seem to want to; trouser legs still wrapped round with cord and one or two with cartridge belts, all talking an incomprehensible dialect.

Amici Miei is a small sit-down eating place in a side street and up some steps onto Catanzaro's second level. The young owner says he would rather be a policeman, because policemen in Italy have power, whereas now he takes orders and doesn't give any. But, he adds ruefully, to get into the police force you have to know somebody, and he doesn't. When I had eaten there three times, unable to find anywhere else, I asked him as politely as I could why any main dish I ordered tasted exactly the same as the one I'd had the day before; to which he answered that it was the Catanzaran way of cooking – everything had to have a strong base of crimson mountain sausage in it. Probably in revenge, next day he gave me some pasta covered in melted cheese and then sprinkled cocoa powder all over it, as if it was a *cappuccino*. This kind of chocolate topping, I've since discovered, was once considered a delicacy in north Italy; on anything, apparently.

As it seems there is nowhere else to eat, I am seldom alone here, and if the behaviour at Tiriolo was considered subversive, you should hear some of these conversations. Garibaldi is the arch-villain of all time who ruined Italy; the government is 'cornuto' and totally corrupt; the Cassa Per Il Mezzogiorno, which was an organisation supposed to bring humanitarian aid to the south and develop its resources, was a complete farce, with only a quarter of any money reaching the area; and for the ruling Demo Cristiani, read Demo Bestiani. And then it all peters out into laughter; it's their own fault, they admit, because they spend their lives talking about it, but never do anything.

I have now discovered somewhere else. This is Manginotte, an evening-only place in a very smart cellar, where the youthful beau monde of Catanzaro can all meet to kiss each other after they've woken from their afternoon slumbers, dressed up chic and needing to be seen. Strutt objected that during his travels he was only permitted to kiss males and never females on arrival and departure, and Ramage had the same experience. Here, anybody can kiss anybody, myself excluded. The men come in down the steps, hiding behind black sunglasses, wobbling their shoulders and trying to look like bull-fighters; the girls trip in looking for a photo-call and expecting to go on the catwalk. It's an 'I love me, don't you?' exhibition, restoring self-confidence and projecting an image of self-assurance. Hollow as a drum, but very good theatre. One girl has just come in, a Bardot lookalike with close-cropped blonde hair wearing a well-cut fawn uniform, almost military, with her waist caught in a rabbit snare, the kind that Octavian might wear when presenting the rose, only in white, and she kissed all the girls first.

Things went badly wrong today; I was going up into the Sila for some peace. There is a small old-fashioned railway from Catanzaro that goes up into the mountains and the forests, and I took the first train. It was a steam train, pulled by one puffing engine and pushed by another, as the climb is steep and the bends endless; alpine heights on one side and suicide ravines on the other. In my carriage was a very intense young German, a railway enthusiast, taking down engine and carriage numbers, gauge measurements and gradient readings. He was extremely excited because when we got to wherever we were going, he intended to walk all the way back to Catanzaro along the line, as this was the only railway in Europe you could walk on safely without being arrested for trespassing. The rest of the carriage was in a state of juvenile pandemonium: a school outing of some sort, highly mobile and noisy; a tribe of some forty squealing girls aged about four to fourteen, with five or six equally clamorous and deafening adults trying to control them. Suddenly the ringmaster, determined to establish some order in this chaos of exuberation and excitement, stood on a seat and demanded that each member of the group shut up and declare herself. This passed with much jollity plus titters and applause, until he spied me sitting in a corner.

'And who are you?' he demanded loudly.

'I'm English,' I replied, hoping for some decorous and astonished silence.

'And where are you going?' he asked.

'I don't know,' I answered, giving the requisite Italian shrug of stupid incomprehension, whereupon there was uproar from some forty throats and I heard him shouting, 'Then you're coming with us', followed by a caterwaul of shrill assent. And that was how, instead of exploring the Sila on my own, I was locked in for the day with a highly effervescent Calabrian St Trinian's.

Then when we arrived at somewhere in the Sila – I've forgotten where – I felt guilty and muted as I watched their happiness. They were from Catanzaro's girls' orphanage and were having their monthly treat. How does one apologise to oneself? That happiness was like a geyser; it just spurted everywhere. They kissed the two porters on the station, they ran up and kissed the engine driver, they ran back to kiss the guard; some of them even kissed the level-crossing gates. Then they bounded off into the fields and trees like spring rabbits chasing each other, the older ones stopping to help and mother the young ones; all different, yet like a family.

'Girls,' sighed the ringmaster ruefully, watching from the platform. 'Always girls.' I let him go on. 'They don't want girls, even the legitimate ones; there's no work for them, so what do they do? They bring them to us. They bring them from the villages: babies sometimes; illegitimates as well; we have to take them in.'

'Don't people adopt?' I asked, and he shrugged.

'They've got children, most of them. Adoption's not easy here: papers, permissions, endless investigations. It's easier to go out to Brazil and adopt one there than it is to do it in Italy. We've got two Brazilian girls with us now, on trial for a month, and their new Italian parents.'

'It seems a bit better than the old "wheel" system,' I said.

'Just a little,' he answered. 'At least we know something about most of them. There are recognised orphanages now – they're not just dumped on the doorstep of a convent at midnight.'

There used to be about 2,000 'wheels' in Italy until they were outlawed after unification. They were small openings in convent walls where a mother could put her unwanted baby – conceived 'fuori letto' (on the wrong side of the blanket) – through the hole onto a tray and then ring a bell. Moments later the tray plus contents would disappear inside, taken by unseen hands, and the mother – also unseen – would know her baby was safe. Those were the *Marriage of Figaro* days when aristos could knock off their serving girls with impunity, which doesn't happen quite so much today. That luxury is left to film stars, rich industrialists, Mafia bosses and members of Parliament. About a thousand babies are abandoned each year in Italy, I've been told.

Later there was a pre-arranged booking at a restaurant in the village: a long table for forty; wine and soft drinks. I'd expected chaos, a mini-maenad riot, but it wasn't. It was just happiness; tremors and fidgets of barely controlled excitement. The waiters had to be kissed before we sat down, some of them again afterwards; small people got piggy-backs all round the room; one with a waiter carrying plates of spaghetti at the same time. The big ones sat almost quietly, as if some voice had reminded them that they were privileged; saved from death; wanted after all. Pasta came, veal slices, endless ice-cream and place changes; gradual quietness as their puppy-skins filled, containing their bursting wildness. I had to make a speech; drowned after half a sentence, and featherweight kisses from the under-tens. A Brazilian crawled into my lap, trying funny husky Italian in a voice as if she'd been gargling with sandpaper and had bubbles of jelly in her throat. She probably did. She had big Copacabana eyes, black as midnight. A micro man-eater.

They wanted me to photograph them afterwards, so I did, and tomorrow I'll have to find the orphanage and give the pictures out. They were quieter on the way back in the train, some of them asleep. Happiness was over. When we got back, the ringmaster asked if I'd like to take some of them home with me. 'They'd like England better than Catanzaro,' he said.

By local standards Catanzaro is not old; probably a bit more than a thousand years, and probably Byzantine-Arabic; *kata* meaning 'under' and *anzarion* meaning a 'terrace', so Signor Mulè says. There's certainly nothing Greek up this high. He regrets that what was left of the Norman castle had to be destroyed so that a new road could be built.

Today he took me a few miles along the coast to visit a ruin. It was less than a mile from the sea and surrounded by olives and oak trees; the remains of an enormous abbey. It was a shell; its size incredible; gaping and roofless, with some walls still reaching for the sky where ravens and pigeons made nests in the brickwork. One end bulged out in a semi-circle and there were the remains of further curves close to it, obviously apses; so I made a guess at Byzantium, but the bricks were all thin and rusty-red, looking Roman. It had been superbly and strongly built, meant to last till eternity and, looked at through the trees, some of it reared over the tops as if it was a mammoth approaching. Nobody really knows what the ruin is or was, because, Lenormant says, of this *'nuage de falsifications'* that permeates history here like a disease. It is called Santa Maria della Roccella locally or the Bishop of Squillace's palace, Squillace being a town on a hill about ten miles away; but that seems a bit far-fetched. Funnily enough, one of the people who has written most about it is Peter Nichols, a former correspondent for *The Times* in Rome. In his historical romance *Ruffo in Calabria* he describes 'the great apse and the walls with their rounded windows' as being Romanesque, and says it was probably built 'on the foundations of a Roman temple which, in its turn, covered a Greek temple'.

I think he's right, though there weren't any signs of it being Greek or Roman in origin. The two French antiquarians disagree about it. Lenormant says it is very early Christian, while Bertaux thinks it is eleventh century. There certainly wasn't any possible connection with real antiquity for ten minutes until Signor Mulè took me up through the trees to climb an embankment and then fall down the bank the other side into thirty yards of solid Roman road which led straight into the partially excavated remains of a very considerable town. There was even part of a theatre, and the outline of an amphitheatre; which could only mean that we were in all that was left of the Roman town of Scolacium, which they had built on top of the Greek Skylletion in 124 BC. As usual, it had all been abandoned at some stage because of malaria or pirate attacks, so they had taken the name ten miles uphill to modern Squillace. It all looked a bit dusty and abandoned, with olive trees still growing in it. So as Peter Nichols says, somewhere under the remains of this vast abbey, now a towering skeleton half-hidden by trees and once a glory of Byzantium, is almost certainly what's left of a Greek temple.

The problem is that Italy has always been useful and accessible; always popular, and always for the wrong reasons. As a stepping stone, as a junction, as a refuge, as a resort, as a looters' and rapists' paradise, as a convenience, as a rubbish dump, and sometimes as a joke. It has been a lot of people's punch-bag for 2,000 years and it shows the scars.

SEVENTEEN

Squillace to Locri

I did not enjoy my visit to Squillace. Its appearance is off-putting for a start, a dark shape squatting in a hollow three-quarters of the way up a hill. It looked sinister and threatening. Some villages sparkle with invitation, but Squillace didn't. One of the first things I saw on entering was a Devil's Bridge with a menacing, pointed arch to it. The name Squillace is hardly encouraging: onomatopoeic and sounding like squelch, which Gissing discovered as he stepped into ankle-deep mud here, and which I discovered inside a roll of newspaper handed to me by a local lunatic who said it was my lunch. Unfortunately one comes across curious people in these parts occasionally, perhaps because of inbreeding or lack of medical attention fifty or sixty years ago. She was certainly one of them.

She latched on to me as soon as I rattled in on AB, running along beside us and cackling excitedly until we stopped. What a greeting! She was old and shabby, without many teeth, and was making incomprehensible noises at very high speed as she danced up and down, then started to paw me. Panic set it. Then I made a mistake by saying *'pane'* and *'vino'*, because I was looking for lunch, where-upon she galloped away as if the words had triggered something in her mind, only to reappear moments later with an offering wrapped up in newspaper. Taking me by the hand, she led me into a square until we stood in front of the cathedral and she began to babble about seeing the *'vescovo'*. 'Oh God!' I thought as she walked me up the steps, 'she's taking me to see the bishop.' But there isn't one; the last Bishop of Squillace lived about 500 years ago. Luckily the door was locked, so she did a little jig and pushed the newspaper package at me, carefully pulling some of the folds back. In the bottom was a soggy mess looking like recent dog's vomit after a hearty meal and I suddenly realised she was offering me lunch and wanted me to eat it. Worse still, an audience was now gathering to watch her antics and I was being scrutinised by some of her tribesmen. 'Yes,' I said weakly, surveying the bilious concoction now leaking through the paper as desperation set in; and '*vino*' I added, in a flash of inspiration, which sent her scuttling away again, just giving me time to empty the newspaper beside the building before she ran back with a grimy tumbler half-full of dark-red something. This time I didn't care. '*Salute*,' I said, downing it in one gulp to the muttered approval of the viewers, before handing the glass back with a smile as she gave another jig of happiness. And I was happy too. I was leaving Squillace straight away. This very minute.

There's an enormously long stretch of road now towards Locri, through innumerable same-looking villages and by the same-looking sea and past endless piles of same-looking rubbish. At one point of land I saw stumps of buildings outlined in the grass that could have been part of the Greek city of Caulonia. A rectangular shape suggested the foundations of a temple, and again it was on a spur of land jutting out into the sea; sublime in its years of triumph, yet easy prey to enemies in the hills behind or to invaders from along the coast. The mountains on the right changed a lot; sometimes shallow sweeps with trees and flowers on them, soft land bulges; then a crag out of nowhere, steep and rugged in white and grey; and then a real crush of falling-over mountains sheer as icebergs, with broken-off bits lying in the road. They really look threatening sometimes: powerful and angry. I don't think they have dustmen in south Italy; there's litter everywhere. Signor Mulè will never get Calabria looking beautiful at this rate. Tin cans, bottles, plastic bags, old clothes, mattresses, tyres, card-board boxes, bed springs, umbrellas, old carpets and the odd dead cat. They're all along the roadside, on the beaches, in the fields and woods, and piled up in ditches. There are one or two signs up begging for cleanliness: *'Rispetta i tuoi ambiente; non gettate rifiuti'*, but the only sense of beauty people have is when it comes to their personal appearance.

A little further along, a dog – actually the size of a pony and looking like a cross between an Alsatian and Cerberus – took a violent dislike to me and shot out of a gateway with the speed of an ejaculation but very different sentiments. I managed to goad AB to an astonishing 10 mph, encouraged by some very nasty-looking white teeth only inches from my leg, until they eventually fell behind. On stopping to inspect the damage, I looked back to see the beast trying the same thing with a large lorry, but this time it had met its match and disappeared under the wheels with a shriek of surprise and lots of blood and mess. It wasn't very nice, but I decided that pulped Alsatian was better than piranha Alsatian.

A number of Italians like to keep large dogs with them, usually Boxers or Rottweilers with cropped ears to make them look more menacing. It's this 'impression management' again; the ego-boost. I once knew a man in Naples who kept a lion in his apartment.

I have now deviated to Stilo, which is up in the mountains again, because Signor Mulè told me to go and see the *farmacista* who knows the area. He very kindly gave me lunch, during which his son of twelve was completely silent until he spoke three astonishing sentences towards the end of the meal, one after the other – 'Take the underground to Charing Cross', 'Where is the Post Office?' and 'Can you tell me the time?' Having got this trio off his chest, he went on repeating them till I began to wish that 'English by radio' had never been invented.

I'm getting into Edward Lear country now, all Jumblies and Bong Trees growing. He's another one who thoroughly enjoyed himself in south Italy, as he was an artist like Arthur Strutt and was blessed with a sense of the ridiculous; he was also fortunate enough to be here when there were still a few well-to-do hosts to call on, even if he had to extract a sheep from under his bed one night. A number of people say he's guilty of artistic licence; that he took liberties with the scenery and his illustrations are only his impressions of what was there. I don't think it matters; he's very probably guilty of literary licence as well, but what travel writer isn't? *A Journal of a Landscape Painter in Calabria* is both fascinating and funny. He's observant, whimsical, full of anecdotes, interested in everything, eccentric, extremely tolerant and, as somebody said, 'amiably preposterous'. Lear also likes people, which is more than Swinburne and Craven seem to have done, and being in the south in 1847 (six years later than Strutt), was very sensitive to the growing political unrest and to the concerns people had about the future. He could feel the tension everywhere; tremors that preceded the political earthquake. Accompanied by his engaging muleteer Ciccio, whose conversation seemed only to consist of '*Dogo, Dighi, Daghi, Da*', Lear left Reggio on 29 July to wander through as many towns and villages in Calabria as he pleased before returning to Reggio in early September. He was then greeted by a drunken waiter in Giordano's Hotel, who shouted that there were no more keys to rooms and 'no more passports, no more kings, no more laws, no more judges, no more nothing. Nothing but love and liberty, friendship and the Constitution.'

But Lear could also be serious. It wasn't always sons of his hosts falling into dishes of macaroni, or having a Barbary ape as company at the dinner table, or trying to eat 'an antique fowl that baffled knives and forks'. He was adept at describing scenery and atmosphere: 'grotesque festoons' of vegetables, 'the broad dark shades of morning' and 'golden abstract visions of the hanging woods'. He gives intimate and sympathetic details of the people he met and some-times stayed with, and his gratitude for their hospitality is always sincere. His whole journey is full of his delight in Calabria and in its inhabitants; and, in spite of his belief in the absurdity of the human condition, his enjoyment of wandering among the people who lived in such amazing scenery runs through his account like a warm thread of affection and understanding. Even towards the 'mahogany cupids' and 'naked berry-brown children' that watched him as he sketched.

He says he liked Stilo and he sketched the main entrance gate with lots of peasants standing in the foreground, all the girls in traditional dress. But he missed the only building that Stilo is really famous for, which is not surprising considering that it didn't become famous until 1911, when the Italian archaeologist Paolo Orsi came across it stuck on a ledge just above the town: a tiny square Byzantine church, which they now call, somewhat perversely, La Cattolica. You have to climb to get to it as it was deliberately positioned out of harm's way. This would explain its reasonable state of preservation in spite of some recent restoration. Sudden beauty is the best way of describing it; a complete surprise; dark red and perched on a narrow track alone in the mountains, small and elegant without being vain; just deliberately and modestly delicate. It is trium-phant without trying, and calmly self-assured in its loneli-ness. It is comfortably compact and almost square, as if confident of immortality; the brickwork – some of it arranged in diamond patterns – is a glowing reddish-brown, and there is a close pattern of five identical circular roofs, the centre ones slightly higher than the others, and all immaculately tiled as if they were sets of seashells laid out in the sun. The small arched windows in the cupolas give a surprising amount of light to the interior, but only a few signs of any frescoes remain; among them are parts of three saints, one possibly St John Chrysostom with a particularly mean and ruthless expression – most unsaintly, in spite of his halo.

The *farmacista* showed me the 'well kept' house where Lear stayed, and where he was given two rooms and his own servant, but where he found the constant fly-swatting during mealtimes disconcerting. Then we looked at the view of the town he had sketched at the entrance gate, but it was hardly recognisable; only the vast background of grey mountains still dominated the town. Wanderers such as Lear, Ramage and Craven can't travel any more via letters of introduction because there is nobody left to be introduced to; though should there by any chance be some residue of the Old World left somewhere, the owner is likely to be terrified that you are a Mafioso and to greet you with a gun in his hand.

It was the Battle of Stilo that the *farmacista* really wanted to talk about: the great occasion in 982 when the hard-pressed Byzantines in the south defeated the Catholics from the north and so managed to hold their ground for a few years. Their foothold in south Italy was hardly secure anyway, and Pope Benedict in Rome now wanted them driven out completely so he invited the German Emperor Otto II to march down and do it for him. With a mixed army of Germans, Swedes, Lombards and Italians, the Emperor quickly overcame neighbouring Catanzaro and Rossano and had a successful first skirmish with the local Byzantines on the plain just below Stilo. However, he was unaware that the Byzantines had found some unlikely allies in the Arabs from Sicily, who hated Rome as much as they did; and Otto, now at rest on the plain, had no idea that a large Muslim army was hiding in the hills just above him. When it swept down on him unexpectedly his forces were cut to pieces; his dream of conquest was over and he himself had to flee for protection to Rome, where he died a year later.

So Byzantium breathed again for a while. And above the battlefield, perched on a ledge on the overhanging cliffs, is the tiny tenth-century church that proves it. One could even say that Allah might be partly responsible for its preservation.

I have made it to Siderno in a drizzle. It was a grey mist of wetness dribbling from scudding clouds and the puddles it formed gave AB a coughing fit. I think it might just make Reggio before it dies. Only seventy miles. The rain meant that the cars threw up hissing fans of spray like peacock tails and thoroughly soaked us. Somebody told me not to bother with a hotel, but to try so-and-so's, a sort of bed-and-breakfast establishment. The owner was small and frail and, before opening her door, shouted through the keyhole asking who I was, and why, and where from, and if I was a 'gente di malavita' – i.e. a badman. After opening the door a crack she gave me a large bedroom and a lavatory with no seat, then introduced me to her collection of birds. There are about ten cages of these hanging in the hall: the Sidernian variety of budgerigars and canaries, all extremely shrill and fluttery. The only louder thing in the establishment is her brother (I think), who doesn't speak, he roars. She calls him 'Il Barone'. I have also met the other B-and-B occupant who is a painter. 'Ah!' I thought, 'creativity at last; a drinking companion in tavernas; a man of the artistic underworld.' No such luck. He touches up cupids and angels in old churches.

I have found something extraordinary round the corner. It is a bookshop. No, it is not a bookshop; it may once have been a bookshop; it is now a conversation shop where anyone with anything sensible to say comes in to discuss it with the bookseller.

'Have you a guide to Siderno?' I asked.

'No such thing exists,' he said. 'This is the Styx. We are

unknown. Here, look at these,' and he pushed two paper-backs at me. *Love and War in the Apennines* and *Slowly Down the Ganges*. I had a quick look inside. Both were inscribed 'To Mario Gentile with very best wishes from Eric Newby. May 7th 1991.' Bloody hell! What was he doing here? There were hardly any books on the shelves, but some good photographs on the walls, and they were signed too: Alberto Moravia, Gerhardt Rohlfs, Benedetto Croce.

'Wow,' I must have said, 'not bad', because he answered in English.

'English weather,' he remarked, looking pleased with himself. 'It droppeth as the gentle rain from heaven.'

This morning I went to see the painter in the cathedral. Cathedrals, you must remember, are to be found in most towns and villages in Italy; even in late-lamented Squillace with its 3,000 inhabitants and its dog's vomit. It's 'impression management' again. *Illustrissimolitis*. He was way up the scaffold doing something to the ceiling and wearing a white coat like a doctor. We shouted greetings to each other. He is obviously of the St Theodor of Brindisi school; a vulgarian; a lover of bright colours; anything godly must be garish. And the Lord spake unto him and said: 'All angels shall be Barbie dolls.' I did notice at one end of an aisle a slot-machine Mary and Jesus, both of whom lit up if you put the correct coin in. This could have hideous consequences if some anarchic Marcinkus type started developing holy pinball games – a hundred for knocking Herod off his throne; game over if you hit the crib.

At some stage a service seemed to start. As usual it was very informal and full of movement, people entering and leaving as they wished; a performance of casual jollity rather than piety. I noticed that the priest's cassock was much too small for him; as it was tight under the arms he couldn't wave about much and he had monstrous police-man's boots on, with leather disappearing up his calves like a despatch rider. He might just have driven in. He seemed to be in a hurry too; everything he said was like a reading from the Sitwell-Walton *Façade*. It's just as the novelist Tim Parks said somewhere: they enjoy their religion for its fun; they ignore its precepts. That is because they are cynics; and with a history like theirs, and laws like theirs, and a government like theirs, who wouldn't be? Bettino Craxi fled the country after putting millions into his pocket, and what did Margaret Thatcher say about Giulio Andreotti? – 'calculated ambiguity and lots of confusion and guile'. And Craxi is rumoured to have had 200 mistresses. They all know what their priests are up to cloaked in their dark uniforms of purity, and about the young Brazilian transvestites hanging round St Peter's Square at night. They call them 'Vatican angels', but instead of '*Vaticano*' they say '*vaticulo*'.

There was a sulk this evening at supper. I was asking the painter about his vocation and his training and why he did it, to which he answered that he was self-taught in the Renaissance style, particularly that of Giotto, and he did it for the love of God; to which Mrs Not-so-frail-so-and-so snapped, 'No, you don't; you do it for the love of money.' I then caused her further displeasure when she deposited a plate of cold whitebait (or similar) in front of me and I said that in England we usually fried them, which caused another snap that I don't know good food when I see it. So I ate them obediently.

Signor Gentile doesn't want me to go to Locri. 'Beware of Locri,' he said emphatically like a soothsayer. Apparently this is because Locri is the High-Noon capital of Calabria, is full of gun-slingers, mass murderers, kidnappers, mutilators, blood-drinkers, cement coffin-makers and has no sheriff. I intend to go nevertheless, but not today because he is now taking me up to Gerace – and I really mean up – to see the largest cathedral in Calabria. And this is enormous.

It is nearly a hundred yards long. There is an underground crypt too, at the entrance; it is almost a cellar cathedral, like the one in Otranto, with the real one on top. And some of the columns inside are of marble and can only have come up from old Locri, which is – or was – at the bottom of the hill, five miles away. Two of these columns are supposed to change colour according to the weather. The cathedral is mainly Byzantine – the origin of the name being *kyriaki*, meaning hawk-land – with three apses and long naves. It was altered and added to by the Normans, and then rebuilt after the devastating earthquake of 1783. Footsteps echo ominously.

Rather like Squillace, there are only 3,000 inhabitants now, and the place has a jaded and dejected look about it, as if it knows it once had a past but there is no real present. It must have been considerably larger when Ramage was here as he found a 'respectable house' with a genial host, and Lear actually refers to it as a city and says he ate 'ices in a café' when he stayed here. In fact he enjoyed his visit so much that he came back later for more. He wouldn't want to do that now; not into this unkempt squalor with mud in the streets and sad empty buildings with broken windows. There's a tiny square by the cathedral with two more churches in it, one looking distinctly Byzantine. Signor Gentile got angry when the only shop didn't have any booklet about the cathedral; not even a leaflet; and then not even any postcards. 'Abandoned,' he hrumphed. 'Disgraceful. We don't exist down here. Rome doesn't care; nor does anyone. The north wanted us once; now we're just an embarrassment. It was all a terrible mistake.' He was talking about unification and its aftermath; the depression that set in after the euphoria, as the south lost its identity and people became bewildered and began to desert; not just the peasants and workers, but even what gentry there might have been; the local employers. They all gave up and slid off into the pages of history and into fantasy memories;

because Rome was supreme and wouldn't tolerate any rivals, so that errant one-time capital called Naples had to be run down and marginalised, allowed to wither away until it was only a chimera, and all its semblance of royalty and importance, and its tentacles of influence, had to wither away too.

It was hard to stop him now; he was really angry. 'They hate us in Rome,' he said. 'Despise us. We gave them all our money towards unification, millions of pounds; our history is older than theirs; we gave them popes, philosophers, poets, artists; we had doctors down here, writers, Olympic athletes, huge buildings and temples while they lived in mud-huts; we even gave them the name Italy – from Vitulus, our herds of cows; and what do they do for us? Nothing. We never see any members of Parliament here (there are over nine hundred of them); they're too busy travelling first-class round Europe with their mistresses, bribing people, eating in the best restaurants, earning huge salaries. We're a banana republic.'

I think it was depression rather than anger. He looked beaten; as if the whole weight of the south was on his shoulders and he felt powerless. Then he gave a little laugh. 'Take but degree away,' he said, 'and hark! what discord follows.' He keeps coming out with odd bits of Shakespeare now and then. King Edward Lear is his favourite joke. When we got up to the remains of the Norman castle he started on 'Once more unto the breach' and then wished all the youth of Calabria was on fire. It was as if the wind had suddenly blown away all his anger and he was happy again.

The one good thing to be said about Gerace is the view it provides. This is spectacular. A shimmering sea stretching for miles with the silver glint of sun on it; a mystery without end; like a mirror reflecting infinity. And then the mountains and cliffs behind, as if the earth had just exploded and wanted to remind you of the power it had, because it would last and you wouldn't. It makes you shiver sometimes. And then the land shapes rolling and bounding down to the sea, as if they want to get into it and swim away but keep hesitating; hillocks, chasms, bumps, hummocks and pimples, and all odd colours and shapes, and rough and smooth. A kaleidoscope of happy chaos and incredibly beautiful. Lear said it was all 'delicate fawn-hued cliffs' and purple mountains, and everything was 'coloured on purpose for artists'. It's a pity I can't paint.

Sometimes I wish they wouldn't moan so much, and do something instead; but they're trained in rhetoric and inactivity. They've been overrun too often; trodden down. Northerners don't call them *'cafoni'* (Kaffir) any more, but the *'mene fregisti'* – the couldn't-care-less people. But then can you blame them when they see the 'Clean Hands' investigation going on in the north and Milan being called Tangentopolis – Bribesville?

Today in the bookshop they were all talking about an Italian who was part of the European Commission in Brussels and who had just committed suicide over accusations of fraud. After that it soon got on to dear old Andreotti again and all his problems. Signor Gentile says the animosity between north and south goes back to the referendum of 1946, which was fixed by the republicans in the north while the monarchists in the south didn't have their votes counted properly, and the result was never officially declared, meaning that Italy's constitution today is illegal.

They go on like this for hours every day: multi-million-lire bribes, members of Parliament on double salaries, pension scandals, corruption, Mafia connections, mistresses, Swiss bank accounts, and now there's some mega-rich tycoon who wants to be Prime Minister even though he's under investigation for allegations of false accounting and tax evasion. You start to wonder as you listen to all this whether it represents Gissing's 'philosophical discussions' or proof of Ramage's opinion that they're not yet ready 'for any form of representative government'.

Yesterday I saw a large painted graffito on Siderno railway station which said – in English and in capital letters – 'FUCK THE GOVERNMENT'.

I've decided that in essence the Italians are not really patriotic. They're stuck with it, but would rather be somewhere else. As the artist in Brindisi said, 'We hate each other. This is Italy.'

I am now in Locri waiting to be gunned down, but so far nothing. There is a slightly intimidating air about it, I must admit, though this could be my imagination. The pavements seem to be crowded with stationary men all shabbily dressed and wearing cloth caps, all standing and waiting expectantly. The roaring baron in Siderno said it was all rubbish about Locri being dangerous; he said it was only twenty local families trying to kill each other and the sooner they did it, the better.

Locri was the smallest of all the Greek cities in Magna Graecia and was supposedly the most democratic and the best organised. This, so it is said, is because it was founded by women; aristocratic women from Greece who were all kidnapped one day by their slaves while their husbands were away fighting, and then taken by boat to south Italy. Captive or not, these ladies soon took control of matters and established a small city, and who could have been a better deity to put in supreme charge of their lives and affairs than Persephone, who had herself been abducted by Hades. The temple they erected to her is supposed to have been one of the most splendid in Magna Graecia.

Once established as a city, Locri became famous for being the first of the Greek colonies to have a written code of laws published, thought up by a certain Zaleucus – the first on record after the Ten Commandments, and perhaps more realistic in some parts. Ownership of slaves was forbidden, so was renunciation of citizenship; personal vendettas were outlawed – quarrels had to go to arbitration, adulterers had their eyes put out, thieves were put to death, and young unmarried women were not allowed to wear brightly coloured clothes. One unusual edict was that any person coming before the senate to make a plea or suggestion, even if it was a senator himself, had to stand before the assembly with a noose round his neck; if the request or proposition failed, the noose was summarily tightened. A kind of Locrian roulette for would-be reformers. It is said that Zaleucus fell foul of one of his own laws when his son committed adultery; he offered one of his own eyes in place of both his son's, and his offer was accepted.

Perhaps on account of the legendary aura of femininity hanging round the city – Athene became the next important deity after Persephone – virginity appears to have been of considerable interest, but it is unclear whether this mainly concerned sacrificing virgins, worshipping them or just deflowering them. When Dionysius the Younger from Sicily took over Locri in about 350 BC, his view became obvious as he and his supporters set about raping and ravishing any females they pleased, particularly the more important ones, though this did not go unpunished. When the Locrians rose up and overcame him a few years later they apparently took him and his family alive, tied them up in the *agora* and let the inhabitants fuck them to death.

One thing known about Locri is that it defeated nearby Crotone with its small army of 10,000 against an opposition of more than 100,000, but no one knows exactly when this happened. It could be that the dissolute habits they had learned after defeating Sybaris had rendered the Crotoniates helpless. It could also be that the Locrians were helped by the Dioscuri, as the twins Castor and Pollux were seen on horseback in the sky urging them on. It is much more likely

that the numbers are complete fantasy, or more of Lenormant's *'fausses chroniques'*, or that supporters arrived to
help them.

The ruins of Locri are quite extensive as the city was five
miles in circumference; now mainly foundations, stumps of
pillars, slabs of roadway and the occasional trace of mosaic
floor. As it is now a very large olive grove, it is peaceful and
quiet to walk in. 'Not always peaceful,' Signor Gentile told
me, 'the land is owned by three different farmers and if they
don't like the look of you they are quite liable to take a
shot. In fact they did at an inspector not long ago.' Like
everything else ancient along the coast, whoever demolished it did the job properly – Pyrrhus, Hannibal, tribesmen,
pirates – as the roots of the olive trees are three feet above
the foundations, each one having been carefully dug round
by archaeologists to appease the landowners. A local road
cuts through it from east to west, and beyond it, among the
ruins, is the theatre, now partially excavated and well
preserved; so I sat in the centre of the top tier in the sun as
sweat dripped, and I looked down over a carpet of olive tops
at the sea and thought how futile all those ancient efforts
had been, yet how stupendous; but was anything ever worth
it, because more powerful than any striving for fame or
power or empire was the silent heartbeat of time, the
invincible and destructive predator that had no conscience,
that moved on through success and failure and through
happiness and despair without looking back. The everlasting leveller.

You go through a small museum to reach the ruins,
disturbing two rather surprised attendants. When I went up
this morning for my second visit I was amazed to see a
crowd of people gathered by the gates and for a moment
thought there had been a cultural revolution and they were
queuing to get in. They weren't. It was Sunday morning and
the ritual time of the weekly cycle race, and this stretch of
road past the museum happened to be about a mile long and

absolutely straight. Soon there were squeals of delight and
handclaps as these bent-over racers hurtled past, with legs
pumping and tiny bottoms peekabooing behind them
hugged by black elasticated pants. I wasn't surprised to see,
as each head-down torpedo shot past to shrieks of joy, that
the audience was mainly female.

There's a female room in the museum as well, a small
one given over to Persephone, though not as full as one
might expect; the museum is only twenty years old, and
before this time any finds tended to disappear. The most
significant of these, a marble statue of Persephone seated in
a chair, is in a Berlin museum. There were some good black-
and red-figure vases in cabinets, one with a spectacular
dancing Silenus, several well-preserved bronze mirrors and
some tiles showing animals fighting, but the rest of the
display was largely a collection of fragments or broken
pieces of statue, though there were coins incused with the
flying horse of the Dioscuri.

Signor Gentile says the archaeologists have terrible
problems getting permission to dig at Locri as the landowners' only interest is in money. They try to charge them
for admission to the site, for how long they stay, and then
charge them for any damage to trees or crops. I'd have
thought they'd have made enough money from the things
they find themselves and then sell on to collectors.

Now another traveller has turned up, but whereas Lear
wanted to be here, Philip Elmhirst certainly didn't. He was
captured. This all happened in 1809 when he was a young
naval officer and was shipwrecked a few miles down the
coast and promptly taken prisoner by the French, who then
occupied the Bourbon kingdom. While Courier was writing
his letters home about the delights and glories of Calabria,
Elmhirst, in his account, found it extremely inglorious.
*Occurrences during a six month residence in the province
of Calabria Ulteriore in the Kingdom of Naples in the years*

1809, 1810 paints a frighteningly realistic picture of conditions in the south under French domination; details of hardships and cruelties, examples of generosity and courage, and insights into the lives and feelings of the oppressors and the oppressed; and never forgetting the private armies of brigands whose loyalty to their king drove them to acts of savagery on the enemy.

Elmhirst is rather like an early war correspondent describing each day's events as he was marched a hundred miles inland under guard through rugged, mountainous terrain, suffering from constant thirst, being drenched by storms, boiled by the sun and having to sleep on piles of straw. But at the same time he is recording what he sees: the French requiring 'an abject submission from all classes of men' and the Italians adopting 'an artful system of dissimulation'.

It is painfully vivid in places. Once he had been marched up through the mountains and had arrived at Monte Leone (today called Vibo Valentia), his captors granted him parole, so he could wander the streets and talk to people. He marvels at Calabria's landscapes of 'the most luxuriant imagination' full of 'bold and stupendous scenery'; he visits a house for supper, after which the ladies sing with 'a horrible screeching' and 'the loudest or the shrillest noise being most applauded'; he sees a French soldier needlessly stabbing someone's heavily pregnant pet bitch; he watches brigands who are captured being tortured and hanged, embracing 'the gallows with an appearance of joy' as the soldiers fire at them.

Living in the town for the best part of five months, Elmhirst had time to study it and write its history from the earliest times to the present, and he had time to study the people. He describes ladies who were 'discreet before marriage but not so afterwards'; Italian aristocrats who were 'haughty and cruel'; priests who practised 'gross mummery', did little to 'restrain their libidinous propensities' and used the confessional as a route to seduction; and brigands who made their captives eat their own ears and fingers before killing them. He hates the 'monstrous system of ecclesiastical tyranny' he finds in the south and, while admiring the resilience of people under occupation, cannot get over the dirt he often finds in their houses – dirt that 'would disgust an English woman of even common neatness', where cobwebs in rooms are 'so thickly matted with dirt that they have the appearance of drapery'.

Elmhirst's account of the south as a prisoner of war is obviously very different from those of most other travellers, but it gives a precise description of the conditions in which people lived 200 years ago. His final analysis of the southern situation even outdoes those of Swinburne and Ramage: 'an unpolitic government, the feudal system, and a superstitious and intolerant religion have restrained the powers of the mind, depressed genius, and destroyed emulation'.

EIGHTEEN

The Mountains and Pentedattilo

I'm leaving Siderno now; leaving the roaring baron as he flicks his remote control to get even fuzzier pictures of fifty options, or thumps his new pinball machine; leaving the ceaseless shriek of birds – one dead on its back this morning, eyes and beak serenely closed and stiff pin-thin legs pointing to the sky; leaving gentle Gentile with his quotes and misquotes and his bookshop with no books in it. We had a pizza together last night, the thing Augustus Hare called 'a loathsome condiment'.

'Anything but a Margherita,' Gentile said, making his order.

'Why?' I asked.

'Too patriotic,' he answered, smiling. 'Red, white and green, the Italian colours; tomato, cheese and basil; King Umberto's wife. You know it's Arabic,' he went on.

'What is?'

'The pizza.'

'No, it's not. It's Neapolitan.'

'A slab of dough put on a stone for the sun to cook. The Romans got it from Africa. Cicero talks about it, covered in fish paste. There are ovens in Pompeii. Unleavened bread; you can spread anything on it.'

'Why is it called pizza?'

'Maybe it was cut in slices – pointed; easier to eat. Perhaps because it was pressed flat . . .'

'The Romans didn't have tomatoes.'

'They used anything: cheese, honey, eggs, olives, sour milk . . . like an open sandwich. Cato wrote about it. A kind of pancake with topping . . .'

'Cato's pancake,' I said. 'So we're eating Cato's pancakes.'

I was trying desperately to keep him off politics, the verbal disease. I'd had enough of it.

'I can't understand the language down here,' I ventured. 'Where's it from?'

'Nor can I,' he said. 'If I go twenty miles away I can't understand a word. It's like being in a foreign country . . .'

'Is it Greek?'

'No. It's territorial; to do with ownership and isolated communities. Under the Angevins and the Spanish, people weren't allowed to move. Even under the Bourbons sometimes. There was no transport anyway. Villagers belonged to their local duke or prince. That's why they had different costumes, for identification. In a close-knit community a kind of patois developed with bits of French or Spanish in it. You'll hear *"besoin"*, *"compledo"*, *"tenyo"* and *"nous"* down here.'

'Will it last?'

'Yes. They're very proud of it. It's their secret that identifies them; sets them apart. You have cockney people in England, don't you, doing the same?'

'Yes. They're impossible. Rhyming slang.'

'*Coquus*,' he said. 'It's Latin; *"coquus"* – a cook.'

'What?'

'A Roman cook. Kitchen is *"cucina"*.'

'What are you saying?'

'*Cuquina*. Cookery. Cockney.'

I stared at him.

'Yes. Cockneys are the old Roman cooks,' he said, 'we didn't just give you Hadrian's Wall.'

Christ! First pizzas and then etymology. I rather like Signor Gentile. He actually wanted me to keep the two Eric Newbys, but I couldn't.

I haven't been done since that silly night in Taranto, but I was yesterday. I stopped at a reasonable-looking hotel as it was time I had a bath. The first thing I noticed was that the official prices for a room displayed on the reception desk had been altered upwards in ink.

'Why?' I asked.

'New regulations,' came the emphatic answer.

It's no use arguing. Tangling with a loquacious Italian on his home ground is like standing under a waterfall; you can't even draw breath. They're trained in rhetoric and how to fill silence. In my room the door fell off the wardrobe, the mini-bar was empty and the shower didn't work.

I was still angry when I got to Melito in the morning, which is where Garibaldi landed on 19 August 1860 with his 'thousand' to make a mess of Italy. I stood looking at the long, low brick-built cattle-shed in a field where they are supposed to have spent the night. It must have been quite a squash. The locals refer to it with notable lack of enthusiasm as '*La Caserma dei Mille*', and there certainly isn't any plaque or memorial on it. So it remains a remarkably undistinguished cow-shed, which is what it should be. Next day he wheeled left, took Reggio and started his triumphant progress up Italy towards Naples, which he entered to ecstatic jubilation exactly two weeks later; though rather short-lived jubilation, as once they had stolen his horse (the city has the only statue of Garibaldi not on horseback) and suffered two days of chaotic rioting without any leadership, they began to wish he had never arrived.

Ask almost anyone in the south and Garibaldi, in retrospect, was not a success. But he certainly was at the time; even the thought of him was euphoric; people were so excited they called him the 'second Jesus Christ', but it ended up worse than the *Life of Brian*. Massimo d'Azeglio, the Prime Minister, said that Garibaldi had 'the brains of an ox', somebody else called him 'a comedian', Tennyson said he had 'the divine stupidity of a hero' and Lampedusa called him 'a simple little boy'. All the same, when the wreckage was over he was fêted in England as some kind of divinity and people even collected locks of his hair. Queen Victoria, however, very sensibly declined to meet him, and Karl Marx described Garibaldi's triumphant progress through London as 'a miserable spectacle of imbecility'.

The problem is that the Italians like change. They get bored easily. Let's have something different: a new government, new mistress, new lover, new car. The need for variety is in their nature; something different must be better. Forty million of them were Fascist one day and the same forty million were anti-Fascist the next. So what? They did it to Julius Caesar, Savonarola, Mussolini, the King, so why not Garibaldi? It's exciting. So are Italian politics; they change governments every year. Ramage was right and so was Elmhirst.

Garibaldi landed at Melito twice in fact, but his second arrival was less of a success. The politicians who were trying to organise the new country got sick of him after a few months and wanted him locked up. Once he had marched the length of Italy with his 'redshirts', defeated the Bourbons and declared Italy was united, he swaggered into Parliament in Turin, said he was going to kick the Pope out of Rome and then take over. This didn't go down well, as the assembly didn't enjoy being spoken to as if they were part of his rabble army, with the result that insults and accusations flew around like a swarm of bees. When Garibaldi realised he wasn't all that popular after all, and was thought of as an ignorant and dangerous megalomaniac, he decided to go south again and start another revolution. But when he landed at Melito this time he found considerable government forces waiting for him, and on 29 August 1861 he was captured. He was then sent back to his house on Caprera to write his life story, look after his potatoes, and finally marry Francesca Armosino, who may – or may not – have been introduced to him by a tailor in Catanzaro.

The scenery inland is ferociously mountainous now; savage and threatening, with towering peaks and grey splits of defiles that soar away into dark forests. It's very masculine; unfriendly and cruel; sometimes it feels full of hate and is challenging you to step closer so that it can suck you in and crush you. It's rather sinister having angry mountains watch you as you pop along past them. You can't help thinking of death as you look at them; death and violence. Some of the old writers expressed it best. Thomas Hoby in 1550 talked of 'great thick' woods 'jeopardous to pass . . . many a man is there robbed and slain'; George Sandys a few years later said 'no night doth pass without murder' and warned about tarantulas that 'lurk in sinks and privies'; John Raymond in 1646 saw 'a pocket church book' that fired a bullet when a certain page was turned. So even then the south was 'much possessed by death'.

It isn't all horror. There are field strips of vines and splashes of orange trees and ragged groups of olives always looking a bit desolate as if nobody wants them. And it's obvious I must be getting closer to civilisation as bits of buildings start to appear; but only bits of them; and whatever they're meant to be, or hope to be, they're all half-constructed or quarter-constructed or one-tenth-constructed. Just a cobweb of rusty scaffolding with a few layers of breeze-blocks. They're eyesores; abandoned; like overgrown lumps of litter, just plonked down in open land beside the road. Most of them are illegal and being built without permission, and one keeps hearing that the government is taking steps to demolish them, but nothing happens. It doesn't only occur near Reggio; there are illegal homes along the Appian Way in Rome and more in Sicily, near the Valley of the Temples at Agrigento. An ulcerous growth that decorates the landscape like picked-at scabs on a beauty queen. It's strange that with their amazing and unique eye for aesthetics and their brilliance at design, they can't see the wanton ugliness of things like this.

So I went up a winding road to Pentedattilo, which means

five fingers, because it's a village built round and into a remarkable outcrop of grey rocks that stick up in the air out of nowhere and look like a misshapen hand with its fingers stretched out. The guide book suggests it was a Byzantine settlement in the thirteenth century. Lear called this 'the beau ideal of the terrible' and found it looked so dramatic that he couldn't wait to sketch it; obviously a dramatic event in itself, as some of the inhabitants ran screaming back to their houses when they saw him sitting on a rock and sketching the scenery. It is not quite abandoned now; some 200 empty houses nestling together and still clinging round the rocks like limpets, but only about eight inhabitants, as most of them accepted the offer made by the local authority in 1967 to move down to a new village nearer the sea. There's an eccentric university professor from Reggio in residence, an eccentric Frenchman, three eccentric Germans and a handful of rather bemused original inhabitants. Apparently an international army of young 'greens' or conservationists descends on Pentedattilo every summer, complete with cement, paint and weedkiller to help stop the whole place falling down; an invasion, a gap-toothed local said, which was really a bunch of hippies having fun. He also said I could buy any of the houses I liked for £100.

So I wandered around them, still remarkably preserved in spite of being empty for so long; over red-brown pantiled roofs, along walls, through doors into abandoned gardens. It was eerie and silent, deadened by the sun. Lizards shot here and there into bolt-holes, scorpions hid under stones, wands of tall foxgloves waved, abandoned and free, straggly vines clambered over walls and chimneys, steps led down to lower tiers, more rows of empty houses locked together, wedged tight against the sinews of the mountain. I saw a sign somewhere on one of the walls: 'This village is not abandoned. With few inhabitants and enormous energy we are keeping it alive. Please respect this place and the magic of its silence.' I liked it; the peace, the contrast, almost the humour of it when compared with the shoreline; a gentle defiance seemingly without effort. Another group of quiet enthusiasts like those of that church at Cerate.

There has to be a legend about a place as unique as this; about a remote village almost crushed against a fearsome mountain with the remains of an ancient castle perched towards one of the peaks. There has to be blood and death; and hatred between two neighbouring mountains, Pentedattilo and Montebello, owned by medieval lords who loathed each other – and there is. It started when Montebello's lovesick son fell for Pentedattilo's beautiful daughter and stole by night into Pentedattilo's castle to carry her away, but was apprehended; and in the ensuing struggle in the dark he severely wounded the Pentedattilo father. He, for some reason, thought his wife had done it, so he promptly killed her and moments later he himself died of his wounds. This left Pentedattilo's daughter happy in the arms of her lover but sad at having two dead parents and, considering that it was all her fault, she eventually took a large dose of poison. This would have left Montebello's son all right, with something to look forward to – in spite of being without his lady-friend – had not a young Pentedattilo son sworn revenge, gained access to Montebello's castle dressed as a page and then managed to imprison Montebello's son in one of his own dungeons without food or water. As nobody knew quite how to end this double tragedy – a Calabrian variation of Romeo and Juliet but with more dead bodies – fate provided an earthquake, which buried all the remaining Montebellos and Pentedattilos in the rubble of their castles, never to be heard of again. And to prove it is all true, say the remaining inhabitants here, there are small crimson flowers the size of buttercups growing between the stones and up some of the banks, and they're called 'scude'. They represent the blood of the two families seeping out of the earth.

What excites people considerably more here is a modern legend: the Versace family. Gianni and Donatella grew up in a small village down the road called Lazzaro, and apparently his craze for fashion started then. He used to dress his sister up in outrageous clothes and microscopic skirts for fun, because their mother was a seamstress and there were always yards of material lying around for them both to play with. And so started another legend. But this is Calabria. Yet another one had to end in blood.

NINETEEN

Reggio

I can't wait to get right into Reggio now, before AB dies under me. It gets hiccoughs, fits of choking and asthmatic wheezes. I must look extremely funny trying to bounce it along by bumping my bottom on the saddle. Sometimes I could walk faster.

When Vivant Denon wrote his account for the Abbé Saint-Non waiting in Rome, he said that entering Reggio in 1778 with his motley crew of adventurers, artists and amateur geographers was like a Bacchic triumph. '*Le chemin nous semblait préparé pour un triomphe de Bacchus.*' No such luck for me; I was positively unnoticed. And Reggio is a monstrous sprawl and obviously doesn't care what it looks like any more as it has been beaten up, invaded, razed to the ground, ruined, smashed to pieces and virtually obliterated so often that it can't be bothered to look nice. It is a harbour, a port, a railway terminus, a tourist trap, a metropolis, a human ant-heap, and if there was a chance of a *fata Morgana*, you either wouldn't see it for the smoke and haze or it would be obliterated by concrete tower-blocks. It has been hammered umpteen times by Greeks, Sicilians, pirates, Carthaginians, Turks, Normans, Genoese, Pisans, and the odd battery of Germans and Americans, plus earthquakes, so it has given up trying. The only fraction of visible antiquity is a few yards from the sea-front: a short length of the foundations of a Greek wall, and the remains of some Roman baths with a notice saying, 'Cleanliness and quiet are two precious commodities. Look after them.' Yet Lear called Reggio a vast garden and 'one of the loveliest spots to be seen on earth', Swinburne said it was full of 'oranges and their kindred fruits', and even Gissing called its beauties 'indescribable'.

I have taken up temporary residence in a very poor-man's hotel in a back street near the museum. It is shabby and unfriendly and I obviously look highly suspicious, very unusual and a nuisance; as is AB propped up in the lobby for people to fall over. Two sour-looking men appear to run the hotel from behind a door with a one-way mirror in it, aided or abetted by a highly mobile Filipino maid with an obliging and occasionally guilty expression, who might have been attractive once and now wriggles her body like a caterpillar to prove there's some life in it yet. I assume she is employed to do the rooms. The only thing she's done in the half-day I have been here is remove the extremely hard-core porn magazine I found in the bedside locker on arrival, which isn't there now. Breakfast is out of the question; there is a machine by the desk downstairs seeping out treacly coffee into minute paper cups, a sort of demi-espresso; and beside it on the wall another machine offering all the rubber-works so far invented, with a cartoon pinned to it saying, 'When jumping for pleasure always wear a parachute.'

On 16 August 1972, a few miles down the coast from here, a young scuba-diver called Stefano Mariottini was some way underwater with his harpoon gun looking for a fish to kill when he saw an arm sticking up out of the sand below him. He promptly thought he had found a corpse and that somebody had drowned. But they hadn't; not in today's sense. That body, and another one beside it, had been lying on the sea-bed for 2,500 years, buried in sand and gravel. They were, and are, the Riace Bronzes: life-like figures of two warriors straight from the best period of classical Greek sculpture. It then took most of a week for the authorities to retrieve them by carefully attaching balloons to each body, slowly filling them with oxygen so that the bronzes could be raised twenty feet to the surface, then having boats ready to pull them ashore. Once in Reggio, both figures were descaled a little so that the archaeologists could begin to see what they'd got: two spectacular and naked Greek warriors, each about two yards tall and symbolising an ideal – the grace, beauty, power and athleticism of the male body. The perfect man.

After Reggio had completed the initial cleaning, both were taken to Florence and Rome for more extensive work on the insides by making small holes in the heads and soles of the feet so that tubes could be inserted to remove any sand and deposits. This took three years, following which crusts of clay had to be extracted to allow for the insertion of endoscopes to inspect for corrosion or signs of damage. Finally, after eight years, the bronzes were returned to Reggio for display in the museum, after Rome and Florence had each tried very hard to keep them for themselves on the grounds that they would look after them properly and had more tourists who would enjoy seeing them.

But Reggio insisted on keeping them, and they now have a large basement room to themselves in the museum; two splendidly imposing Greek warriors standing on a central dais so that they can be admired from all angles. If their expressions were fierce, they'd be Lear's 'beau ideal of the terrible' again, but they're not; they are precise, sinister and inscrutable, mindless even, gazing ahead as if lost in another world, allowing you to think or feel for them. They have perfectly shaped male bodies – the beau ideal – firm and muscular all over with one foot slightly forward, posed for physical effect, seriousness and determination. They have been deliberately formed to represent the faultless body that belonged not to man but only to certain gods; powerful gods braced for action, well bearded and stern-eyed in hard stony faces, their shoulders squared, with breath gently drawn in to inflate their chests, and their muscular arms actively poised for gripping the weapons they once held in their hands. Their stomachs are athletically hard and flat, and their genitals small and insignificant; they are not sex or pleasure gods; they're gods of wonder and reverence, even fear; their stares fixed on something more distant and lasting than human weakness: heroism, victory, justice, freedom, the search for perfection and their right to immortality. Their stance is one of pride, not vanity; a commanding dignity that is unlikely to be challenged. Muscular thighs taper to well-shaped legs, and the forward foot serves to emphasise the grace and proportions of the entire physique, making the buttocks suggestively uneven, yet perfectly matched in shape and in the firmness of the curves.

When school parties arrive, that is where the girls go to admire and giggle. Two beautifully compact Nureyev bums in glossy bronze, without an inch of shame. The boys would rather not bother; it might cause comment. They're fascinated by the front, smirking with incredulity and hardly believing how lucky they are. They haven't really got time for Greek gods; Olympians from another world setting standards of physical power and beauty; something to aspire to and wonder at. They're thinking about other things . . .

No one knows whether they were gods or not; in fact they're a mystery; no maker, no provenance, not even a definite date, though very probably dating from around 450 BC and contemporary with the Chatsworth Head from Cyprus. They could equally be Magna Graecian or from mainland Greece, and were very likely being taken to Rome by boat as booty to decorate some victorious general's palace when a storm took care of them. They could be the twin gods of Locri, who helped the inhabitants to victory over Crotone when they were so outnumbered – Castor the dextrous one and Pollux the brave. Or they could just be anonymous warriors; two heroes, two valorous ''Ndrangheta'. It's probable that nobody ever will know; all they show is how great the Greeks could be in their art and craftsmanship in the midst of all their centuries of degradation and fighting; and how even then gods were made in the image of man.

I was honoured this evening; invited behind the one-way mirror by the owners to watch television because there was a football match and an English team was playing. I didn't see or hear much of it because both of them refereed the encounter throughout and, when anything remotely interesting happened, they stood up and screamed. Football here is gladiatorial; hysteria sets in; apoplexy almost; the difference being that the Romans didn't have repeats, reruns, inquests and post-mortems. When it was over and some measure of calm had settled, the owners fiddled around until they found a recording of a concert given by the Three Tenors, and then sat back smiling seraphically. Now if anyone can murder good music, that trio can. The noise they make reminds me of Elmhirst's 'screeching' ladies; something Lear had to put up with as well, his after-dinner hostess singing 'with terrible energy'. I think they're a comedy trio; a circus act; an offence to the Italian musical tradition; made worse by the expressions of joy on their faces. Naturally. While they make a noise like three waste-disposals chewing up china, their bank balances disappear off the decibel range. They suffer from another of the national diseases – they can't stand silence.

My second visit to the museum today. The first time I went in there were half a dozen layabouts in the entrance hall chatting and smoking; these were the official attendants – no uniforms, no badges, just old clothes and holding fags behind their backs; and the old woman at the kiosk preferred to knit rather than sell me a ticket. I made them all jump a bit when I said I knew the director and had an appointment tomorrow. I was immediately elevated to

'Professore', which in fact only means schoolteacher. I'd have preferred *'Illustrissimo'* or *'Eminenza'*.

Actually the museum, apart from the bronzes, is a shambles. There are builders everywhere, not really doing anything that one can see, except move piles of bricks or sand around or shift bits of scaffolding rather slowly. It's cronyism and the hand of the Mafia gone mad. A building firm has got the repairs or improvements sewn up, and the attendants have got the running of the museum sewn up. If they don't want to open one of the rooms, they don't, because they can't be bothered to man it. If they want to shut off a whole floor, they do so; supervising it would be too much trouble. The director can't do a thing: one squeak of complaint and they'd all down fags and walk out; or the builders would make a hole in the roof. You can actually sense the power they have; see the shifty looks in their eyes and the smugness on their faces.

After my mention of the director, the *'capo'* of the group was fawning around me like a sick spaniel.

'What would you like to see?' he asked.

'The Dioscuri,' I answered.

This meant unlocking one of the closed rooms. *'In restauro,'* he announced, which is the everlasting excuse, pointing at a remarkably small, less-than-lifesize figure of a frightened-looking horse with a naked youth on its back, both of them uncomfortably balanced on a female sphinx. The room resembled a warehouse; stacks of miscellaneous remains everywhere. 'We're reorganising,' he said proudly, 'we have so many treasures', smiling as if he owned them. There was another Dioscuri in the room; this time the horse supported by a sea-serpent with a human head and the rider holding the bridle as he dismounted. 'Locri,' he said. 'You know Locri, don't you? Persephone and Pluto living in Hades together for six months a year. What a life!'

He offered to open more rooms; locked because of the builders, he explained; they're so ignorant.

'Look. Our collection of five thousand coins; Sybaris, Crotone, Metapontum.'

The cabinets were full of them, and on a pedestal a remarkable bronze head that had recently been found underwater and could have been anyone's great-grandfather today, nearly balding with a lined forehead and a severe, deep-eyed expression with a tight mouth, thick moustache and long, well-kept beard. Everything about the face was pure Victorian; it could easily have been Tennyson or Darwin, except that it was 2,500 years old and just called 'the Philosopher'. There were collections of clay figures in cabinets, rows of identical smiling goddesses with plaited hair, seated in chairs and wearing long skirts that only let their toes peep out. They looked strangely Egyptian. Best of all perhaps was a long section of frieze from a temple, still showing the coloured paintwork and floral designs and key pattern, with wide open-mouthed lions' heads at intervals acting as water-spouts, all showing delighted expressions as if happy to be of help.

Tucked away at the top was the art gallery of three connecting rooms, where the pictures were either sombre oil paintings of Old Testament stories of martyrdoms or miracles, or else violently heroic episodes of the Risorgimento. I had hoped there would be a picture of St Francis of Paola sailing across to Sicily on his cloak after some boatmen had refused to row him across, but there wasn't. This remarkable man from up the road had raised at least a dozen people from the dead by the time he was fifteen and then went on to perform more than another 13,000 miracles before he died, which works out at one a day for about forty years.

I was rather glad to get out and away from the slow-moving builders; out into some fresh air and sunlight. A group of visiting school children were having the same idea; a susurrating crowd of small bodies milling around the exit in high-pitched bedlam. This gave the 'capo' a real chance to do his stuff. Biff! . . . Smack! . . . Wallop! . . . 'What a job we've got, *Professore*,' he gasped, flailing his hands. Bang! . . . Thump! . . . 'Always keeping these ignorant kids in order. Just look at them.' Wham! . . . Crack! . . . 'Worse than animals. Bad for tourism.' Crash! As another ten-year-old reeled round the entrance holding his head and the bruised girls snivelled. I didn't know whose side I was on: the kids' or the '*capo*'s. I rather wished they'd turned on him like a hive of Furies attacking Orestes. He deserved it. It was time to leave.

No one I spoke to knew when the last *fata Morgana* had been seen. My question led to a number of strange expressions and rather clipped answers before they hurried on. A bookseller was more helpful and said the only such mirage he knew about had happened in 1643 which a priest called Angelucci had described. He then scrabbled around in a back room to look for evidence, which he found in a tattered magazine: a reprint of Father Angelucci's experience. It said it happened on 15 August. The sea was like 'a polished mirror', it went on. 'I saw a string of several thousand pillars . . . Then they lost half their height and bent into arcades . . . Then a cornice appeared on top and above that lots of identical castles, which soon split into towers and long colonnades with windows in them . . . Then everything disappeared among pine-trees and cypresses . . .' This must have been one of the double-type of mirages, or 'superiores', mentioned by Galateo back in Puglia.

Swinburne gives instructions of how you can see a *fata Morgana*. Stand on a hilltop outside Reggio and look west, he says, and hope there's no wind, a calm sea and a high tide. Then 'as soon as the sun surmounts the eastern hills and rises to an angle of forty-five degrees . . . every object existing or moving at Reggio will be repeated a thousand fold upon this marine looking-glass'. A description that sounds to me more like a simple reflection than a mirage.

A number of people like to bring King Arthur into it, or rather his evil sister Morgan le Fay; they say that's where the name comes from, imported by Anglo-Norman knights when they invaded Sicily with their troubadours, singing songs of great kings and heroic deeds. That's probably how Arthur got onto the floor of Otranto Cathedral as well. If the name is not from Arthurian legend, then it could come from *maga*, meaning witch.

The director is the archaeological head of all Calabria and has an office up on the top floor of the museum, out of harm's way, where there are Saint-Non engravings on the walls; one or two nice ones of Reggio made to look as if it were only a village, which some people say are artistic fantasy. All very romantic. As he hadn't been here long, he knew what I was going to ask, so I did – was it better here than in Basilicata?

'Different,' he said, 'very different. Not so friendly.'

'People? . . . Or pressures?'

'A bit of both,' he sighed. 'They're not so interested. Archaeology is not popular, so I'm not,' and he smiled. 'I'm a minor concern – even a nuisance . . .'

'What's the major one?'

'Building. Always more houses. If I tell them it's an archaeological site, they don't care . . . It doesn't matter.'

'Can't you stop them?'

He actually laughed. 'How? We haven't any power. By the time I get a committee in Rome to have a meeting, the bulldozers are in and they've started building a road. There's a site we're trying to protect now not far away . . . I get telephone calls saying I'm wasting my time; then they pay the farmer to keep us out . . .' He looked depressed and I felt it.

'Do you get threatened?'

'I've had one telephone call, maybe two.'

'What happened at Locri?'

'Yes. Our inspector was shot at by one of the farmers. We knew he'd been digging things up. It's his land anyway; we just wanted to see what it was. When the inspector went to ask him, he shot at him.'

'It must be a rich site,' I said.

'Fabulous. We can't do anything because of the land disputes. They just rifle the place,' and he gave a shrug. 'That's the way we are here; the poor relation . . . We're not as high on the list as Florence or Rome when it comes to handing the money out. We haven't got anything to show.'

'Doesn't it make you angry?'

'Of course it does, but what's the point? I can't do anything if they break open every tomb in Locri. By the time we get there it's too late; even if we hear about it. Art thieving has been going on for centuries and always will. The stuff that has gone missing over the past three years would fill five museums. At least most thieves look after the stuff properly, which is more than we do sometimes.'

'How's the museum going?' I asked weakly.

'You've seen it, haven't you? The builders have been in for two months. I didn't want them in anyway; only for a small repair on the roof. Someone decided everything needed doing. I wasn't asked. They didn't even put tenders out. I came in one morning and they were here.'

I didn't say anything; just felt a wave of depression, that something so exciting could be strangled so easily by bumbling bureaucracy, greed and secret deals. Was any-where free of it? When will today's Diogenes find his honest man? I pulled a small and rather beautiful pot out of the bag I was carrying and put it on his desk, and he smiled.

'Yes,' he said. 'It's nice. Fifth century. You got it in Ciro, didn't you? They told me. It's quite well done,' and he was turning it over slowly. 'Yes, I like it,' he said, then added slowly, 'There's only ever been one civilisation in south Italy. That was the Greeks.'

RIP AB on a crackly line.

'Hello, Aldo. I'm in Reggio.'

'Who?'

'Me. I'm in Reggio with your bike.'

'Where?'

'Calabria. I'm sending it back.'

'What?'

'Sending your bike back.'

'What bike?'

'The one you lent me. I'm sending it back . . .'

'Oh. Where are you?'

'Reggio.'

Silence.

'What are you doing?'

'Sending your bike back. Going home . . .'

'I don't want a bike.'

'Well, I've sent it . . . it's yours. It'll take about a week.'

'Why? You can keep it.'

'I've just told you . . . I've sent it.'

'Oh.'

Silence again.

'Are you in Reggio now?'

'Yes.'

'Why don't you keep it?'

'I can't. It's yours. I'm going home. I don't need it.'

'Where is it?'

'Here at the station. It was fine. You'll have it in a week.'

Then the line went dead.

I went back through the maze of empty offices to find the shirt-sleeved man I'd paid £30 to in exchange for nearly a ream of paperwork, and who hadn't smiled once.

'Can I cancel it all?' I said. 'There's a problem. I've changed my mind.'

'What problem?' he asked. 'You've paid. It's booked.'

'I've decided not to send it.'

'Not possible. It's gone.'

'No, it hasn't. It's over there. I can see it.'

'It's on its way. Where was it going? Taranto?'

'Otranto. I want to keep it.'

'Why?'

'Because I don't want to send it. Can I have my money back if I take it away?'

'You've already paid.'

'I know. I'm going to take it back to England.'

'England? You can't. You'll need to go through customs.'

'Why can't I have it back?'

'You can't. You've signed the papers,' and he started looking for his copy through another ream of rubbish. He found something. 'Yes. Value, one hundred pounds. Is it your bike?'

'No . . . Yes . . . The owner doesn't want it.'

'Why not?'

'He's got another one. He lent it to me to ride all along the coast. He says I can keep it.'

He turned and looked at AB thoughtfully, propped against a wall. I had a wave of mixed feelings: loathing and desertion, fury and exasperation, followed by desperate inspiration.

'Do you want it?' I asked.

'Why? Is it stolen?'

'No. He doesn't want it. He's got a new one. That one's old.'

'So it's nobody's, if he doesn't want it.'

'Looks like it. Sort of.'

'That's a problem then,' he said emphatically, 'sending nobody's bike to Taranto.'

'Otranto.'

He turned to look at it again, stroking his chin. 'A real problem,' he said.

'All I want is my money back,' I said weakly. 'Why don't you have it?'

He looked at me and began shuffling the papers away. 'Tomorrow,' he said. 'Come back tomorrow ... We'll have to see ... Perhaps we can do something,' and he turned away.

I'm on the train now coming home. I should have known. He wasn't there when I went back this morning and nor was AB. Not a sign. This is Italy.

Bibliography

Barzini, Luigi. *The Italians*. London, 1966

Bertaux, Emile. *L'Art dans l'Italie Meridionale*. Paris, 1904

Bertholdi, Giuseppe (attrib.). *Memoirs of the Secret Societies of the South of Italy, particularly the Carbonari*. London, 1821

Blewitt, Octavian. *Murray's Handbook for Travellers in Southern Italy*. London, 1853

Breval, John. *Remarks on Several parts of Europe*. London, 1738

Briggs, Martin J. *In the Heel of Italy*. London, 1910

Brydone, *A Tour through Sicily and Malta*. London, 1773

Bryson, Bill. *Neither Here nor There*. London, 1991

Chaney, Edward. *The Evolution of the Grand Tour*. London, 1998

Church, E. M. *Sir Richard Church in Italy and Greece*. London, 1895

Clay, Edith. *Ramage in South Italy*. London, 1965

Courier, Paul-Louis. *Oeuvres Completes*. Paris, 1951

Douglas, Norman. *Old Calabria*. London, 1915

Elmhirst, P. J. *Occurrences during a six months' residence in the province of Calabria Ulteriore in the Kingdom of Naples*. London, 1819

Gissing, George. *By the Ionian Sea*. London, 1901

Graves, Robert. *The Greek Myths*. London, 1979

Gunn, Peter. *The Companion Guide to Southern Italy*. London, 1969

Hare, Augustus J. C. *Cities of Southern Italy and Sicily*.

Hibbert, Christopher. *Garibaldi and his Enemies*. London, 1965

Hutton, Edward. *Naples and Southern Italy*. London, 1915

Bibliography

James, Nicolette. *Inglesi a Gallipoli*. Lecce, 1993

Keates, Jonathan. *Italian Journeys*. London, 1991

Keppel Craven, Richard. *A Tour through the Southern Provinces of the Kingdom of Naples*. London, 1821

Lear, Edward. *Journal of a Landscape Painter in southern Calabria*. London, 1852

Lenormant, Francois. *La Grande-Grece*. Paris, 1881

Lowe, Emily. *Unprotected Females in Sicily, Calabria & on top of Mount Etna*. 1859

Luce, A. A. & Jessop, T. E. *The Works of George Berkeley*. London, 1955

Macaulay, Rose. *Pleasure of Ruins*. London, 1953

MacFarlane, Charles. *Popular Customs, Sports and Recollections of the South of Italy*. London, 1846

Moens, W. J. C. *English Tavellers and Italian Brigands*. London, 1866

Morton, H. V. *A Traveller in Southern Italy*. London, 1969

Norwich, John J. *The Normans in the South*. London, 1967

Orioli, G. *Moving Along*. London, 1934

Parks, Tim. *Italian Neighbours*. London, 1992

Ramage, Craufurd Tait. *The Nooks and Byways of Italy*. Liverpool, 1868

Revel, Jean-François. *As for Italy*. London, 1959

Rohlfs, Gerhard. *Vocabulario dei dialetti Salentini*. Monaco, 1956

Ross, Janet. *The Land of Manfred*. London, 1889

Saint Non, L'Abbe de. *Voyage Pittoresque de Naples et de Sicile*. Paris, 1781

Sitwell, Sacheverell. *Southern Baroque Art*. London, 1927

Strutt, Arthur John. *A Pedestrian Tour in Calabria and Sicily*. London, 1842

Swinburne, Henry. *Travels in the Two Sicilies*. London, 1790

Index

Index

Index

273

Index

Index